OVER THERE

OVER THERE

From the Bronx to Baghdad

ALAN FEUER

COUNTERPOINT
A Member of the Perseus Books Group
New York

This is a book of recollected memory, not recorded fact. It is one man's attempt to re-create events that touched the lives of others, some of them his colleagues, some his friends. The situations, people, and places described within it are real. Some dialogue has been created to move the story forward, the act of bringing back the past being a creative act.

Designed by Brent Wilcox
Text set in 11.6 point Adobe Caslon

Library of Congress Cataloging-in-Publication Data
Feuer, Alan, 1971–
    Over there : from the Bronx to Baghdad / Alan Feuer
       p.   cm.
    ISBN 1-58243-327-5 (alk. paper)
    1. Feuer, Alan, 1971–.   2. Iraq War, 2003—Personal narratives, American.   I. Title.

DS79.76.F48   2005
956.7044'3'092—dc22

                                                                                          2004027149

05 06 07 / 10 9 8 7 6 5 4 3 2 1

Denise

"There is an old proverb that a girl may sleep with one man without being a trollop, but let a man cover one little war and he is a war correspondent. I belong to the one-war category."

A.J. LIEBLING

"The only people who ever loved war for long were profiteers, generals, staff officers and whores. They all had the best and finest times of their lives and most of them made the most money they had ever made."

HEMINGWAY
in a letter to *Esquire*, 1936,
forgetting to include reporters in his list

"The practice of journalism is seldom as useful for telling others about the world as it is for teaching oneself about the world."

MURRAY KEMPTON

A PROTAGONIST IS BORN

As GENERAL POLICY, the *New York Times* frowns upon the use of first person in its news stories. The following passage is drawn from correspondence with Allan M. Siegal, assistant managing editor for standards.

"In a genuinely personal piece," Mr. Siegal writes, "there's nothing wrong with 'I.'" He continues:

> A few writers can't bring themselves to use it, and we're indulgent about letting them say "this reporter" or "this writer." In a piece that's otherwise written as an outsider, about people other than the writer, I find "this reporter" more graceful.

Mr. Siegal may indeed be on to something here. Not everyone feels comfortable in the bespoke suit of the first person. Some feel more at ease in the costume, as he puts it, of the outsider.

At any rate, one could certainly do worse than to defer to his indulgence and sense of grace. Thus, without undue delay, the curtain now is raised on a trying two months in the life of This Reporter.

OVER THERE

BOOK ONE

ENGLAND

Chapter 1

THE LIST

O NE LATE FRIDAY afternoon in March 2003, some fifteen days before the outbreak of the Second Gulf War in Iraq, the pager in his pocket buzzed and T.R., reaching for it with a customary mix of guilt and dread, saw it was a call from the metropolitan desk of the *New York Times*. This was hardly a surprise. Only two parties used the pager with any regularity—the paper and his wife. Because it was a Friday, it could not be his wife— she was working at her restaurant—which left the paper as the only viable alternative. It was not a pleasant alternative, however. At half past three on a Friday afternoon, when typically he would be wrapping up business at the bureau in the Bronx, there was only one good reason why the editors would call—there was a breaking story to be covered.

Unlike most reporters, who seemed to thrive on the fresh-pressed juices of the news, T.R. hated breaking stories. As with unexpected guests (or car alarms at midnight) they intruded on the happy rhythms of the day. So T.R. did his damnedest to avoid them. He often hid out in the bureau as the weekend approached, and sometimes went so far as to ignore the telephone after three. At best, a breaking story meant that you would labor for a few hours on a murder case that would be utterly forgotten in a week; at worst, you could wind up in the wilds of Queens at a scaffolding collapse. How many times had he received such calls and spent the better portions of an evening in the lobby of a flame-wracked apartment building talking to the victims of a gas fire? Or tracking down the uncle of a dead man's second cousin for a quote? And for what? A front-page byline or a squib in the metro briefs? The problem was that the effort was the same despite the outcome, and you never knew which outcome to expect. In either case, a breaking story tended to upset his stomach in a fashion roughly equal to ingesting sixteen cups of coffee on a starter plate of Benzedrine. Everything about such stories spoke of speed, scrambling, urgency, and the compression of your finest nerves. It was precisely what you did not want on a Friday afternoon.

For a news reporter, T.R. had an admittedly shameful lack of tolerance for pressure. It was no doubt why he refused to carry a cellular phone. Among his reporter friends, it was no small source of humor that he would call them from a pay phone, if indeed a working pay phone could be found in the city. Behind his back they almost certainly referred to him as a Luddite, but this was only true in part. He did not fear technology so much as object to the constant inroads it made on an otherwise dreamy personal life.

Submission to the pager was bad enough. There were times, in fact, he fantasized about destroying it—smashing it to bits with a hammer, drowning it in the sink, or throwing it off the railing of the boat basin to the currents of the Hudson. As a type who might be called self-consciously old-fashioned, T.R. even avoided having cable television. It was only natural then that every month or so he somehow managed to accidentally drop his pager—whoops!—onto the hardwood floors of his apartment. It was a testament to the Jesuit in his private self.

So there was the dread. The guilt was just as bad. The guilt arose from the fact that, even as the page came in, T.R. was playing hooky from his job. He was not in the Bronx at all; he was in Times Square on the lam from his employers. More precisely, he was strolling in a light spring breeze down Forty-second Street, having just left Kaufman's Army-Navy with a friend and colleague at the *Times*, Charlie LeDuff. LeDuff had visited this store and bought all manner of supplies to ship off to Iraq. The war was coming, the president had all but formally declared it, the armies in Kuwait were marshaled on the border, the press corps in New York was ready to depart, and this fine fellow would be going along. Until two weeks before, T.R. himself was going to Iraq, but then without warning he was bumped from the list. So it was not just guilt and dread he felt, but professional bitterness and a lingering despair. And when the number of the metro desk lit up his pager's screen, he sighed profoundly on the bricks of Forty-second Street. Not only was a breaking story coming in; he was a solid forty minutes from the Bronx.

But on this Friday afternoon, the breaking story had nothing to do with the Bronx.

Of course, at that point, there was no way to tell. And, calling the desk (with Charlie's cell phone, naturally), he asked the clerk to tell him who had called. It had been Jon Landman, the metropolitan editor. This was something strange. Only two hours earlier, T.R. had eaten lunch with Landman at a Times Square rib joint—indeed, it was over lunch that Landman had informed him of the politics behind his getting bumped from the coverage of Iraq. Landman had explained that a pair of colleagues had complained themselves of getting bumped, and that their patrons on the masthead had removed T.R. from the all-important list. The squeaky wheels had nabbed his place. With customary kindness, Landman offered his apologies, but such matters, he explained, were out of his control.

"What we'll do instead is give you something juicy in the Bronx," he had said. "You'll win a Pulitzer." Whether this was true or not, T.R. felt justified to take revenge; encountering LeDuff in the *Times* main office after lunch, he had gone with LeDuff to the Army-Navy store to purchase the duffel bags, canteens, and so on that he himself no longer needed for Iraq. Why Landman should be calling now, however, was a mystery. And in the shadow of this mystery, T.R. waited on the phone.

In truth, Landman was among the few *Times* editors whom T.R. unequivocally admired. He was, first of all, an honest man—a faculty that flourished in the paper's newsroom about as well as a climbing rose at Fresh Kills—and his impassioned, factual intelligence was that of a Talmudic scholar hired by the Tweed Ring after leaving the yeshiva. He was something of a nebbish, stiff-backed and bespectacled, and yet his nerdy manner was the basis of his strength. Clearly, Landman was the smartest kid in school, but he was still no wuss; he could beat you on the track the same as at debate. In fact, he was remarkably physically fit. Landman was a marathoner with a runner's lean hard body, spare without an extra gram of fat. Moreover, he never seemed to sweat. Though he might betray his bookish disposition by wearing a sports strap on his glasses at the gym, he was stubborn, tough-minded and astutely energetic—a product of Amherst and the *Daily News* copy desk who had not yet reached the blossom of his powers even as a section head at the *New York Times.*

As for honesty, Landman seemed to grasp that moral honesty, intellectual honesty, even journalistic honesty did not, at all times and in every case, require a strict adherence to the facts. Which is not to say that Landman lied. He was rather that rare soul who seemed to comprehend that good reporting was not an end in itself but served the purpose of the story, and who understood that underneath the epistemic truth of any story lay a different truth, a difficult and human truth, that did not match, or could not always be contained by, the cold arithmetic of fact. It was Landman, after all, who had overseen production of the "Portraits of Grief," those tenderly evocative obituary-poems for the dead of 9/11. In another man's hand, these pieces might have read like death notices; instead, they breathed with life. And their breath was no more than the breath of honesty allowed free passage through the lungs of his reporters. Landman's honesty was an impressionistic honesty. Let the breath in, let the light in, let the strokes go blurry, so long as the larger truth remained. Most interesting of all was that this expansiveness existed in conjunction with a personality exacting as a razor blade. It was quite interesting—and quite unlike the *Times.*

It was Landman who had hired T.R. four years before—another act unlike the *Times.* T.R., after all, had never worked as a reporter. At the time he had been working as a stringer for the paper, mostly in New Jersey, but Landman, sensing something in his young disciple's energy, if not in his experience, decided he would buck all trends and take the risk. The deal was sealed in 1999 at a bagel shop uptown. The two both lived nearby and, waiting for their pumpernickel schmears, Landman had enticed T.R. with the tastiest of treats: Would he care to join the staff and write about the mob? He would, he would indeed, despite the fact that he was working on a novel (a novel that was comatose, if not completely dead). While T.R. was terrified of the nine-to-five, reporting on Cosa Nostra was a meat too sweet to pass. In short order, he signed the papers. Hello, paycheck. Adios, siestas and the Nobel Prize!

So there T.R. was now on a borrowed cell phone waiting for the man who had brought him to the *Times*. The job at the *Times* had brought him into contact with every sort of meathead, gindaloon, Don Wannabe, and flimflam artist—an astounding education in the city's underworld, a universe that in a few more years would surely disappear. The Mafia at the millennium was not unlike the Hapsburgs at the end of World War I: decadent, irrelevant, and rotten to its core. It was also a case study in authenticity and one neat beat for a cub reporter like T.R. The trouble was that once the paychecks started rolling, the *Times* owned his hide. It could send him to Albany or Hartford at the ficklest of whims. One day in his second year, Landman called to say, "Pack your bags, you're headed to the Bronx." And that is where he found himself as war approached in March. Random shootings in the projects, domestic violence on the Concourse, stabbings in Crotona Park, dead babies, welfare mothers, prison inmates, dealers, rapists—he was swimming in the chaos of the Bronx. It was a far cry from the seedy elegance of the Bonanno family and also from the discarded dreamings of his book.

Whenever T.R. spoke with Landman, he was somewhat bitter at having given up such pleasures and always somewhat worried at whatever redeployment might be coming at him next.

From the start, then, their conversation was marked by a defensive tone. Even as he greeted Landman he was skeptical. It turned out rightly so, given the orders coming down: Landman had just finished saying he had spoken with the Pentagon and that the Pentagon had offered to the *Times* a new embedded slot. So after all the disappointment and the dumping, Landman said, T.R., for absolutely certain, was back on the list.

Two blocks north of the Port Authority Bus Terminal, T.R. said: "The list?"

"The list," said Landman with his energetic brusqueness. "You're on the list!"

"I'm on the list?" The Times Square sky was sunny. LeDuff was standing on the corner with a smoke.

"Look, I just spoke with the Pentagon," said Landman. "They have another slot. Congratulations, Mr. War Correspondent. You're on the list."

The list. A taxicab drove by. The cab was yellow. Its driver was an Arab. LeDuff said, "Are they breaking your fucking balls?" T.R. shook his head. He was on the list.

"Jesus, Jon, that's a surprise. So what's the plan? When do I leave?" He was on the *list*.

"Well, Defense needs your passport number in about"—a shuffling of papers—"an hour. And you'll have to be in London for the satellite phone training. So," he figured, "Friday afternoon to Saturday . . . Tomorrow night, I guess."

Tomorrow night, he said, all right, and then hung up the phone. He stood in the sunshine on the curb at Forty-second

Street. LeDuff asked, "What's the matter?" T.R. told him. "I'm on the fucking list."

"You're on the fucking list? You're on the fucking *list?* Dude, that's great! Beers in Baghdad! You're on the *fucking* list!"

T.R. drove home. In his car, which he adored, in the sanctuary of his car, it started sinking in. He was leaving for the war tomorrow night—he had made it on the list. The problems were enormous. They started with the fact that, two weeks earlier, when he was *not* on the list, he had told his wife that he was not on the list. Now he would have to break the news and, as he took Eighth Avenue uptown toward the corner of the park, he wondered how he would accomplish that grim task. It would be grim, apocalyptic grim, and yet he found he did not care. He was on the list. He was going to war.* But there was sickness in this thought, there was true perversity, since what sane man could *want* to go to war? And not just sickness, selfishness: It was the ultimate untrammeled burst of ego, we go, he goes off to war. At Lincoln Square on Broadway, it occurred to him that if he truly was to leave tomorrow night, there were duffel bags, canteens, and so on to buy, and bills to pay, and airline tickets to arrange; and there were passports, visas, hugs, tears, explanations, and many preparations to be made. T.R. was only sick and selfish to a point and on the stoop of his apartment—no, forget the stoop. Step inside and hear . . .

"Jon," he said to Landman's voice mail, sitting on a kitchen chair. "I'm not sure how to say this. It may be one of the hardest things I've ever said. But it's not fair to me, or my wife, to

---

*As Hemingway had gone to war, as Mailer had gone to war, as all the writers he adored who had gone to war had gone to war.

leave tomorrow night. It's too soon. I'm not going. Can't go. Won't go. I'm sorry. Call back. But in the meantime, take me off the list."

He then proceeded to the bar where he consumed—without pause and in a most efficient manner—a pair of double bourbons, neat.

A half-hour later his pager started to buzz. The whiskey had just begun to take hold and T.R. considered it prudent business not to loosen its grip too much by looking after who had called.

Ten more minutes and it buzzed again. This time T.R. glanced to see that it was not Jon Landman calling but Jennifer Preston—the administrator of the *Times*'s coverage of Iraq. Gloomily, he wandered toward the pay phone prepared to take his lumps—would he be scolded? excommunicated? exiled to Connecticut? marooned at City Hall? Not at all: Preston, much to his surprise, was gentler than a lamb. Good gracious, Preston said, don't leave tomorrow night. Leave Tuesday night for goodness sake, or no, leave Wednesday—and please, please take your wife. (Ha, ha! Henny Youngman had come to crack a joke!) And yet it was no joke. This offering from Preston was for real. T.R. was amazed. For it was nothing but amazing that the surest way to win concessions from the *Times* was to raise one's moral hackles: A behemoth, though a liberal behemoth, the *Times* was still susceptible to small fries wagging fingers in its face.

T.R.'s victory was small but secure. He now had four days in London with his wife. If he was headed off to battle in Iraq, it felt good in the extreme to leave without a battle here at home.

Chapter 2

GOAT FUCK

LONDON, AS IT happened, was the battle. If they were not exactly at each other's throats, they were upset, mutually upset—T.R.'s wife because he was preoccupied and distant, T.R. because his wife possessed the nerve to point these failings out. The act of feeling separate in each other's presence could, of course, be augured as an omen of their parting in a few more days, although it is just as likely that a four-day trans-Atlantic trip, like a ballgame called by rain, is too little of a lovely thing to be worthwhile. Still, they managed to view the Palace, drink at Irish pubs, and walk the gardens of St. James' Park. Their final day in town, they were thrilled at their hotel—the Crown St. James—to discover LeDuff at the check-in desk. (T.R. and his wife were good friends with LeDuff and his wife, and nearly at once the former decided this familiar face was just what they required to free themselves of their marital funk.)

At the hotel bar, LeDuff spoke of the week of military training he had just received from a team of SAS commandos in the countryside—a boot camp for the press that, seminar-style, could have borne the title "How Not to Get One's Ass Shot Off in Seven Days or Less." T.R. had attended something similar with the Marines at Command Base Quantico, Virginia. Largely for insurance purposes, the chieftains of the press had paid top dollar for their armies of reporters to be taught the rudiments of land navigation, tent pitching, combat medicine, latrine construction, and infantry technique. ("In case of nuclear attack, place feet toward blast and kiss ass good-bye!") There had also been helicopter rides and a course in how to use the gas mask. (T.R. found it fearsome strange that, half his family having died at Auschwitz, he had willingly—no, happily—entered the chamber with his mask.) It was all good preparation for the war, said LeDuff, but it had mostly been a chance for cutting-up.*

LeDuff was a tall, good-looking native of Detroit with a class clown's ribald nature, somewhat wild, always entertaining, whose taste for the outrageous hid the fact he owned the heart of a man who may have put in thirty years of swing shifts at the Ford plant. Yet, with his goateed mug and stylish dress, he looked, if anything, like Paco, dealer from Miami Beach.

National correspondent in Los Angeles and the inventor of the paper's much-loved Bending Elbows bar report (which had

---

*The average news reporter "cut up" on a regular basis. Tasteless jokes were his bread and butter, and a self-conscious, manufactured variety of hard-boiled disaffection served as the primary system of emotional defense. At a crime scene in the Bronx, for instance, where a nine-year-old had been shot to death, T.R. prayed aloud with colleagues that the neighbors might say, for once, "We hated him" or else "The kid was annoying," instead of the usual recitation of shock and praise. "You know," the guy from the *Daily News* went on, "we could do a front page saying, DEAD TOT HAD IT COMING: LOCAL BOY A SHIT, NEIGHBORS SAY. Wouldn't that be refreshing?" Hearing LeDuff recount his adventures with the SAS, T.R. imagined there would be many an opportunity for cutups in Iraq.

led T.R. and him into many strange adventures, the latter as the evening's comic talent, the former as the straight man of the team) LeDuff was already planning capers for Iraq. Over drinks, he explained that he would write about Marines, whorehouses, corpses—everything visceral and vivid—and talked with a passionate foul mouth of desiring no less than to knock his stories out of the fucking park.

The bar was in a back room of the quaint hotel, and gave off a quiet tension, much the same quality that was plaguing T.R. in relation to his wife. Indeed, as LeDuff went on, there was a pause in conversation as the three old friends conspired to sip their drinks through a murderous dip in talk. As he often did, LeDuff stepped in to fill this silence, telling dirty jokes. What difference if they were not all that funny after all? They got one past the fatal moment.

Thus recovered, LeDuff was explaining that the war would be "a goat fuck." Unlike in Afghanistan, in this war, the Pentagon had managed to co-opt the press through the embedding process—a brilliant move that rewrote the old saw to the tune of the Stockholm Syndrome: "If you cannot beat them, take them hostage and make them love you." Upwards of seven hundred news reporters would follow in the military's wake. This did not include the others—the unilaterals, so they were called—who would bide their time in Turkey, Jordan, Syria, Saudi Arabia, Kuwait, or Iran before rushing into Baghdad when the city finally fell. Even in London, the thought of Baghdad swarming with pockmarked correspondents and boozy producers, each one scratching for a story in the same half-inch of dirt, placed an undeniable chill in T.R's heart. Discussing the ins and outs of this mess, he and LeDuff agreed that all they wanted, and it wasn't much, were two small stakes of virgin soil on which to work.

At present both men were slated to embed, LeDuff with the First Cavalry Division, which his brother had served with coincidentally for a tour, and T.R. with the First Armored, Old Ironsides, which in the first Gulf War had made a ninety-hour blitz across the desert. The two were pleased with their assignments, these were frontline units, and their strategy, as it developed at the bar, was to record the intimacies of the fighting, not the overarching context of the war. As best they could, they would avoid reportorial harrumphing—"Under the glare of mortar and artillery fire, Bravo Company moved toward Hilla yesterday . . ."—and they would avoid the mob. Should the great white whale of the media spread its fatty ballast in their stories, they in turn would hang back, eel-like, and strike at the tiny tales—what the troops might say as they rolled into battle, how the chow tasted, or else the sounds of the desert on a silent night. They had been training for just this sort of thing. Their careers had been spent in the margins of the news, on page B5 to put it bluntly, where everything depended on the details—or, as LeDuff now said, the "deets." That was one way to avoid the mob. The other was to find what they had come to call *a guy*. On metro stories *a guy* might be a sympathetic cop, a happy bum, or an eloquent drunk—someone through whose eyes a story might be told in human terms. In Iraq, *guys* would come from the ranks of the troops. "Always go left," LeDuff advised, signaling the barkeep. "When the crowd goes right, go left."

T.R. said, "No doubt." He knew this was good advice, but also knew its limitations. One of the absurdities of this war would surely be the follies of the press. With such a mass of stumbling reporters on the ground in the war zone, the media would surely be the message. And yet the crowd, he thought, like anything else viewed properly, held fascinations of its own.

By now it was after eight, the dinner hour, and they found a restaurant near Leicester Square that was dark, French, and pleasantly busy. London, with its tables filled, bore little sign of war. The faint salts of its harmless air, its lingering sense of fustiness (the youth of London, or the rich white youth, seemed comfortable and plump), its boundless peace, its royal gardens, even its ill-concealed superiority (like a pale aristocrat who barely tolerates your impudence at tea) held nothing of the brewings overseas. Over dinner, T.R. drank a bit more than he should have: He was reaching for solidity. London's fog had somehow got in his brain and the war seemed far away. Like the city itself, he could not convince himself of the nearness of the storm.

In fact, for years he had sought to rid himself of just this sort of dreaminess. He often noticed, for example, that he lacked attention to the details (yes, the deets!) and had the damnable habit of seeing into all sides, all angles, until his vision was completely blurred. In charitable moods, he flattered himself that he possessed what Scott Fitzgerald had once called the mark of a first-rate intellect—the ability to hold in mind, at once, two completely opposite ideas. But there were more occasions on which he knew that he was callow, uncommitted, craving the certainty of bold ideas. Walking home that night, the thought had dawned on him that the war might hold a cure for this disease. Surely, it would drive some spike of cold reality into his brain. (A brain that sometimes might go days without a thought about the world. It was strange for a reporter, was it not?) He had no choice but to accept this schizophrenia, for clearly it was his. Clearly, it was his next morning when he placed his wife in a taxicab for Heathrow, feeling sad but much relieved, morose but eager. Once she left he bought a pack of cigarettes, went up to his room, took a shower, dressed, and straightened his bags—needless, nervous tasks, for sure, but then he was alone now, inching ever closer to his leaving in a few more days for the Middle East.

Chapter 3

DRINKING WITH HIPSTERS

H E W A S N O T alone for long. Later that evening, LeDuff called to suggest a drink.

T.R. was not in the mood for drinking, at least not public drinking. He could have stood a whiskey at the hotel bar, but even that was questionable. If anything did not blend well with bourbon, it was self-pity; if gloominess were added to the mix, the perils were increased. He therefore accepted the invitation with a measure of reluctance. In the absence of his wife, T.R. felt gloomy (her departure boded lonely nights to come, but more importantly his *own* departure). His gloominess was all the worse when LeDuff informed him that a friend now planned to join them, a friend who had invited friends of his own.

"They're sort of hipster types," LeDuff had said. "Come on, we'll have a gas."*

---

*The pattern of his evenings with LeDuff had been set on their first night out together, years ago, when, at an art show in Brooklyn, they had wrestled one another on the street. T.R. could not recall if there had been an argument—

At any rate, it was not good news about the hipsters. T.R. had always disliked hipsters. In zoological terms, he meant the sort of young, attractive, wealthy, clever, high-ironic city type to be found in any of several Lower East Side ratholes with a feed-store gimme cap, a vintage T-shirt, a job in the production end of anything, a habit for quoting television shows, and a bad Chinese tattoo. One could slice them in a hundred ways, it did not matter; like the towns they were raised in, they lacked some hard rich core of personality, some iron ore of self. So they were reaching, always reaching, for identity, for history, for the lost remote control. Even their politics were much the same—they reached for them like hand-me-downs. Just last month T.R. had seen a group of hipsters at an anti-war march in New York. There they were—Greens, queers, whalers, Naderites, pro-Palestinians, anti-globalists, free-trade haters, late converts to Marx—they had that patchwork quality of a freshman campus activity fair. As they marched down Second Avenue, a fire truck had tried to cut through the crowd on its way to fight a fire. The hipsters, assuming that any city vehicle with lights and sirens was an evil detachment, had thus seen fit to block its progress. This very company had lost a half-dozen men on 9/11. And when the firemen hollered out that there were lives

---

it was likely they had simply fought. Boorish pranks, fueled by alcohol, became their modus operandi. On one occasion, a Friday night, they scaled the walls of the Columbia Journalism School, having seen lights burning in a study hall, and shouted to whoever had been toiling away at the weekend to come out, come out, and join the world. They shared the recognition that a pair of grown men, under the influence of whiskey and adolescent antics, could never have more fun than while doing things they would later disavow to their wives. T.R. and LeDuff brought out the worse in one another, although it might have been the best.

in danger—move!—the hipsters hollered back that the firemen were . . . *fascists!*

Having grown up east of Cleveland, T.R. had watched a score of his high-school classmates graduate from college, head for cities like London and New York, and there become hipsters. It seemed the thing to do. That he had never done so was attributable to his peculiar relation with the past. A hipster longed for the nostalgia of his childhood, but T.R. longed for the childhoods of men now dead for half a century or more. That evening, on the Tube to Hackney, he had felt a twinge of envy at the station names appearing on the map—Wembley, Piccadilly, Kilburn, Willesden Green. They seemed to come from another era; they were certainly unlike the stations of his childhood, Lee, Ashby, Drexmore, East Seventy-ninth. They were authentic London, chummy ascot London. This bar in Hackney, which they entered now by a narrow, ill-lit, shabby flight of stairs, was London of a different sort.

It was no great show. The bar was a boxy cavern of a room with concrete floors, purple lighting, and the sort of spare décor that says, What need for furniture when you are cool? The drinkers were mostly black men, Africans and Islanders, some skinny thrift-store whites, and a few attractive girls, some very attractive, who seemed to have come straight from jobs at high-end advertising firms and glossy magazines. The men—the whites especially—bounced to the music in jerky motion that seemed some strained Caucasian metaphor of funk. Only the blacks seemed natural, webbing the women with their moves or letting them writhe atop the sofas of their cool. Not for nothing did T.R. avoid hipster bars. The vintage clothing, Ecstasy, and afro-beats were not his world. (It should be said as well that he was ten years older than the crowd and, justly so, they made him feel like a crank.)

So there he was with LeDuff and his friends, who were also older than the crowd. One was a slender academic sort named James, who made his living teaching and writing on "the sporting life." He wore thick Buddy Holly glasses and had taken a first in English *litrachuh* at Oxford, or maybe Cambridge, where he had made acquaintances with Tom, a bankerish blond with whom he had played on the cricket squad. Tom made his own money in a high-minded corner of the finance game, but he was likable. The third of the group was Steve—shortly to be known as Steve-o!—a lank, light-skinned black man who owned an Internet firm and claimed to have the power to elicit rainstorms with his mind. All in all, an ecumenical group that had as commonalities a programmatic liberal bent, a taste for good books, wives and girlfriends with socially progressive careers, and a firmly principled stance against the war.

Even now James handed T.R. a beer, an opportunity he used to sniff the reporter's ass about the war. It was not indecision that made T.R. hedge his bets. By then, he was working on his third round and had recalled Jake Barnes's admonition not to let emotions spoil your drink. This, of course, was a cop-out: T.R. was indecisive as to the war's complexity because its complicated origins made easy answers so alluring. In fact, he had arrived at the thought that the war in Iraq was not an oil-grab or a fight for liberation, as the hipsters had alleged, but rather something altogether on a different plane.

As he conceived of it, the war was being fought on two separate planes. The first—the realist plane, it could be said—had been hatched inside the brain of some strategic coterie within the

Pentagon that had decided that the status quo no longer worked in the Middle East. The Middle East was broken, and it needed fixing. Forward-thinking, breathlessly ambitious, and completely unafraid to use the country's gathered might, these men had decided the United States could no longer trust the Saudis, was in need of a new military base and a newfound source of oil. What better option than Iraq for such a base: Iraq was in the center of the map, blessed with oil, a pariah state unloved by everyone, including many Arabs, and had already gassed some thousands of its own, therefore offering a compelling rationale for the attack.

The realists had well-developed reasons for invading, whereas the moralists—the second plane—had worked on the push of instinct alone. Led by a president with an instinct for instincts, the moralists had felt no solid rationale to fight; instead they felt the need to send a message. And the message they desired to send was from the gut—it claimed that the United States would brook no bloody nose, that far from being decadent or weak, it would answer every threat with a swift decisive blow.

The war in Iraq was therefore both a carefully considered plan *and* a barroom brawl. It was confusing, which is why T.R. had sidestepped James's question. Now running the risk of looking like a fool, he tried to lumber past the moment, summoning machismo from his beer. "The situation is completely FUBAR overseas," he said.

"FUBAR?" James asked.

"Yeah, fucked up beyond all recognition," T.R. said, his built-in shit detector going off. The instrument (lifted from Hemingway on the same raid that garnered him the Jake Barnes quote) was sensitive to all occasions where he substituted bluster for propriety or covered up some indecision with a rude, foul-mouthed remark. Such remarks he used especially with hipsters. Hipsters styled themselves as rebels, claimed to celebrate the concupiscence of the sewer with such discursive flair that it was a pleasure to explode a well-placed *fuck* on the pastures of a good debate and watch their eyes go narrow, as if one had just squatted bare-assed to deposit a full intestinal load on the very quads of Yale. Now T.R. loved the sewer too—if anything, his writing for the paper bore this out—but he admitted that his character changed as often as an actor in a one-man play. If on occasion he reached for obscenity, a second later he might use a phrase so stiff or precious one might guess he had been educated in a rhetoric class at Eton. Bold declarations, bad jokes, stretched metaphors, and witticisms cribbed from smarter fellows than himself disfigured the surface of his conversation much like driftwood on a river, and his underlying mental state was never more like a marionette trying to control its own strings than when speaking with a hipster. The truth, of course, was that he feared being taken for a hipster and did his best to counteract their irony with earnestness, to humanize their most pontifical arguments with fistfuls of shit—that is, he zigged when they zagged, broke left whenever they broke right. (It was at this point in his perorations that his wife would often tell him to shut up.)

"Pip me!" LeDuff said. "Come on, boys, Pip me!"

T.R. turned. Across the room LeDuff had started lip-synching like Gladys Knight, peering over his shoulder at Tom and Steve-o spinning their hands in a desperate attempt to resemble the Pips. Soon after, he organized a conga line of aging hipsters: Tom, Steve-o, even James had joined by now. The young hipsters did not partake in the reveling. They danced on, coolly ignoring the older men who snaked between them.

Leave it to LeDuff to demonstrate with a brief four-minute conga line what it had taken T.R. paragraphs to say: One had to take oneself, at all times, with a healthy grain of salt.

LeDuff, whose energies were nothing less than startling, touched, as they were, with lightning quickness, depth, vigor, endurance, and a herky-jerky grace like a college football halfback unleashed across the field, was already entertaining thoughts of where to take the party next. "Steve-o thinks we ought to go to Brixton," he was saying at the bar. "What do you think?"

"I don't know. Steve-o says he's only half black."

"Steve-o, is it true you're only half black?"

Confused looks from Steve-o. Dark and mildly irritated looks.

"To Steve-o!"

"To Steve-o!"

"To Steve-o!"

Their glasses in the air.

Soon they would be off and running. T.R. knew he would have to counteract the virus fast. He was quick to realize—for he had seen it many times—that without the proper antidote the manic juice in LeDuff's heart would spread through his entire system. It would render him insane.

Before the antidote could be administered, however, something happened. A large Arab bumped into LeDuff at the bar and LeDuff, waiting for the man's apology, placed himself directly in his face. The two stood nose to nose, breath to breath, LeDuff demanding an excuse me, the Arab refusing. Nodding at the door, it was LeDuff who suggested that perhaps they ought to step outside. The Arab readily accepted.

"I will kill you," the Arab whispered now, drawing a finger past his throat. "I will kill you dead."

"Look, Ali, you're messing with the wrong motherfucker."

"What's going on?" asked James, curious as to what the noise was. "What on earth is Charlie saying to that man?"

"He just said Ali messed with the wrong motherfucker."

"What—are they going to fight?" James asked, a tremor of the palest English terror in his voice. Tom had edged a little closer, wanting to be privy but keeping a comfortable distance. Steve-o, meanwhile, had vanished. "Don't you think," James said, appearing to swallow and exhale at once, "don't you think we ought to break them up?"

It was put forth that active pacifism might do more harm than good. At this stage, T.R. ventured, it was better to let things run their course. He trusted LeDuff. Moreover, there were betting odds that if James intervened, he might end up with a broken nose. No, it was best to keep a watchful eye on the proceedings, then to step in should stepping-in be needed.

So T.R. watched. In truth, he felt small confidence in his decision. He was not convinced of the inherent wisdom of a bar fight. It was also clear that to tussle with an Arab might easily be mistaken in the politics of the present day. Of course, by now he had a personal stake in the matter. Satisfaction having been demanded, the principals were casting about for seconds—if T.R. was LeDuff's choice, the Arab's eye had fallen on his large, spectacularly muscled friend. "I drew *you*, ha, ha?" T.R. imagined saying on the street with a diversionary prick of humor. Still, he could report he felt no fear. Rather, he felt a quiet resignation that a solid beating might soon be thrown his way.

This inner dialogue required the time it took for LeDuff to pull back from the Arab and saunter toward the door. T.R. went with him, not sauntering, and hoping his behavior would not prove weak, embarrassing, or inauthentic, or reemerge in a later version of a bloopers film.

Now they were outside. The cobblestones of Hackney were uneven, wet, darkly industrial. The only light was from a small falafel joint across the street.

"You ready?" LeDuff asked in his gamest voice. He bent down to touch his toes. "Where did James and Tom go? Where's Steve-o? What a bunch of pussies," he exclaimed.

T.R. was certain LeDuff meant this. But he had also observed on occasion that LeDuff could be dared into a fight. It was insufficient that his image advertised his toughness; sometimes the advertisement needed to be reinforced with upraised dukes. Even the outcome hardly mattered. A pretty shiner, after all, did wonders for one's name.

It suddenly occurred to him this quirk held metaphoric insight on Iraq. The American nation was in the hands of cowboys now, roughs, toughs, bugle-blowers, acolytes of the aggressive pose. These men had never been through combat, nor had they felt firsthand the nullities of war. And so a gap existed between their rhetoric and their experience. To close the gap required one of two eventualities: an increase in experience or a decrease in rhetoric. Because America was at the apex of its power and because these men were not the type to carry sticks while speaking softly, subdued rhetoric seemed out of the question. However, they could always raise the bar of their experience by embarking on a war . . .

No doubt this was terribly unfair to LeDuff, who, according to the evidence, was not outside for the sake of his name but rather because he was genuinely pissed (in both the British and American sense). Let us not forget it was T.R. who had scooted into the night concerned by his own behavior. The problem was that he had not partaken in a fight for several years. There had been scraps, shouting matches, and a few adrenaline-flooded standoffs, but as with any physical activity one has long forsaken, T.R. hoped that all his body parts would work.

Courage may indeed be nothing grander than devotion to the moment, but try as he might to be courageous, his brain kept slipping through the cracks of the future. Even as the taxis—big, black, boxy British taxis—pulled to the curb and deposited a fresh load of hipsters, T.R. felt insides going jelly. "You think they're actually coming?" he asked. He disliked the sound of his own voice now—it was plaintive, worried, pinched by a whine. "I don't think they're coming out."

The question was sincere, but its effect was like a breeze that lifts a curtain to reveal a masturbator hard at work. T.R. was caught, the slow leak of his anxiety had been revealed. But LeDuff ignored the flub. "So what," he said with generosity. "If they don't come out, it's the same as having beat them, right?"

After ten or fifteen minutes, it was clear the Arab and his second had refused the challenge. (How T.R. adored these masculine complexities. The intrigues of Rome were never more arcane than the goings-on between two buddies on the street.) Momentarily the hipsters came to join them and the two reporters took the opportunity to gloat. Telling their story from the start, they made specific reference to having waited in the rain for their opponents—for indeed it was raining now, London's specialty, a cold, thin, mealy peacoat rain. But Steve-o cut them off, in fact he seemed impatient: If he had known there was to be a brawl, he said, he would have been there.

"I'm quite good with my hands," Steve-o smirked, laying them with some strange provocation onto T.R.'s shoulders. T.R.

shrugged instinctively to test his grip and then, with a quick wrestler's pivot, spun to tackle Steve-o's legs—with a chuff, they both went down. Soon they were rolling on the sidewalk, back over back, arms, legs, cheekbones pressed to Hackney's ground.

No doubt psychologists among the audience will raise their eyebrows to suggest T.R. was merely seeking to erase his prior cowardice by grappling with Steve-o. But they would only be a quarter to a third correct. In fact, there was a larger point to make. The fullness of his motive had its roots in a conversation that had taken place beyond the earshot of the reader—in the bar, Steve-o had made a passing comment on the foppishness (his word) of men employed by papers like the *Times*. He had taken pleasure in comparing himself to such men, and kept insisting that if they *worked* on the streets, well, he had been *raised* on the streets—a distinction he connected to his downright remarkable talent for attracting women and assured skills in hand-to-hand combat. At any rate, Steve-o was not-so-subtly asserting dominance, and T.R. had the unmistakable impression he'd been branded a wimp. He was shocked. If he were a wimp, he might have let the insult slide from his tweeds, but he was nothing of the sort. (He didn't even own a set of tweeds.) So he decided to be shrewd. Instead of going after Steve-o with an argument that might have begun by saying Steve-o was hardly fit to pick out anyone's supposed faults, having conceded the intellectual high ground, T.R. had lain in wait for the proper moment . . . to drive the poor man's cranium into the curb! Yes, T.R. could be a bugle-blower too. All it took was proper provocation. He had found that provocation in Steve-o's comments, which had implied that (1) all journalists were wimps, and that (2) this wimpishness was somehow related to their social class.

Since boyhood T.R. had been fatefully obsessed with class. No doubt the obsession was related to his middling status. He was too low to claim the haughty honors of the upper class, but still too high for the bitter pride of the working man. So he was trapped in the indeterminacy of the center, in the vast vat of the middle, where despite one's efforts to authenticate one's self with phrases such as might appear on highway signs to suburbs off the interstate—"Franklinburg: *Salt of the Earth*" or "Wankton Heights: *Heart and Soul of America*"—one was always and forever . . . normal. Yes, it was his own normalcy that so enraged T.R. and that erupted at the moment Steve-o had the gall to point it out. "If you must fight, never choose the little fellow sitting in a corner minding his own business," James J. Walker, former mayor of New York, had said. "Chances are he is the ex-welterweight champion of the world." One could only hope. In T.R.'s dream life, he would be that quiet man with the devastating punch, for what he wished most of all was to cut cross-wise against the grain of class; to partake in a cross-pollination. Content to be the plumber's son who went to Harvard or the second Duke of Gravy who resided in the street, he was neither. Instead he was the offspring of a middle-class, midwestern family who pursued the rote of the expected. He had graduated high school as expected, gone off to college as expected, found some suitable employment as expected—everything was expectation, assumed and met. And yet the middle class was home to more than expectation. It was home to ambition (with the fear of poverty below it and the promise of the leisured life above), and so T.R. had grown up burbling with a fierce desire to be something other than he was.

But then there was journalism. Under its mask, he could enter worlds of which he had no firsthand knowledge. What else had he been doing in the Bronx? The Bronx was the projects where a dealer once had showed him a photo of himself lying naked on the bed atop a pile of eighty-thousand dollars. It was the Grand Concourse where Shorty Jones stabbed to death his girlfriend. The medical examiner was smoking and accidentally tipped ash on the corpse, and said, "Fuck it. Ash to ash, dust to dust." Same with the Mafia—another world where he did not belong. And yet, with a pen and notebook, his entry was paid. (Once, on assignment for the gossip column, T.R. had entered the upper stratum. It was a cocktail party at the Plaza where Dr. Ruth had quoted Dr. Kissinger along the lines that, "Power is the ultimate aphrodisiac," unaware that Kissinger himself was standing in the room. Working up an angle, T.R. approached the diplomat to say Dr. Ruth was plagiarizing him, whereupon he sighed and said, "Zat line will haunt me for zee rest of my life . . .") Such were the pleasures of the middle-class reporter: He believed himself to be mobile and sought compensation for his normalcy in dips into the high and low. In fact, he was at best a guest, at worst a pawn. Under the happiest of circumstances it was irritating, but with Steve-o throwing the whole conundrum in his face like some kind of sociological cream pie, it had touched a nerve—and touched indeed, T.R. had jumped.

Nonetheless, T.R. now had Steve-o in what is commonly called the mounted pose. Victory was his, not to make too much of it. As an infrequent fighter, T.R. had suffered his share of losses, which is why he felt confirmed taking satisfaction from his win.

He would have to report he felt rather pleased with himself, and yet embarrassed. In a word he felt *awake*. It had not escaped T.R., even as he rolled with Steve-o, that the war was no more than the next in a line of middle-class diversions. It was perhaps the fullest flower of his desire to be somewhere, someone, else.

He therefore reached for Steve-o's hand and helped him from the ground, and took his offer of a ride to their hotel—it seemed the smartest course. LeDuff said goodnight to Tom and James, then together, they set off in Steve-o's car.

At the hotel they turned on the television set. It was 4 A.M. but both men had a taste for the news. T.R. switched to CNN as LeDuff cracked the mini-bar, choosing rum and coke. T.R. chose a beer. On separate beds, they listened to the headlines from Atlanta. To a backdrop of tanks in the Kuwaiti desert, the newscaster spoke of the failure of diplomacy and the inevitable outbreak of the war.

"We didn't fight the Arab, but we fought ourselves," LeDuff mused at the first commercial. "How's that for weird?"

"For weird, it's pretty good."

LeDuff shook his head. "Steve-*o*," he said beneath his breath.

"Did you hear when Steve-o dropped us off he was asking for a rematch? He wanted to fight in the elevator." He had actually said, the lift. Somehow T.R. felt responsible for this. It was as if he had watched his own foolishness enter Steve-o's body, take root there, goad him on, make him bray, whinny, twist his face—discovering a new host, the foolishness had than refused, contagion-like, to die.

"Well," said LeDuff, "next time you fight, make sure you're wearing that." And he nodded at the flak vest labeled PRESS beside the bed.

If ever there was a time to talk about the war, it was now, but T.R. would not, or could not, muster the attention. The commercial ended and the news returned: a live shot from Kuwait of the 101st Air Assault, camped out under sandstorm-blotted skies.

"Look at that!" LeDuff said.

"Their laundry blew away."

"Forget their laundry, the whole fucking tent is gone!"

"Poor bastards . . ."

"Who's with them? Dwyer?"

"*Is* it Dwyer? I don't know."

They watched TV until the footage changed.

"Well," T.R. began, standing, yawning, rubbing his eyes as if the very grit of the desert was in them. "I guess it's time for bed."

"We'll head over to the bureau in the morning," said LeDuff. "I want to grab a new satellite phone."

"I want to grab some goggles, if they have them," T.R. said. "I haven't got mine yet."

LeDuff looked at him askance.

"Don't worry. I'll pick them up tomorrow."

As he rode the elevator up, T.R. compiled a list of all the other things he did not have, and by the time he reached his empty fourth-floor room it was already worrisome and worrisomely long.

Chapter 4

LONDON CALLING

H E AWOKE NEXT morning with a hangover. It was not a crippling hangover where the brainpan suffers the electric shock of morning and the stomach is full of bitter grieving at the pleasures of the night; it was an ordinary, low-watt hangover that seemed to stuff his head with sand. He had slept in his clothes—that was bad—but shaved, showered, and re-attired, he managed to divest himself of the worst of the hangover and, like a sinner scrubbed for Sunday, went down to the hotel restaurant for breakfast. Breakfast had always been his favorite meal. It spoke to him of penance, possibility, the light of new beginnings—and under the influence of British coffee and the *Guardian* (pale substitutes for their American brethren) he began to feel that system-wide rejuvenation that often came to greet him with the day.

T.R. felt blessed to be a morning person. Nothing was better than to rise from bed and wander to the kitchen, to ingest the nectars of seven o'clock. If one added coffee and a paper to the mix, then it was better—one felt miraculously, even criminally, clean and awake. Several times he had entertained the thought that his career in the news was little more than an avatar of his abiding love for the presence of a paper on his breakfast table and that, consciously or not, he had taken the job at the *Times* so as to dwell in perpetuity within that passionate and civilized exactitude the news provided him each morning. If on this particular morning he was feeling less civilized than usual, no matter—a sparkling tonic was on its way. In another few minutes he would head over to the *Times's* London bureau. But one small thing concerned him. Tonic coming or tonic denied, he was still hung over as a bedsheet on a laundry line.

The bureau lay across the street from his hotel and he walked over Buckingham Gate with the blinking aspect of a vagrant who has spent the evening in a cave. With no small effort, he signed his name to the lobby logbook where the uniformed attendant bid him good morning. In the elevator, his delinquency was reinforced by the mirrored walls that scolded him at each floor with his own bedraggled image. Outside the bureau door, he paused, feeling it wise to conduct a swift bodily inventory. He checked his breath—the sour rebellion of last night's beer had been quashed by toothpaste. Next he took a quick exploratory whiff of the pits to find no damning trace of odor. In all, T.R. felt as if he had regressed to the eleventh grade (not for nothing did the newsroom in New York remind him of a high-school cafeteria full of hives, ticks, acne, rampant insecurity, status checks, and furtive looks) and he scolded himself for being such a ninny. On his head was a pea-green watch cap—his one unmitigated personal flair. Now he cocked it toward a jaunty angle and made his way inside.

In brief, the London bureau of the *New York Times* gave the impression of a lucrative midwestern dental practice. Its large reception desk, its recessed lighting, and its scattered periodicals all hinted of dull terrors that occur in unseen rooms. The corner suite, appropriately windowed, belonged to the bureau chief, while the lesser minions of the news made do with upholstered cubicles stocked with telephones, computers, and high-speed Internet connections. T.R. found it exceedingly depressing. Ever the romantic, he had assumed the London bureau—a phrase of fog and tea, indeed—would have possessed at least a splash of European charm. It did not. Standing in the dull fluorescent gloom, it occurred to him in fact there was a link between the slow demise of the news reporter and his work space. In the same way newsmen were no longer hacks with semiautomatic mouths, so too were news bureaus no longer speakeasies filled with obscenity and booze. The street smarts, the tobacco stains, the *bullshit*, all of it was gone, replaced by the plastic hush of the waiting room. Where he had expected Dunhill smoke and parliamentarians huddled over gin, he had found instead the offices of Kenneth Nussbaum, DDS.

And yet that vanished past was palpable to him. T.R. knew of it, he had read of it, had even sought it out. In A. J. Liebling, for example, the *New Yorker* writer: "Prior to October 1938, my only friends were prizefighter's seconds, Romance philologists, curators of tropical fish, kept women, promoters of spit-and-toilet paper nightclubs, bail bondsmen, press agents for wrestlers, horse clockers, newspaper reporters, and female psychiatrists." What a thrill to spot a news reporter on that list beside a horse clocker, three steps down from a bail bondsman! Impossible today. Today, the news reporter would be listed there among the other pale professionals, the academics and the corporate lawyers, and yet it had not always been that way. T.R.'s mentor, Nora Sayre, had been the daughter of a newsman for the New York *World*, Joel Sayre, who had worked in the era when reporters were assigned famous gangsters as a beat. Sayre had been assigned Legs Diamond, the Albany boss whose claim to fame was getting shot on New Year's Eve. This was in the day when members of the press were still allowed to visit gangsters in the hospital. What then could be better than the stories Nora told about her father standing at Legs's bedside as Legs came out of surgery and, much like Edward Robinson as Little Caesar, said, "Hello there, Sayre. Good to see you. Looks as if those bastards missed again . . ."*

Like all good dental practices, however, the London bureau had a coffeemaker—there it sat in the tiny kitchenette—and T.R. headed for it now, and quickly too, for he is obliged to note that three steps into the place he suddenly found himself the victim of an insurrection from his gut. Nausea, that sly guerrilla force, was steadily advancing on his belly even as dyspepsia was marshaling its armies in the rear. All sludges shifting, T.R. ordered a retreat. He withdrew from the lobby, fell back past the

---

*T.R. had met Nora at a writing class she taught at Columbia. They became friends, an odd couple—he, a young enthusiastic freshman; she, an established author in her sixties. They often met for drinks or went to the movies. "What's the gossip?" she would ask when they got together over wine. She had never extricated herself from the intrigues of the newsroom. Born to parents who split their time between the New York journalism world and Hollywood, Nora had been raised with writing. She worked as the New York correspondent for *The New Statesman* and had written several books. A. J. Liebling was her mentor. Nora's conversation, delivered in a joyous, clucking, Anglophilic voice, was chocked with earthy observations and historical references. A Chinese dinner in her company never failed to send T.R. scurrying off to the encyclopedia. He never understood what he provided in exchange for the free-wheeling education of her barside seminars. Perhaps longevity. Nora died on August 8, 2001, of emphysema. She was sixty-eight.

water cooler, and rushed into the kitchen with a single thought in mind: A cup of coffee was the sole defense to keep attack at bay.

It was not so easy as you might imagine. On its surface, the London bureau may have resembled something to be found in a Milwaukee strip mall; still it was the premiere foreign outpost of the *New York Times*. The hard drives, modems, monitors, and scanners had been purchased from the highest ranks of high technology. The coffee machine was of an equal ilk. No mere pot or percolator, it seemed to him a puzzlement of buttons, hoses, spouts, lights, plastic cups, and packagettes of freeze-dried grounds. It spoke of fuel-injected carburetion, not the morning's simple brew.

In short, T.R. could not get the goddamned thing to work. (Do not forget he was a man for whom the cell phone was anathema.) Nevertheless, keen to make a good impression, he felt a stubborn surge of pride and refused on principle to cast about for help. Pride, however, is the assassin of the amateur, a type who in his ignorance believes that earnest application of his powers will suffice. The less he comprehends, the more complete is the amateur's assurance he can master any task. Why then annoy himself and others by asking for advice?

Thus swollen with pride, hoping that a cup of coffee might restrain the combat in his gut, T.R. was unaware that he stood fifteen steps from imminent embarrassment.

Approaching was a man in a collared shirt and necktie, a journalist no doubt, for the man had the stooped shoulders and the I've-been-shat-on look that often accompanies a long career at the *New York Times*. He was tall, slim, elegant, middle fifties, sandy-haired, with a keen equine face and the pallor of a minor British diplomat—perhaps in a former life he had served with the Foreign Office and been dismissed for mishandling government funds or a bit of hanky-panky with the Secretary's wife.

In any case, the coffeemaker took the moment of this man's arrival to spray a hot brown mess on T.R.'s pants. No chance for escape—the hallway was much too narrow. Besides, the man had seen. He had seen T.R. do battle with the thing. Seen it take its sly revenge. Seen the coffee stains, the soiled pants, the failed attempt to wipe them clean. He had even seen the ridiculous pea-green watch cap, which even now he was assessing with a dry displeased hauteur and a skeptical gaze that fairly seemed to ask, "My word, will they let anyone into the country club these days?"

"I'm Warren Hoge," he said. "The bureau chief."

At this moment, it is permissible to wonder at the thoughts in T.R.'s head. Hoge was staring at him with a quality of bald discernment. It was no stare of confusion; no, he knew exactly who this young man was. It was rather the surly stare of the headmaster forced to reprimand the disobedient troops. Headmaster-like indeed, Hoge had been awaiting him in London. There had been faxes, e-mails, late-night messages—the central cortex of the *New York Times* had beamed its orders over the ocean that a novice correspondent was arriving; it had given Hoge the mission to invest this man with the treasures of the paper, its vaulted gold—airline tickets, laptops, power chargers, power strips, power converters, power itself—and yet to whom? To a bespectacled young runt of a reporter who had never filed a story overseas?

T.R. could smell the musty odor of Hoge's disappointment down the hall. And yet Hoge had a right to feel this way. There was madness in the paper's plans to let a novice like T.R. cover the war. The last story he had written was the four-hundred-word obituary of a travel agent who transformed his "modest storefront underneath the elevated train in the Bronx into the world's largest operator of escorted tours to Italy." (Yes! "Mario Perillo, the silver-haired tour operator whose raspy television pitch, 'Go Perillo to Italy,' persuaded more than a million Americans to visit that country, died Friday at his home in Saddle River, N.J. He was 76. The cause was cancer, his family said . . .") Forty correspondents and photographers had been dispatched to London, there to venture forth to Arab nations, bide their time on flight decks, at the Intercon, in desert wadis, to sneak across the border, infiltrate Islamic armies, sweat (and maybe die) with the Marines. T.R. was the youngest and the greenest of the lot. He knew nothing of Iraq. No, he knew exactly three things. Before departing for the country, T.R. knew it had once been known as Babylon, that its capital was Baghdad, and its ruler, soon to be deposed, was named Saddam. Thus he greeted Hoge with the ingratiating smile of a new recruit, spoke some cheerful self-effacing words, said happily that he looked forward to the great adventure now before him, and pulling down his jacket to disguise the stain that announced his clumsiness, leaned back against a bookshelf, knocked a dictionary to the floor, and, stooping to retrieve it, nearly brought the whole thing down.

"Well, yes, it's wonderful to have you here," Hoge said, observing this with a cringing self-control. "I always like to keep in touch with the . . . ah . . . younger generation. Tell me about yourself."

T.R. had no idea what to say, but willed himself to describe his journey at the paper: the mob, the courts, the various assignments in the Bronx. In truth, he was stalling. The coffee meant to calm his nerves had instead been poured on his lap—he was still hoping to obtain another cup. More to the point, he had wanted to slip into the bureau unnoticed, grab a few more bits of gear (he was not immune to the pleasures of the stuff), and take a gander at its *Times*ian allure (nor was he immune to that). Now, however, he was caught. The harmless pleasures he had planned for this, the morning of his hangover, had been hijacked by his gastric tract and Warren Hoge, who listened to him now as one might listen to the clinically insane. Hoge's lips bore the hints of a dwindling patience—he was plainly sorry to have asked. T.R., in turn, tried to save the moment with a touch of humor. The paper, he said, seemed to think that covering the Bronx was fair training for covering Iraq.

"It's practically a war zone in itself"—ha, ha!—he chuckled with a grin.

Hoge seemed to connect with the analogy. The Bronx to him was Yankee Stadium and Puerto Ricans, perhaps the place where all good Christians locked their doors at night. At best, it would salt the metro pages with a rich whiff of its ethnic flavors. Hoge in fact was too sage to consider this a joke. "So it's your first time overseas?" he asked, not quite grinning back.

"My first time *working* overseas."

"Well, yes, of course," Hoge grinned again—intimations that T.R. was certainly a rube.

Now the bureau chief withdrew a small object from his pocket and began to clip his nails. Standing in the hallway, Hoge moved on to inquiries of when and how T.R. might ship off to the Middle East.

"Your final destination, I assume, is Baghdad?"—all the while conducting a distracted manicure of his slender outstretched hand.

The question, innocent enough, became a cul de sac, or rather a roundabout, for Hoge, clipping, checking his labor, clipping more, then filing rough spots and depositing the trimmings on the floor, now said: "John Burns is in Baghdad, you know. Do you know Burns? God, I remember, it was years ago"—clip, clip—"that Burns was arrested in China and I had to bail him out. Actually, Max Frankel and I had to bail him out. We both had to fly literally"—*litch-rully*—"into the heart of Communist Beijing because Burns, God knows, had ridden his motorcycle through some forbidden Chinese military zone—well, we finally got him out, but suffice to say, it was a staggering ordeal. Oh yes, Burns is quite a character. Still, we're close, quite close. You'll certainly meet him," clip, clip, clip.

It went on like that for five more minutes—T.R. nodding, smiling, acting nervous and polite; Warren Hoge digressing into politics—"Well, the last time I saw the prime minister, when I was actually *with* him . . ." and the like.

At some point both men spotted Charlie LeDuff walking toward them down the hallway—a statement that is both misleading and only partly true. It is misleading because it gives the impression that Hoge and T.R. saw LeDuff at the same time, but that was not the case. The bureau chief was still with the prime minister, and did not notice LeDuff until he caught T.R. in the awkward act of shifting his gaze. For his own part, LeDuff was not quite walking toward them—rather, he was trying at a distance to attract T.R.'s attention. In his grip was a copy of the paper. The front page, global herald of infinite bad news, appeared to have some message to impart.

It was now a matter of breaking free of Hoge, though that was no great task. Hogue was obviously skilled at leaving rooms and excusing himself to hosts; he had been doing it for years. Now that he had seen LeDuff, it could be said he concluded their discussion like a cabinet minister called from cocktails;

there was some brief hint of the same inflated grace. He had to be off, he muttered. The BBC was coming soon to interview him. And shaking hands, he flashed a smile straight from the pages of early Kipling—"Beware the savages, old bean"—and advised T.R. to keep his head down in Iraq.

The following is an excerpt from a story headlined "U.S. Plan Sees GI's Invading as More Arrive" that ran on page A1 of that day's *Times*. At this point, coffee gotten, T.R. has read it once. With LeDuff at his shoulder, he is reading it again:

. . . Three powerful units—the First Cavalry Division, the First Armored Division and the Third Armored Cavalry Regiment— are still in the United States or Europe and will not be in the Persian Gulf region until mid to late April, intended as a postwar stabilization force . . .

Mid to late April? Yes, the message was clear. They were going to miss the war.

"Fuck," said LeDuff.

"A postwar stabilization force?"

"Fuck," said LeDuff. "Fuck. That's fucking us."

Fucked indeed, the two reporters took the paper to the bureau terrace and stepped outside, their well-laid plans scattered like an infantry platoon in need of cover, and sought relief in the unfulfilling solace of a smoke. Mid to late April? Christ! Their vivid articles about the troops in combat, there on the dusty road to Baghdad, the culminating battle of the war . . . let history and all the hacks in Washington determine if the country's might was a force for good or ill, but let the real reporters in the trenches write about the guns, the guys, the gear, good Lord, the *gear*.

All wasted—no choice but to sit around and wait. There it was, extra, extra! It was goddamn fit to print. They were going to miss the war.

They stood exhaling smoke above the rooftops of London. It was sunny, cheerful, mild—the unexpected easement of a blue-skied British day. The weather entered T.R.'s heart. He felt enraged, but also felt relief. *He was going to miss the war.* Suddenly, his brain packed his bags, called a taxi, whisked him to the airport, flew him home, embraced his wife, showered, fed the cats, went out to dinner, expressed a noncommittal disappointment to his friends, drank bourbon, ambled home, ignored entreaties from the bedroom, switched on the television set, and watched with every jealous nerve of wounded pride on fire the great electric oozing eye of the media reporting live from Baghdad every rocket burst and catastrophic shell.

No, he would not go home. He *could* not go home. There was something out there waiting for him in the desert, something nonnegotiable and cruel. It was a force to make him grow; it was an urgency that would confront all fears and inner slack. He almost had it now, or rather it had him, for the force was like a powerful hand that would punch through his scrims of dreaminess, evasion, comfort, laxness . . . Yes, it was a *hand*! Perhaps it was even a fist, the clenched fist of the world come to cold-cock his naïveté, come to deal a knock-out blow to every lingering childhood haunt. T.R. found he was relieved to miss the war, to hear the bout was canceled. Still, he knew that in the dressing room, far from the arena, there awaited him the double-breasted goons of his own conscience (so to speak). It would come to blows in either case—he knew it. Better then to make for the ring and choose the wound that healed.

"Look," he said to LeDuff, "we have to get the desk to send us *somewhere*, at least to the neighborhood," his courage rising on the phrase's terse demotic ring. Slowly he could feel a sense of sureness coming back—and plucked another cigarette from LeDuff's pack. He had entered a strategic mode by now, bolstered by the calm lucidities of nicotine. If nothing else, they would smoke their way into a plan.

"Yes," T.R. exhaled. "We have to call New York."

"All right."

"You want to do it?"

"Sure."

Butts stubbed, they agreed. Entering the bureau from the terrace, LeDuff picked up the phone.

"[Editor], please," he told the clerk when the foreign desk answered. "Tell her it's London calling." Nudge, wink, wink. "Tell her it's LeDuff."

Nervous expectation. A trans-Atlantic pause.

"[Editor], it's Charlie," he began. "No, I'm still in London"—here he flashed a disbelieving eye—"no, he's right here, too." Good Charlie! They were partners to the end! "[Editor]," he said, for it was time to make his point, "have you seen the paper? The units we're embedded with, they aren't moving till the end of April—no, the *end* of April. Look, you have to send us somewhere, you have to send us to the neighborhood," he said, launching an assault that pleased T.R., for as rhetorical ordinance it used the same phrase he had used, "the neighborhood—the *Middle East*." He strained, "No, it doesn't make a difference, Turkey, Jordan, we don't care, we didn't come here to sit around in a fucking hotel—" Incoming! The obscenity burst on the wire—LeDuff winced. He had rolled out the howitzers a bit too soon. Now he would have to make a stealth attack. (Perhaps T.R. should have led the charge himself—his quiet sniping was often more effective than LeDuff's big guns.)

"[Editor]," he cooed, efforts redirected in a bid to calm her nerves; it was a tough bid, too, for the editor accursed becomes The Beast. "All we want is to contribute something here," and threw The Beast some meat. "I mean, come on, we're two of the best reporters on the paper"—yes, a subtle play for dominance to keep The Beast in check—"so all we're asking, [Editor], is that you use us, *use* us"—nice, a masochistic turn. "Consider it an education. The older guys can't do this job forever, it's a young man's game, the younger guys, we have to learn the ropes." Remarkable! Appealing to the paper's future! And now for the kill . . . "So what slots are open?" LeDuff went on. "Really? *Really?* When can we go?"

LeDuff had stormed the breech, he was there in the very gap, and yet there was no sign of close capitulation. Instead, there was a pause—LeDuff nodding, squinting, frowning, T.R. imagining some roster being read. X was in Cairo, Y was in Riyadh, it was tight all over, she was sorry. But in fact it wasn't tight—more than likely, it was the squeak of bureaucratic wheels.

"[Editor]," sighed LeDuff, right hand jamming back his hairline as he scrambled for a notepad with his left, "[Editor]," all worry now, "I don't think you want to do that. No, I just—fuck fair, it isn't right." LeDuff had the notepad. Now he started scribbling on the page. T.R. recognized the old reporter's trick—LeDuff was listening and jotting notes at once.

He wrote: "She . . . wants . . . me . . . go . . . Turkey . . . You . . . stay London . . . stay . . . put."

So that was it, it was over—T.R. had lost. He felt split in two. In one half of his brain he was happy for LeDuff; in the other, there was confirmation of his fears. He was going to be left behind—it was the worst of all contingencies. Stiffening his lip, he glanced at LeDuff with a look designed to banish all hard feelings. Hang up the phone, the look said. Hang it up. I know you tried.

But LeDuff did not hang up. "No," he said. "I think you need to tell him that yourself."

Almost instantly T.R. recoiled, for he felt no need to plead his case. If the paper did not want him, it was their loss. Still, he could not go without a fight. He took the telephone and sat down in a chair. He was mindful to remain polite. "Good morning, [Editor]," he said. "I understand there's a change in plans."

What he should have said was this: It seems ridiculous to keep me here in London, which does neither one of us a bit of good. It also seems ridiculous to send me home. So here's my plan . . .

What he said, of course, was nothing. For he had no plan. Even now, he was riding on the wings of an improvisation. "At the end of the day let's talk. If there's a new assignment, I'll take it. If not . . ." He would let the editor determine if his tone contained a threat.

It was on this note of patient ultimatum he hung up. In the hallway, out of sight, the bureau chief welcomed his camera crew with bellows of the warmest welcome. "Gentlemen, ah, yes, I've always loved the Beeb . . ." His secretary stood at the coffeemaker striking buttons like a woman at an ATM. LeDuff meanwhile sat in a heap at T.R.'s side, his Big Ten arms folded at his chest, captive of a scowl that seemed to offer untold curses—"Editors, go figure," or blunter still, "Those fucks." And yet there was a glint of harried preparation in his eye. Though sympathy demanded that he frown, it was clear that every piston in LeDuff's head was already on fire. Unlike T.R., he was going now, no turning back, and one could see it in the stricken lips, in the mad-dog look of worry. No stranger to the frantic, T.R. did not begrudge him this one lick.

LeDuff indeed looked nervous. His swagger had disappeared and a leanness like a hunted beast had taken up his jaw. T.R. had often noticed that LeDuff grew tense when he was handed an assignment and his breeziness in the field was unformed anxiety before he started on a piece. Something somber overcame him then, a thinning of the jowls; it was possible that he cared deeply for the paper, more deeply than he wanted to admit. It was even possible—one could never tell—that he was bonded to the paper and the conflict it produced in him was nothing less than wild. It could lead to the most astounding bursts of journalistic wickedness. Still there was a price to pay—LeDuff had paid it with his nerves. Having gone to the well so often, so success-fully, he was called upon to always have his buckets brimming full. If this was true in California, it would be triply true at war. His orders to decamp still seemed to ride the ridgeline of his forehead like a freak electrical storm. He would have to deliver again and so was jettisoned into a manic future: the on-rushing need to arrange his travel, the certain strains of a sleepless night, the absurdity of covering the war from Turkey—for Chrissakes, Turkey? Who knew if he would ever get to write, or if he did, would anyone care? LeDuff stood up and expelled a breath. It was an eloquent breath that seemed to say, "I'm sorry, pal," but also, or instead, said, "I brought this on myself, but, Christ, I don't know how much more of it I really care to take."

Rising too, T.R. could sympathize, but only to a point. The truth of the matter was that he lacked LeDuff's commitment to the paper. Sadly, blessedly, it was his secret source of strength. T.R. had not come to the *Times* by an ordinary route. There had been no year in journalism school, no apprenticeship at the Boston *Globe* or the *L.A. Times*. Typically, a *Times* reporter started at a local paper, wrote much, wrote well, got noticed, then got a phone call from the office in New York. Then, if he was lucky, it was on to metro, where for a period of months he slaved away at stories on the new ferry service in Astoria while cooking up a cache of stories of his own. T.R.'s experience in sum, when hired, had comprised six or seven articles for lifestyle magazines, all of them defunct. He was hired by the *Times* to work in Newark, once a week, as a part-time stringer, filing eighty-five-word shorts on bar fights in Passaic and toll hikes on the Garden State. His first day on the job had fairly set the tone. He was told that he would never a write story longer than 150 words—he did. He was told that he would never get his byline on a story—he did. He was told that he would never get a full-time job—when he was offered one, at first he turned it down. (It had been something of scandal. The metro editor, pre-Landman, had in 1998 asked him to take the education beat. He did not want it, he had *literary* aspirations. When the editor had asked him why he did not want it, he had said, quite honestly, with no intention to offend, "I don't want my tombstone to read, 'RIP: He was a great reporter for the *New York Times*.'" Ah, scandal!) When Landman offered him the chance to write about the mob, he took the bait—it was proof he was a dilettante at heart. T.R. was neither braver than LeDuff, nor more intelligent, nor made of harder stuff—he simply could not drum up respect for subjects distant from his heart. Impatience was his trump card, selfishness his hidden ace. Yes, he was monstrously selfish with the *Times*—its appetites were monstrous on their own. Visualize LeDuff. There he stands on the verge of a journalistic coup. He has been chosen, one of the elect, to cover the fighting in Iraq. Why then do his cheeks look hollow? Why do his eyes betray the coming of the noose?

The answer lay in T.R.'s own consternation late that night when he was wakened by a ringing in the dark. Sheets flung back, hands grasping, jolted from a dream, he managed nonetheless to find the phone. The dream had concerned some portions of his wife's anatomy, and poised on the lip of wakefulness he imagined for a moment it was she. Sadly, it was not. The voice, which he could not yet place, had the chipper energies of early afternoon, suggesting that the call was coming from another time zone. But if the voice was still untraceable, the message it was carrying was not.

He was told to leave for Jordan in the morning. He was told to arrange an airline ticket and lodgings in Amman, make contact with the *Times* reporter stationed in the country, and begin all preparations for a western passage to Iraq. Money would be waiting for him at the London bureau—five thousand dollars in one-hundred-dollar bills. If extra filters for his gas mask were required, he could find them in the conference room along with spare ceramic plates for his protective vest. Furthermore, by way of good advice, he should consider picking up a secondary method of communication. There were rumors, after all, that the military planned to jam all satellite connections when the bombs began to fall.

"Which reminds me," the voice said now with disconcerting flatness. "You ought to turn your television on."

Chapter 5

FELINES

He did. The bombs were falling. Now he was awake.

There was suddenly much to do. Not desiring to waste time with hygiene in the morning, he proceeded to the shower, then, still wrapped in a towel, set about the task of policing up his things. The process had the pleasant, forward-looking calm effect of packing for a long vacation, but serenity soon disappeared. T.R. was too dazed to feel anxiety, but he was able to detect within himself the dull sleepy jitters. In the sockets of his eyes, he felt an irritating dryness—aridity, no doubt, from being yanked without warning from the moistest cycles of his sleep.

The television set was not helping. The images, still fresh, were of an urban landscape shot from above with bright parabolas of midnight fire shedding spooky luminescence on strange unfigurable buildings. The camera, holding a steady shot, looked straight at the city—it was Baghdad, said the anchor, where American missile fire was trying to "decapitate the regime." (A nasty bit of diction, this would not be the last to surface in a conflict that produced such works of linguistic

49

origami as "shock and awe"—unfolded: big fucking bombs—or "coalition forces"—American and British troops. One wondered if deep within the entrails of the Pentagon there was an Office of Literary Jingoism full of poets skilled in the art of coming up with these fine gems.)

So the invasion had begun and T.R. watched it, far from the center of the action, on CNN. Earlier that evening he had gone downstairs to bid farewell to LeDuff, LeDuff's belongings, battle helmet, work boots, gas mask, goggles, laptop, and various electrical devices spread like a yard sale on the bed. It was a solemn, distracted, uncomfortable occasion; neither one of them evinced a taste for talk. Instead they drank—not with joy, but with the dull obligatory spirit of partisans who place their faith in alcohol to communicate emotion. For nearly an hour they went at this; perhaps a dozen words were said. Finally LeDuff stood up and the two men looked at one another. In one sense they were brothers and, brother-like, embraced.

"We'll meet for a beer in Baghdad," T.R. joked. (Conscious shades of Harry's Bar.)

"You'll get there."

"I will."

"Good luck to you."

"No, good luck to you."

"Well, see you later."

"See you later."

Now it was later. The First Marines were packed on the border of Kuwait. The Third Infantry was already across. T.R. was nearly packed himself. Woken by the call, he had felt the urge to call LeDuff—but resisted. Surely, they would find each other. He should have called to amend their final words. But he was picking up the foreign correspondent's version of departure. Everything was touched by imminence as if by light, his rucksack leaned against the wall in such a way as to suggest the future, and the backdrop of the British anchor speaking of missiles in the Gulf had all the melancholy grace of world events. In his towel, in his room, in London, he could feel a tightness, a twinge of jealousy at being distant from the center of the fray. Still, he knew that he was on his way, knew he had a *place*. The sweetness was almost unendurable for it was sweetness of the oldest sort, the quiet midnight gathering of men, scrape of footstep, clink of gear, the burning hints of motor oil and waiting cars. Now that the dawn of his departure had arrived, T.R. could appreciate some sense of the weary steps the soldier, rancher, pioneer might take—American *isolatos* all—in the early morning dark.

Before he left, he would have to call his wife. It would not be easy. On the one hand, it would prove enormously upsetting; on the other, it would taint the solitude that he was trying to effect. (T.R. was never quite as lonesome as he thought; still, he could feel departure tugging at his blood.) So he sat down by the telephone and dialed. Two short rings, then his wife was on the line.

He had always loved the sound of her voice, especially on the phone. It had a graceful toughness with a slight midwestern whine, and it was always very calming to his ear. He had fallen in love with her voice years ago when it had seemed he was the one man who could pick up the tenderness in every hard-edged tone. Now her voice had a lovely open-throated innocence, soft, expectant, full of breath, as if she had just rushed in from doing errands, bags and keys in hand. In fact, she had just hung up with LeDuff's wife. Now she was relaxing in the bedroom with the cats. "I'm sorry," she was saying. "You must be sad to see him go."

"Yeah, we just said good-bye a couple hours ago."

"How is he?"

"Nervous, excited. Ready."

He could hear her whisper something to the old cat, Zowie. She often joked that if something happened to him, she would end up one of those ridiculous old women you saw in the park with tote bags and a house of cats. He could picture her like that, and it moved him to respectful silence. He loved her more than any other woman in his life.

"The girls say hi," she told him now, hints of an unseen smile. "They miss you."

"I miss them."

"So," she said—and now the edge came back because she knew T.R. would not call in the middle of the night to chew the fat. "What about you?" she asked. "Where are you going?"

"To Jordan," he said. "In the morning."

She breathed a gentle breath.

"Well, just be careful. Please be careful." A period of disassociation from the threat of danger had already occurred. He had seen her struggle with it on her trip to London: In concert with his own self-absorption, it had brought about their sluggishness and fights. Like many marriages, theirs was caught up in the illusion of inequity. To some outward eyes T.R. was the hero, even the saint. But it was not remotely true. For every adventure he pursued, his wife had stood along the home front. He could do the things he did simply, and solely, because she stood an ever-present guard above their hearts.

"I'll be careful," he said now. "I always am."

She laughed, with perfect skeptical knowledge. "No, you're not," she said.

Laughing, too, he admitted she was right and then she told him briefly of the friends and family who had called to wish him well. Then it was time to go. Hanging up, he was left with the image of her sitting in bed—it burned like a snapshot in his mind. T.R. knew, if he desired, he could have talked with her all night and fallen asleep with the phone at his chin as they had once done long ago, in different days, but it was late and morning was approaching, so he hung up, brushed his teeth, turned out the lights and climbed into bed, alone.

BOOK TWO

JORDAN

Chapter 6

CREDENTIALS

Of all the risks involved in the undertaking of serious journalism, one of the greatest is to let the amateur report on world events. By his very nature the amateur is likely to graft his own desires, needs, and struggles onto history and in the process confuse the global story he is meant to cover with the ongoing fairy tale of his own personal growth. Unlike the professional reporter, who has learned to cage his moral sensibilities, if not his ego, the amateur at every turn is struck by signs and wonders—portents of the most reflexive sort. He is the prisoner of individuality, which is to say he sees things in relation to himself. It may be tempting not to trust him, but this would be to misconceive his nature—for the amateur is no mean egotist; rather he is bursting, undefeated, still possessed of *spiritus mundi*, and perhaps a whiff naive. Still, it must be recognized that his approach presents a danger to the truth, and with this in mind, it would be wise to spend the long dull hours of the flight from London to Amman investigating T.R.'s portfolio of credentials. We ought to make an effort to explain why, despite his disadvantages, he is nonetheless the right man for the job.

The launching of the second Gulf War in Iraq marked a crucial turning point in U.S. foreign policy because it saw the mightiest republic in the history of Earth attack a cruel, if harmless, country not to preserve its interests but to slap an Arab bitch. Beyond all else, the war could be taken as precisely that—the reassertion of national machismo. Deeply wounded, perhaps unmanned by the shock of 9/11, the country was required to send a message that proclaimed in boldest terms, "Do not ever fuck with us again." In the White House sat a man whose own inner turmoil mirrored the turmoil in Iraq. He was a Texan, eager to achieve the muscular bravado of his state—more eager than most, perhaps, for he was not a native but instead a second-generation transplant from the East. So there was much to prove. Indeed, there was everything to prove—he needed to suppress within himself all shadows of the fey aristocratic past; at the same time, his fierce desire to be a Texan forced him to embrace the credo of the Gadsden flag. Whether it was luck, pure coincidence, or some divine and cosmic mystery that *this* man, engaged in private combat with his manhood, happened to be running the country at a time when manhood mattered most may never be known—although the question itself suggests there was a personal tint to the news.

T.R., of course, was attuned to the personal; furthermore, he was attuned to the Texan in the White House for he, too, was embarked on a journey to the proving ground, the battlefield (quite literally) of Iraq. There, courage would stand with cowardice, strength with weakness, and all accounts would finally be known. In the opening phases of a war launched to prove that America had not lost its manhood, T.R. discerned a visceral, a primitive, urge to settle those accounts. And even as the country counterpunched to reassert its might, the Texan raised his own fist: He wished to shatter every last vestigial eastern weakness in his soul. So if there was to be a battle over manhood—a public *and* a private battle—it would make good sense that the correspondent sent to cover it should not only be obsessed with cowardice and courage, but should also be hooked to the live wire of his instincts. In other words, no professional bent on gathering the facts alone but an amateur bent on following the filaments of fear, aggression, foolishness, and wounded pride even as they passed through his head. Send in the cavalry by all means; but if the story smells of the therapist's couch, best to send an amateur as well.

And so it was that, in the cloak of the reporter, T.R. flew to Jordan with a secret mission: He would investigate the contradictions roaring in those around him and himself. He would also cast a weather eye toward the news. But first he had to make it into town. Even now, he was arriving at the airport in Amman, trudging down the jetway, gathering bags. Except for the skinny Arab soldiers checking passports it was not unlike arriving in Detroit. He hailed a taxi with the only Arab words he knew ("Hotel Intercontinental?") and proceeded on a two-lane desert highway through the hills, low white chalky hills with sheep and shepherds from the Bible. Amman was all white dust; it was thickets of antennae, billboards advertising cell phones, auto body shops on narrow side streets that emerged to boulevards with palm trees, fountains, embassies, and, further in, the glass-and-marble towers of international hotels. Pulling up to the

Intercontinental was like pulling up to Vegas: The dust was gone, the shepherd boys were gone, the desert flats were gone. In their place, beneath the palm trees, the parking lot was jammed with Jeeps, Suburbans, four-wheel drives, and television trucks. Here then was the first contradiction, for here in the heart of biblical Amman was an oasis of the news: Danes, Swedes, Frenchmen, Brits, Americans, Koreans, Japanese, all abustle in the sunshine, all abanter on their cell phones in their knee-length khaki shorts. With no small self-disgust, T.R. left the cab and over-tipped his driver.

The cavalry, by all accounts, had already arrived.

Chapter 7

CASABLANCA

At any rate he went inside—rucksack on his back, duffel in hand, laptop slung like a bandolier across his chest. He was stooped beneath the weight of two months' gear and his entire body sagged from seven hours on the flight. The flight had been awful. Leaving London, he had been momentarily amused by the television screens in the airplane aisle, which, beacon-like, had shown the plane's position toward the Q'aaba stone in Mecca so that the passengers could pray in the correct direction as they flew, and the improvisatory style of the Emirates Airline pilots who flew as if already in a war zone. Now, however, he was not amused at all—he was exhausted. T.R. had always hated the anxious expectation of arrivals; arrivals were like waiting for a doctor's visit. They were fretful, full of nerves. He much preferred the sweeter sorrows of departure. After all, departures were a mystery: You never knew what might occur.

He was wearing the one expensive shirt he owned, a purple number bought in London. Below that were the cargo pants that, despite a solid wash, still bore traces of his mishap with the coffee machine. Leather work boots completed the picture, which in all made for an image, much to his liking, very different from that of his colleagues who even now were lingering about the lobby on embroidered sofas and upholstered chairs. In terms of style, T.R. picked up a general safari look. The men were clad in khaki vests that spoke of hippo-hunting on the Kalahari and seemed to hold as their advantage pockets in abundance—far more pockets than one could possibly need. (One could devise a theory that pockets were the glory badges war reporters wore.) The women were of lesser African inflection, but appeared nonetheless to like their cotton shirts unbuttoned just enough to show a suntanned hint of neck. Their pants fell capri-style between the ankle and the knee.

T.R. was not typically attuned to the sartorial, but entering the Intercontinental was like entering an African safari lodge. He had long desired to enter hotels in just this sort of manner. To do so seemed the province of the foreign correspondent. To arrive at the Intercon, to wander toward the check-in desk, to leave one's luggage with the bellhop, to announce one's presence to the lovely female clerk, and then to say, "Good morning, the reservation, I believe, is with the *New York Times*," what could possibly be more refined than that? Of course, that he had *actually* arrived, that was *actually* standing in the lobby now, did little to alter the overpowering sensation that he was in an old-time movie—*Casablanca*, perhaps. And with Hollywood in mind, it might be appropriate to swing the camera lens around and take in the lobby itself with a slow wide-angle pan.

In every war zone, or staging ground for such, there is a place that serves as the unofficial press hotel. In Jordan, the

Intercontinental was that place. Such hotels are often multinational chain hotels that can absorb the instant influx of the press and that possess sufficient infrastructure to serve as the ad hoc bureau for a hundred news shops at once. They are typically awful places filled with hacks, drunks, spooks, smugglers, drivers, smokers, diplomats, photographers, pornographers, hookers, death addicts, and a viciously bitter competitive air—which is to say they are fascinating places if one's view of fascination includes hearing ossified reporters, strung out on cigarettes and gin, saying things like, "Yes, we were all at the Al-Rashid having cocktails on the balcony when the bombs began to fall."

Quite often these hotels are adorned according to indigenous themes. But while they are *in* the country of their origin, they are not *of* it—for they cater to a clientele that is transient by nature. Despite the African accent of its clients, the Intercontinental had a faux Arabian harem leitmotif. And fresh from the foggy civilities of London, T.R. was confronted on arrival by the sight of caftaned bellhops hauling luggage for the press. Worse yet were the cocktail waiters in tasseled fezzes serving vodka tonics to reporters reclined on pasha chairs and fringed settees.

T.R found himself desiring a drink. In the lobby down the hall there was a bar. It was advertised as "Mama Juanita's Mexican Cantina." *No mas!* The cross-cultural trade winds were already stiff, what with the Arab *hamsin* and the deep breaths of the savannah. Now, these breezes blew him toward the check-in desk where he asked for his keys. It seemed dangerous to drink in such absurdity. He would make it to the bar, after he had showered and unpacked.

For some reason, he had assumed the Middle East would be free of the absurdity that seemed to permeate the country back at home. In New York, it often seemed that every other restaurant was a faux French bistro cluttered up with antique posters bought at auction (Lillet, absinthe, Tour de France), and this was nothing to the high-schlock Outback Steakhouse. Such absurdity had recently been captured in a perfect cartoon. The frame, in *The New Yorker* magazine, had showed a couple in a diner. The caption, or at least as he recalled it, read: "I don't think this is a diner about being a diner. I think this is just a diner." Yes! Home run! For in that cartoon was all of America's profound distaste for the grit of the real, a reality of dirt, bad menus, sodomy, body odor, spoiled milk, and immigration, and much too of its nostalgic need to cling to the meat of an authentic culture, albeit a culture stripped of calories and fat. His assumption about the Middle East had been proven wrong at first at the airport in Dubai, where he had spent two hours on a layover smoking in a high depressive state. The indoor palm trees were to blame, but it was not just the trees, for the trees were merely weird in the vaulting neon Vegas-like mall. But the white-robed Arabs and mysterious Caucasians talking on their cell phones as the television sets showed Al-Jazeera broadcasts of the war were past weird. They were exceedingly absurd.

As a journalist, T.R. had professional interest in absurdity, but as a citizen he found a different pleasure in the stuff, some voyeur's high, some unadulterated peek at vertigo, transformative as any drug. He made his way to the elevator now with every neuron in his head on fire, feeling itchy, feeling anxious—no way for a war reporter to feel, unless—forgive him, Father—he was nothing of the sort.

The trouble with absurdity is that it leaves one temporarily inert. It was early morning; by mid-afternoon he would have to get his bearings, get in contact with the *Times*, and get to work. If all he wanted was to take a nap, it was just too bad. He was on a critical assignment, such as he had never had before. T.R. tried to concentrate. He was a touch concerned about accomplishing this task.

The room, however, helped. It was sunny, well-appointed, and immaculately clean. A clean hotel room being tonic for the soul, he set up shop and so enjoyed the various hookings of his camera to his laptop, his laptop to the phone, the phone to his converter that he soon began to feel as if this room was an office here in exile. Foreign correspondents surely loved their gear because it made them feel at home.

In the bathroom was a lovely robe, fresh towels, and, best of all, a telephone beside the pot, which spoke of deadline matters so severe as to require conversation despite the urgency of bodily needs. What luxury, what power, to discuss one's lead with an editor while engaged in the relieving of one's bowels! Needless to say, there were no such amenities in the Bronx, where T.R.'s office on Fordham Road possessed a broken wall clock, views of the bus stop, infrequent visits by the janitorial staff, and all the off-white institutional charms of a public hospital—a place to severely lessen one's reserves of *joie de vivre*.

The plan from the outset had been for him to settle in Amman and then call Ian Fisher, the senior *Times*man in Jordan. In a typical display of his lazy attitude toward the detailed logistics needed to carry out such plans, he had written Fisher's number in one of his notepads, along with those of Charlie LeDuff, the *Times*'s computer guru, an Iraqi he had met in London, and a half-dozen other sources. Now he had to rifle through his luggage for the pad. T.R. had always admired colleagues who could use devices like a Palm Pilot—wedded to the deep security of paper, he could not. Even in the Bronx he kept his sources in the classic small black book (which, organized by code, might list Anthony Spero under M for *Mafia*). It seemed to work in New York City, so he saw no need to change it overseas. In truth he was secretly fond of this old-fashioned method and, at times, alone of an evening over drinks, he would turn the pages of the book, and the list of names inside—Carl Bernstein, Bill Bratton, Jimmy Breslin, Little Joe Corozzo, Bruce Cutler, Stanley Friedman, Nat Hentoff, Johnny C, Ray Kelly, Spike Lee, Bones Malone, Burt Pugach, Danny Provenzano, Charles Rangel, Al Sharpton, Russell Simmons, and someone simply jotted down as Woody—were both a pleasure to read and a history of his travels through a certain stratum of New York.

But now he worried that his fetish for disorganization might prove a liability. He was concerned that his tendency for working off the cuff might bring him trouble overseas and that his habit of making conversation out of interviews, of entering his subject's lives as best he could, might contradict the realities of war. Things would get too crazy. If he was on a secret mission to detect all contradictions, he was nonetheless aware that the *New York Times* was footing the bill. Quite possibly it would require an alteration of his style, and T.R. wasn't sure that he could manage such a task. He liked his style—others, too, apparently, for here he was—and yet he had been brooding more and more in recent days that he was too relaxed for war reporting, too soft, too sloppy, too intrigued by the minor key. Perhaps he even lacked the necessary crispness to produce stories filed on deadline for the front page. His slow approach, his personable manner, his desire to wait to get things right—would they work in Iraq?

In the Bronx his method was to riff with people, jazz awhile, until they coughed up a gem worth putting in the paper. "Check it, Queefa, you know like I do, whatever goes into prison must come out. So what's it like when your husband finally comes home?" How was he supposed to do that with an Arab? The Marines at least spoke English. So he sensed a crisis coming. He was too entrenched in his belief that people responded best to jazz to suddenly become all business, yet business he would have to be. His bosses would expect it, the situation would demand it, and he would be thrust back on his own ingenuity, cunning, and wit to work out a compromise in which the paper got its copy and he did not betray that jazz which had served him well up-town, that de-coagulation of the spirit that had flourished in the Bronx: improv, dirty jokes, bullshit, jive, slang, drinks, sarcasm, finger-pointing, cheekiness, and notes taken down on missing pads. It had served him well before, but would it serve him now? Even now, hunting in his luggage, he allowed himself a private smile, for if he had remembered this internal dialogue in London he might, just might, have given Warren Hoge a little of the old Bronx jazz. "Tell ya, War, it's sort of like this," he might have said. "I'm the kind of guy who tends to lose his notebooks, har, har, har! I just find this whole verbatim thing a little overrated, don't you think?"

Anyhow, in the grand discomfort of arriving in Amman, T.R. found some humor in such imaginary replays. And, finally re-trieving Fisher's number from his bag, he dialed and entered into something like the following chat:

"Is this Ian?"

"Yes, who is this?"

T.R. introduced himself.

"Oh, hey. You're in Amman? Wow. Terrific. That was fast. Welcome. You're at the Intercontinental, right? How is it?"

T.R. told him that the crowd was fair to middling, the accommodations seemed OK. He held back on the *Casablanca* details—the taxi drivers smoking in the lobby, the seedy grandeur, the air of intrigue, the muttered conversations over drinks—he did not desire to seem naive.

"Look," said Fisher, trying to be polite, for he was clearly busy, "I'm in the middle of something now. Actually I'm in Ruweished. On the border. Not pretty. Well, it doesn't matter. Never mind. So what are your plans? I'll be back in a day. Maybe two."

T.R. said he had no plans. He had yet to speak with the desk.

"You know what you have to do? You have to get a press card. Don't worry. It's easy. Take this number. It's a guy from NPR. He's nice, very nice. He'll help you. Got a pen?"

And paper, T.R. said. Fisher gave him the number.

"All right," Fisher said, for he was clearly busy. "What? No. Yes. No. Yes. What? I told you, in a second." He was talking to someone else, but now came back. "All right. Sorry. Yes. The Intercontinental isn't bad, but the food's better at the Hyatt. Anyhow you have to get a press card. And a translator. You have to get a translator. And a driver. But first a translator. Look. What? No. Look. I have to go. Call me later? We'll talk when I get back. In a day or two. Or three. Whatever. What? Not sure. OK? Did you hear me? Right. Good-bye."

T.R. had barely time to say good-bye himself before the line went dead.

Chapter 8

THE TRANSLATOR

Now he went downstairs to have that drink. He needed it. Having first unpacked, then shaved and showered and replaced his purple Oxford with a T-shirt (would he ever quit exhibiting his love for the informal on his sleeve?), he had managed to eliminate the outer shell of his anxiety. As T.R. entered the bar, he felt as fresh and wholesome as a set of laundered sheets.

Mama Juanita's was a dim-lit cavern with tortilla chips and salsa, two-for-one tequilas, and a bank of television sets bolted to the walls on which there played the endless loop of cable news. It had the sad dank air of a permanent happy hour such as one might find in any airport bar. There was, in fact, a happy hour afoot as he came in. The happy hour was no more than several young reporters standing in their khakis at the bar or sitting glumly on the wagon-wheel stools. T.R. took a seat apart from them to listen. By their chummy conversation, it was clear these men knew each other, if only from previous happy hours in Amman. They seemed to have reached that point of boredom at which men will talk of anything. The man talking most, as T.R.

quickly learned, was named Robert Pelton, a middle-aged American with heavy mustache, a pair of wire-rimmed glasses, full in the jaw, big-boned, wearing khaki pants and the standard-issue tan safari vest. Pelton spoke in a loud, broad, deep sarcastic voice and at the end of every sentence lifted his beer to his mouth with a gnarled, mysteriously bandaged hand. He was coming to the end of a long story about the gunfights he had seen in Chechnya.

"The Republican Guard are nasty guys," he was saying, "in fact, they're *really* nasty guys"—and here he took a lubricating swig—"but never, *ever* have you seen a guy so nasty as a Chechen rebel with a loaded AK." He lit a cigarette and shook his head. "A company of Chechens, no, a small *platoon*, could waste the best Saddam has got . . ."

This speech attracted an admiring silence from his audience since most had never been to Chechnya, had no desire to go, and might indeed take Pelton's word for it, perhaps to repeat his story somewhere down the line ("Dude, the Chechens are *nasty!*") to erect the right veneer of authenticity when authenticity was needed most.

They were a funny group. Clearly they were not the shock troops of the press, for those men were already with the real troops. But they were not quite slouches either; after all, they had made it to Amman. Listening at the bar, T.R. decided they were acolytes, young acolytes, for they were jaded, humorless, and smug enough to suggest that if they had not seen it all, they had still seen much. Surely, they had seen more than their college roommates in New York who were grinding out their own days at investments banks and legal firms. And yet among them only Robert Pelton had the spice, the raw salts, of the old-time correspondent who would cut through jungles for a story, hacking vines, slapping flies, slipping across the border only to appear much later at the press hotel, exhausted, dirty, but ready to indulge in carnivals of drinking. He alone (as Pelton now was claiming to have done) would fill the swimming pool with waiters, naked flight attendants, and every mode of hotel furniture for an all-night poolside bash. Pelton was the eldest of the group, and yet the wildest too, and by degrees that seemed to shock and please the acolytes around him. They seemed to revel in his presence—here was a man who had been to Chechnya, who had been to Bogota, who had been *kidnapped* in Bogota. Every time the acolytes spoke, it seemed designed to impress Pelton, but their speech did nothing of the sort. If anything, the fawning only honed the blade of his superiority—but the acolytes gave it their best. Some spoke of working in the Gaza Strip; others of midnight tank rides in Hebron. A few of the better-traveled types had been to sub-Saharan Africa. One chubby fellow, working on his third or fourth White Russian, said he had once seen a collaborator killed in Ivory Coast.

T.R. drank his whiskey. Down the bar was another pair of men. He moved to sit beside them now to eavesdrop. (On his first night in Amman, T.R. had planned an evening of reconnaissance, arrival's first rule being: Get to know the land.) These men had the unwashed heads and smockish shirts of neo-Hippies— pastel Hindu shirts of a heavy muslin cloth. As soon as T.R. sat beside them, he could smell the oily odor of patchouli through the heavy scent of beer.

They were discussing visas for Iraq.

"I'm running out of money," one of them said, a young man in his twenties with a rat goatee and long, dark, stringy, dirty hair. "I thought your father's friend in the embassy was gonna hook us up?"

"He *will*," his partner said. "But I can't burst in there saying, 'Hi, I'm Jason Dalton—Jeff Dalton's son? Could I get a visa for Iraq?'"

"Why not?" asked Rat Goatee. "We gotta get in country."

"Dude, I know we gotta get in country. Relax. The country is at fucking war."

It developed they were human shields. T.R. had read about them in the papers in New York. The shields had come to Jordan, hoping for a passage to Iraq, where they would place themselves in front of orphanages, schools, and hospitals to protect these institutions from the bombs. That these two shields were drinking in Amman did little to diminish T.R.'s fascination. He was tantalized by human shields, none the least because he wondered what colossal fool might actually believe the U.S. Air Force would not obliterate a building in Iraq because a Phish fan from Vermont had chained his body to the door. T.R. was on the verge of striking up a conversation with the shields when a small detachment of the acolytes appeared. Apparently they smelled a story, for they bought the shields another round and then began an interview, some with brandished pens.

"So after graduating Reed you went where? Really? 'A capitalist empire bent on global domination?' Can I quote that?"

Around the moment T.R. decided he was being terribly unfair to the acolytes (because of their safari vests, the five-gear drive of their ambition, their tales of war and interest in the human shields) something happened to confirm his views. The shields went back to their hotel, the acolytes went back to drinking. But as the happy hour began to dissolve, the acolytes began to pass their business cards around. Some of these had local contact numbers and satellite and e-mail links; some had Arabic translations on the flip side. No one seemed to think it strange that trading cards—the dullest mode of professional rapport—was precisely the glad-handing all of them had sought to flee by coming overseas.

At any rate, it soon came time for Robert Pelton to display his own card. Since he had finished his lecture on Chechnya—"It's not a *major* scar"—and not-so-subtly suggested that in terms of war reporting he was the most experienced man for miles, the acolytes now stood around him, pressing close to get this card. But Pelton shook his head. "I don't carry cards," he said. "I mean, I'm not a journalist, guys. I'm—well, I'm just *me*." Sooner tell the pope that Christ was just a carpenter's son! That Robert Pelton had no card was heresy; the shock it caused was intense. All of a sudden each card tucked in a wallet or slipped in the pocket of a vest took on a radioactive stink that smelled of boardrooms and the catered lunch. It ran against the image of the foreign correspondent as a maverick, speed freak, devil, as a loose cannon with his barrels pointed at the bottom line. What on earth did a war reporter need with business cards when he had danger, cash, adrenaline, an intimate relationship with death? The business card was a refutation of his freedom—"Look here, Ahmed, I'll be out, but you can reach me at this number." It was also a reminder of the cattle calls and press events he had suffered, all that schlepping and shmoozing and shmying about. Taken to its logical end, the business card was the very mindset rooted in the synergy of news and network; it was the integrated masthead, where the corporate chieftains put their names above the editors, where they ran roughshod over editors, where every article was checked against the bottom line. The business card was *business*—that was Pelton's message. If he himself had come to Jordan on a tasty deal with CBS, so what? It compromised him only to a point. Self-inflation to the side, Robert Pelton had a knack for reawakening one's better virtues. For that alone, he was a handy man to have around.

Now he was drinking up and making noise about retiring upstairs to call his wife. Half his seminar had already dispersed. T.R. had a mind to join those who remained on the proposition that, over drinks, dull conversation is better than none, but lacked the necessary heart. Journalists, observant on the job, often took a holiday from observation in civilian life. It was the same mechanism that accounted for chefs who ordered takeout, or plumbers who had leaky pipes: One liked to leave one's labors at the office. In just that spirit, T.R. found an empty stool and ordered one last drink. He would enjoy the solitude and let the last of his arrival jitters melt in the ice.

As always in a quiet moment, his mind began to drift toward thoughts of love and work. If T.R. wasn't working, there were odds he was in love; if not in love, he was probably at work. At the moment, he was neither (his wife was in New York, he had no story in Amman), and the emptiness had given him a niggling inner ache. He did not know if the best course was to cultivate a social life in Jordan while he still had time or to concentrate on getting stories in the paper. Normally he would pursue the two at once, but he had found himself imprisoned by the new reporter's paradox: Since he did not know a soul in town, he had no clue of where to look for stories, and since he had no story in his pocket, how was he to find the proper source?

In New York, T.R. had developed something of a reputation for turning bad ideas into printable stories—chicken shit to chicken salad, as his uncle might have said. These transformations often happened on the weekends, dog days of the news, when the paper, lacking news, needed to be filled. On Saturdays, he was often greeted in the newsroom by the wild eyes of the assignment editor, eyes that glittered even as they said, "Now let the alchemy begin!" "Know what day it is?" the editor might ask. "The winter solstice. Shortest of the year. Give me seven hundred words by three o'clock." T.R. would then begin to rack his brains to discover any news in this insanity to print. He paid a visit to a lamp store. ("Say, friend, it's the winter solstice—any spike in sales?") He went to the bar to see if the extended darkness led to drinking. In a pinch, he left a message with a vampire club in northern Jersey. ("It seemed a sure bet that vampires would appreciate a long, dark night.")*

For the innocent, however, salvation often comes (like a late commuter train) when one gives up all hope. If T.R. was not hopeless, he had nonetheless decided that the best method to defeat the new reporter's paradox was to embrace it. Trusting in the future, he would wait for something to occur. Just then, a young woman took a seat beside him at the bar. She was dressed rather shabbily in sweatpants, T-shirt, and a baseball cap, which is not to slight her style but to distinguish her from the reporters in the bar trussed up in Afro-desert modes of chic.

---

*These adventures in editorial ass-saving had begun two years ago when the Saturday editor greeted T.R. one morning by holding up a plain white Chinese food container. "Know what this is?" she had asked. "Your dinner?" "Look," the editor said, turning the carton so that an advertisement for a cell phone company now showed, "advertising on a Chinese food container. Never seen that before. Seven hundred words by three o'clock."

"I'm covered in sand," the woman said. It was a good opening line.

"I'm sorry to hear that," T.R. said, being earnest since his brain was free of wit.

The woman seemed to appreciate the thought. "It's just that I spent the day at a refugee camp, at the border, in Ruweished"—this with a perfect Arab accent—"and the sandstorms there were crazy." T.R. flashed on the name. It was the same town where Ian Fisher spent the night. He smiled at once to the gods of luck.

The woman was smiling, too, although it seemed not born of coyness or flirtation—it seemed her natural state. She lit a cigarette and waved away the smoke.

"So," she asked, "you're a journalist?"

T.R. confessed he was. And she?

She shook her head. "No," she said, "I'm a translator. At least I'm trying to be a translator. I work for the CBC—the Canadian Broadcast Company or Corporation or whatever. But I'm Jordanian. I live in Amman."

The woman's name was Nadia al-Huraimi. She was short, sweet, light-skinned, pretty, and twenty-four years old. Her English, nearly flawless, had been acquired, she said, in Buffalo, where she had studied at Canisius College, duped by its brochure into believing it was somewhere one might want to be. Her Muslim parents had forbidden her from living in Manhattan. With shameful honesty, the deans of Canisius had touted Buffalo as the second-largest city in the state.

Already there were numerous indications that T.R. had found his translator over whiskey at a Mexican bar. The notion had a certain swing he liked. With unpretentious charm, Nadia went on to describe her disappointments with the CBC, her manner straight, engaging, funny, her insights deft and to the point. Despite appearances, she clearly knew her way around. She had a way of speaking that was reminiscent of a freshman at a small midwestern college—Antioch, or Oberlin perhaps. It blended nicely with her Arab recognition that the world could not be changed by idealists alone; it might require blood. Clearly an optimist, she was also no one's fool. In simplest terms Nadia was the product of her childhood for, as it happened, she was Palestinian by birth, and if she seemed particularly suited for a bullshit session on the quad, she still maintained some shadow of her father's suffering born in the early stages of the P.L.O.

Best of all, of course, she was an amateur, and even as she spoke T.R. began concocting stratagems to woo her from her job. He asked if the Canadians were going to Iraq. She did not know. He asked if she would like to go herself. Indeed she would. No doubt there will be cynics sniping from the gutter that Our Questioner was looking after pleasure. Let us nip that falsehood in the bud. While Nadia was sweet, she also had that carnal reticence often found in women of an idealistic bent. She emitted not the shock waves of sex, but calmer currents of sisterhood and Plato, which is not to say that she was unattractive—she was; that is, was *not*—but there were hints in her of inexperience. You had the sense that she would hardly stoop to an affair (no prude, she managed to suggest this without uttering a word), but would wait instead until the right man happened by to introduce her to her own secret turmoils and, in the process, sweep her off her feet.

Who that man might be and when he might arrive was none of T.R.'s business. The worst he could say for himself was that he found a certain solace in the presence of the girl. Though his condition would worsen in Iraq, in Jordan he could already feel his human batteries running low. It was a feeling not unlike a mild depression, as if his soul had caught a cold. To have a woman around would not only counteract the high testosterone of all the men he would encounter; it would also keep the sugar in his blood from heading south.

So after one last drink, they made a date to head for Ruweished in the morning. Their plan was to get up early, since the drive to the border would require at least three hours. As for compensation, they decided to defer until they saw how well, or not, they got along. It seemed most fair. In fact, it seemed exceedingly generous—T.R. could not believe his luck. As an atheist, he had always thought of luck as the secular equivalent to grace—it came to your life when you were ready to accept it. As he paid the bar tab, bid goodnight to Nadia, and watched her navigate the crowd, T.R. felt lucky in the merriest extreme.

Chapter 9

ZEE INTERNET

AT FIRST LIGHT, he saw his luck had not diminished. Nadia was waiting in the lot behind the wheel of what appeared to be a brand-new car. She had brought along a full supply of cigarettes. They were not his brand, but how could a moocher possibly complain? Even the photographer he had asked to come along had shown up early—grouchy, sleep-deprived, but early— no mean feat for a type that typically shunned the clarities of morning. The photographer had brought along a friend, another photographer, which meant the pool of pictures to accompany his story had just increased by two. There was no doubt about it. The day was off to a capital start.

When T.R. had first heard of Ruweished, images had come to mind of gold, lush, rolling sand dunes of the sort that T.E. Lawrence might have crested on a camel. But as they made their way on the highway from Amman there was not a dune in sight, nor hardly any sand. Beyond the capital, the desert was a field of black volcanic rock that stretched like shattered bowling balls to the horizon, broken only by the marching armies of steel electric towers. The only life was the carrion birds drawn by the occasional dead dog rotting on the road. Every now and then, a Bedouin in robes led his flock across the asphalt then vanished quickly into the dust. All else on the road was sun, light, scrub, black rock, and the morning heat that shimmered underneath the downturned bowl of the enormous desert sky.

Even at half past six, it was hot enough that when Nadia rolled her window down to smoke, the heat rushed in like wool. They had the air-conditioning on—that, at least, was comfortable and cool. The radio was on as well: some old tune of nasal Arab strings. Singing along, Nadia held both hands on the wheel and told a story of camping in the desert as a child. The danger was not the heat, she said, it was the jackals, which would eat a man alive. And yet there was a happy feeling in the car recalling all the road trips T.R. had taken as a college dropout through the foreign country of the West. One season he had driven 15,000 miles across America, with strangers, hitchhikers, hitching himself when the car had died. Now that feeling of mobility came back. Alan Chin, the *Times* photographer, disheveled veteran of many wars, had ensconced himself in back and was taking pictures of the desert from the window. His partner was a close-cropped kid from Oklahoma on assignment with the Getty agency. His name was Morrison, Graeme Morrison. He had a nasty scar on his cheek, and smoked, then slept, then rose again to smoke.

Riding shotgun, T.R. was attempting to assimilate the landscape while beating back the brush fires of anxiety at being on his first assignment overseas. He had been to the desert—mainly Arizona and New Mexico—and had come to love it as a visitor, if not a friend. The American desert dweller was a laconic type whose system of emotional response reacted slower than the city dweller's did. In the desert, speech and feelings dissolved into empty tracts of land; the buildings of a city trapped them like a horsefly in the fist. He had boiled it to a slogan: Deserts echo, cities buzz. He had no clue if this would prove as true in Jordan—though he was picking up the sense that arriving in Ruweished would be much like arriving in Kingman, Arizona, or the California flats—the isolation of geography would likely be the same.

The first inkling that this theory was about to be disproved came as they entered Ruweished proper, which appeared from the desert out of nowhere as a lonely roadside billboard, then a service station, then a few young boys pedaling along the berm, and finally a smattering of small, low, shabby buildings thrown together on either side of the narrow pitted road. They parked outside what looked to be a restaurant, a low-slung desert pile of bricks. A sign in English hung from its eaves—"Abu Sayef's Roasted Chicken Place." The first thought was to have a meal and then proceed to work, but T.R. saw that the thought was not unique. In front of the restaurant was a motor pool of at least a half-dozen Chevrolet Suburbans, their doors and windows plastered with precautionary messages in thick black strips of tape.

TV, the messages read. And, *PRESS*.

Evermore uncertain, the travelers stepped inside to a long, high-ceilinged dining room in which a grainy sunshine fell from skylights onto white plastic furniture that could have been purchased from the patio section of any discontinued home-and-garden magazine. The white room smelled of olive oil and smoke. The grill in back was tended by a stooped old man in a checkered headscarf; a younger man stood post at the register halfway toward the front. The register itself, an ancient hulk of iron, stood before a window to the kitchen, which even now dispensed a busy stream of hummus, shwarma, lamb kebabs, and chicken platters, not to local clientele but to a sunburned standing army of reporters. There were perhaps two dozen of them on the patio chairs—"Fries, please!" "Another Coke!" "We'll take the check!"—and T.R. shared a look of puzzlement with Alan Chin. "Goddamn," said the look, "we drive a hundred miles across the desert for a diner in New York?"

Ruweished, T.R. rapidly discerned, was now the staging ground for embarkation to Iraq, and these reporters stationed here were languishing like sailors in a port. Like sailors they had even left their mark, for on the wall behind the register there was a strange mosaic. Taped to the wall in a staggered mural-like display were several dozen business cards.

As the rest of the party claimed a table, T.R. went to inspect this work of art. In it was the arc of Ruweished's economic history. The oldest cards, starting on the left, were from indigenous concerns—tanneries, mechanics, import-export shops. And yet the new cards, straggling like hieroglyphics to the right, were from the latest chiefs of commerce: CNN, NBC, and CBS.

Well, he had certainly found his story. Never one to miss the follies of the press, T.R. could now write a piece on how the great white hunters of the media had taken over the town. The desk might scoff at such a story, but there it was on the wall. It was a journalistic Cavern of Lascaux.

"Great chicken sandwiches!" an ITN reporter had scribbled on a card.

"Four stars!" a wag from ABC had written on his own.

Forgoing breakfast, T.R. introduced himself to the man behind the register and asked what economic engines drove the town. The man explained that Ruweished was a rest stop for a troop of smugglers whose specialty, he said, was skirting U.S. sanctions on Iraq. "They smuggle everything—guns, food, oil, sheep," said the man, whose name was Mahmoud Al-Laham. Al-Laham went on to say that everything that one could imagine crossed the border in the smuggler's nightly desert runs.

And what was it like now that the international press corps had arrived?

"I find the journalists have much better manners than the smugglers. Besides," he shrugged, "they have more cash."

T.R.'s journalistic jowls were damp with drool. To have landed such a quote—and on his first attempt—was too good to be true. He took leave of Al-Laham and next approached a portly aging fellow drinking tea with friends on a hunch this man would prove a citizen of note. He did. And T.R. asked him now about the rents in town, for surely all these journalists encamped to penetrate Iraq would be in need of rooms.

Yes, said the man, rents indeed had gone through the roof. A modest flat now let for five hundred dollars a month while a "more substantial" house, retro-fit with power lines and central air, was twice that price. And this in Ruweished, where, the man explained, salaries did not rise much above a thousand dollars a year. With no small pride, he said that he had personally signed four leases in a week and stood to sign another seven more. T.R. turned to Nadia to double-check this fact—she began to nod her head. It was in fact amazing, for whom had they discovered in Ruweished but a desert Donald Trump.

By the time they left Abu Sayef's, T.R.'s notebook was chock-ablock with evidence of an all-out media invasion. The press had now become a full-employment act in town. Out-of-work Ruweishans had been hired as fixers and interpreters; several more had been hired for their cars. Then there was the service station on the main road, closed eight years ago, reopened to accommodate the hacks. Outside, T.R. stood beside the car and jotted in his notebook *boomtown, Klondike, Gold Rush days*. A family passed him as he flipped his notebook closed. Its two young boys had Fox News ballcaps on their heads.

In passing, Donald Trump had mentioned that a cousin of the country's foreign minister had come to town last week to build a press hotel—Great Scott!—and now they made for this hotel along a narrow side street winding through the dingy neck of town. Ruweished, in its poorer quarters, was a dusty slum of open sewage pits and mud-brick huts and dirty laundry hanging over sun-baked desert alleys. Driving the streets, T.R. could not help thinking that the cash infusions of the press would dry up soon and, when the journalists left town, Ruweished would return to this: a dusty slum. After all, the media were even more efficient than the government at conning people with their money and consumer goods, corrupting modes of commerce, and reducing ancient culture into photographs and tape, while claiming to expose all evils in an altruistic way. He could imagine what would happen when the media pulled out. There would be the awful sucking sound of money leaving town.

Even now on a back street, they came across a house that rivaled something one might find in the gated suburbs of Los Angeles. It sat down a dusty alley—full two-car garage, trellised yard, a satellite receiver on the roof. T.R. later learned it was the house that CNN had built and saw the image of a young producer from Atlanta pointing one slim finger at a mud-brick hut and three days later doing live shots from the roof. There was a massive camper idling in the drive, as big as any Airstream. The house was of the Mediterranean style with red-tiled roof, protective foliage, and stucco walls. Next door was a mud-brick hut, as yet unreconstructed, where some dirty children happened to be throwing pebbles at a tired, mangy dog.

At last they pulled up to the Arab Beach Hotel, or rather —— el, according to its broken sign. This was a building four full stories high, made of stone, with the sad-sack look of a fleabag on the northern Jersey Shore. It stood beyond an open gravel lot where a tent had been erected—stakes and rolled-up flaps—a large, wide canvas tent that one might find at a carnival or church revival. A wide-berth motor coach was parked before the tent.

Chin was the first to comment on the sight—"What the *hell*," he asked, "is that?" And indeed it was strange, since not only were the bus and tent the same bright candy-apple color; they were both festooned with banners that proclaimed them property of Jordan Telecom, the country's largest Internet concern.

T.R. stepped from the car, Chin went with him, and together they walked across the gravel toward the bus. Passing the tent, they saw beneath its canvas roof a set of folding tables, laden with computers and encircled by a complement of chairs. Shaking heads at this display, they were unprepared for the short thick man in spectacles who ambushed them, approaching from the entrance of the tent with outstretched arms, and an accent that was obviously French.

"You want to make zee Internet? Please, come, my friends. We make zee Internet right now."

The man, no more than five feet tall, stood before them rubbing hands with an eagerness that brought to mind the seamier side of profit. Reaching out, he placed one hand on T.R.'s back and tried to steer him toward the tent—T.R. did not approve. Chin, perhaps suspecting that the man might draw a punch, had dropped back silently to take some pictures. The man meanwhile had dropped back himself and produced a slender card. The card announced him as Pierre Mattei, Jordan Telecom's president and CEO.

T.R. was amused, but more amazed, for it was one thing for Donald Trump to rent houses at exorbitant rates, but it was madness of a wholly different sort for the chief executive of Jordan's major telecom company to have personally hauled a dozen hard drives deep to the desert. Such madness was a singular force—it brought to mind the tidal pull of markets, and the floods of money to be made at war. (For the record, Monsieur Mattei was the only man for perhaps a hundred miles in a tie and three-piece suit.)

The bus, which was enormous, brightly lit, air-conditioned, carpeted, its windows tinted to dissuade the sun, contained another shiny score of new computers. Each one had before its terminal a comfy-looking stool. Mattei sat down to show them how it worked. "You see," he said, tapping gleefully upon the keys, "zee Internet! We make it nice!" T.R. wrote this in his notepad. He asked the Frenchman why he had brought his bus to town. It seemed there was a pair of rationales. "First," Mattei began, "for zee journalists, of course, like you, who must to make zee Internet to, how you say it, file your stor-ees." No doubt this was true. The second concerned some refugees who were living in a U.N. camp a dozen miles from town. Zee Internet, Mattei explained, was the only chance such people had to communicate with family members stranded in Iraq. Unclear to him perhaps was that the telephones across Iraq were down and so zee Internet had all the chance of two tin cans connected by a string of reaching anyone at all. Of course such technicalities were nothing to the Frenchman's zeal, which was the zeal of any businessmen at war and for which, it should be said, he was charging only a dollar a minute, far below his normal rate.

"I tell you zis," Mattei went on, as they climbed down the steps of the bus and stood once more in the sunny gravel lot, "political problems, zese are good for Telecom. When you cannot travel, you must talk."

In the middle of his speech, Alan Chin walked up. He had been hanging back in his normal ghostly manner (the best of all photographers were ghosts) to photograph Mattei. Chin had shot an entire roll. Now he held his camera with a shy disgraceful touch that bordered on disgust, as if the images it held were a particularly nasty breed of insect he had been ordered to collect but did not have to like. "I've never seen it quite this bad," Chin said with a shake of his head that gave the impression life still had the power to revolt him. "I've never seen it quite this bad, and this is the fifth war I've covered," he went on with a heartsick weary edge. "I was in Bosnia, I was in Kosovo, Afghanistan, man. But it was never *this* bad. Does he really think a bunch of Arab refugees are going to send their cousins e-mail on a bus? What the hell? Are you getting all this down?"

T.R. was getting it down. Moreover, he was getting some small sense of how it worked. Beneath the soaring rents, the soaring payrolls, the soaring misplaced faith in every last technology, he caught a whiff of the same absurdity as at the Intercontinental—

the ingredients were the same, the smell was the same. It smelled, in fact, like blood being let from a fatted calf. And yet there was no blood in Ruweished; the blood was in Iraq. Could it be that Jordan at peace was stranger than Iraq at war? If that were so, the suggestion was that deep within the violence lay a calm like the eye of a hurricane. A violent calm? Perhaps, because the center of the hurricane was focused on the fight. Yes, there would be no scrambling for money, rents, and profits in Iraq—there would only be the war. It was the outskirts of the war, untouched by combat, that would bubble with insanity and greed. At least until the war was over, the outskirts alone would be absurd.

Surely this accounted for the Arab Beach, which T.R. made for now. He was joined by Chin, then Morrison, then Nadia, who said she was acquainted with the hotel's owner—she had just now seen him parking his car. "His name is Samer Mouasher," she reported, then went on to say that not only was he cousin to the foreign minister, he was one of the most eligible bachelors in Amman.

"They wrote some story on him in a magazine," she said. "He's actually kind of cute."

Entering the Arab Beach, T.R. was not surprised to find a snack bar called the Baghdad Cafe, nor was he shocked to find a laundry service in "The Clubhouse" with a billiards table, television set, and public hookah pipe. Somewhat south of expectations was the flyer on the wall announcing imminent construction of a full-scale gymnasium with Swedish massage. The flyer offered DVD machines complete with discs. "Any film, new or old," it said. "Even *Lord of the Rings II.*"

Presently the man behind such amenities appeared in the door. He fixed his guests with an ever-ready grin and approached to greet them with a handshake honed in many backroom deals. Samer Mouasher had the happy jaw and can-do manner of a pledge chair for the Delta Kappa Eps at Rush Week—he was that good, and that good-looking. Taking a seat, he ordered coffee and proceeded to expound in perfect English on his vision for the Arab Beach.

"I guess I see it as a full-service multifaceted hotel, not only for the press," he said, pausing to sip his drink and then to sign some documents placed at his wrist by an eager silent member of his staff, "but—thank you, Musti—for the NGOs that are sure to use Ruweished as their gateway to Iraq. Look," he said, "this town is poor," requiring no question to continue, "it's an old-fashioned smugglers' town, but people here, they know Iraq. They want to work, I want them to work, so if the World Food Program or the *Washington Post*, whoever, needs a place to stay, a guide to get them into Baghdad, a driver or a man who speaks the language, I provide. You see, my background"—and here without a break in rhythm he leaned to offer Nadia a light— "my background is in the film industry. I happen to own the largest production company in Jordan. We're used to doing desert shoots—we take entire film crews to the desert for a month with trailers, caterers, the works. I also run an ecological travel agency for tourists who want to see the wilderness in style, plus some other small concerns, so"—breathing now—"I have to say, in truth, if I could, and it *is* true, that I'm the perfect man to do the job."

For the first time Mouasher spread his gaze around the room, where a dozen reporters in safari gear and hiking boots drank tea, smoked cigarettes, consulted maps, ate omelettes, read, talked, napped, and played a rotating friendly game of eight-ball on the billiards table, one eye on their business, the other cocked toward the never-ending loop of cable news—and smiled his Pledge Week smile. "Besides," he said, as if it only now had struck him, "what a great place to hang out. I could leave tomorrow, but you know, I'm having fun."

Until that moment, T.R. had never considered the role of fun in any of this—it seemed a secondary motive to the exercise of greed. Nonetheless, Mouasher had confessed to his enjoyment so readily that T.R.'s brain picked up the trail. Perhaps it *was* fun to have a hangout for the press with all of its construction projects, marketing strategies, and in-bound shipments of tobacco, food, and booze. Perhaps, as well, there was fun in the logistics needed to plan and prosecute a war. Even in New York, he had never quite believed the argument that Iraq had been invaded for the money—as *casus belli*, it seemed too dull and too obtuse. Besides, the billions being spent each month to fuel the war would eventually outstrip whatever Halliburton and Bechtel would make. There were deeper drives afoot. If these included a desire to smack the Arabs, show them who was boss, to drive a spike of power through their hearts, and then to arrange the map so as to shift troops from Saudi Arabia, eliminate a peril facing Israel, and put a little pressure on Iran, they also might include the best chance yet for America to exercise its muscle in a fight against an enemy that had no friends, no allies, no one at its back—and, in the process, yes, to have a little fun. One had only to observe the president in discussions of the war to see that he was in his element. Confident, engaged, untouched by ambiguity, buoyed by every chance to show his balls—indeed, his words were those of a man enjoying sweets of newfound pleasure. Whether he enjoyed the war in truth or whether it was merely a facade hardly mattered, for that was the image he had chosen to emit. It might be stretching this connection to suggest there was a similarity between such presidential pleasure and Mouasher's own great happiness. Still, Mouasher seemed to be having quite a ball at his makeshift Hilton in the dust.

Now Mouasher rose and led them up a rickety flight of stairs to a long wooden hallway where single rooms and suites had been erected and where, he said with pride, Dan Rather himself would stay in two or three weeks' time when the border would be safe enough for news anchors to travel to Iraq. Mouasher had hung a CBS sign on the door to Rather's room to protect his "reservation," and asked if T.R. might include this in his notes. Even as he did so, T.R. felt a sudden profundity of shame, because he also felt profoundly hypocritical. Here he was making notes on a story that would roast Mouasher, just as it would roast the correspondents renting videos and playing pool, Dan Rather too, but it would not roast himself, and that was hypocritical, because if their crime was to revel in the pleasure of their own agenda, T.R. was equally guilty, and phony. His own agenda, after all, was to point out the flaws in those unlucky enough to have crossed his path. So as he stood and listened to Mouasher tell him of his good relationship with all three television networks, T.R. felt that it was far too easy to eviscerate this man, and that to do so, to eviscerate the whole damn town for its insanity and silliness, and greed, was perhaps a low blow that would say less about Ruweished than about his own reserves of bitterness and bile.

T.R. often felt the need to savage his surroundings, usually by means of nastiness in print. It was never meant to be malicious; often it was meant to define himself among the men he ran with as tougher than the rest. For years, in fact, he had set about to make himself a rebel in the field, a roughrider on the fringes of the city, or a man's man with the strength to match his wit. He had mocked the pampered life of the reporter with its cocktail parties and political talk, its televised appearances, its half-a-faggot restaurants, its easy living, easy money, easy workdays in the office on the phone. More than mock it, he had openly despised it; it was no more than a con man's life where one could win acclaim with minor effort, where a few well-chosen words could make it seem like danger hung about one's throat. Had he not done this himself? He was in Jordan, after all, with a comfortable room, a pleasant bar, a nice toilet to sit on, and a telephone beside it, far from the guns and bombs, and far from death. He was living the exact same life he so despised. No rebel, certainly no roughrider, he had satisfied himself by detecting and deflating all pretension. That alone had been his task.

As Mouasher went downstairs to entertain his guests, T.R. watched as Alan Chin took twenty-four more pictures of the Arab Beach and listened in the car as Nadia spoke of the inequities in town, and felt compelled to speak of them himself, and spoke in a tone of voice so muted he was thankful they had turned off the radio or else his words might have been lost. He only shared a portion of his thoughts—that on this afternoon he had realized the press would have to finally confront the damage it inflicted on the places that it went and the people that it met, and this was no mean task since it would take relinquishing the fantasy that one could cover a story without affecting it. And clearly one could not. The war in Iraq was damaging enough— it was still unknown what damage it would cause—but those entrusted with its history, he said, might do well to tread as lightly as they could. On little more than fumes, he took himself to task for sharing in this mess and caring more about his reputation and his writing than the people and the places he described. Then he shut up and drove the car and soon they were back in Amman.

They returned after dark, the dirt of the day was on their skin. They were fatigued and Nadia, looking drawn, went home to get some rest. With Chin and Morrison, T.R. went down to Mama Juanita's first for one drink, then another, then, starting to enjoy themselves, they ordered meals. Despite his bitterness, T.R. had managed to maintain his appetite. Ruweished was a horror show and an embarrassment, but it was also one hell of a story. He watched his intake. He wanted to write well that night.

Chapter 10

THE GOOD SOLDIER

H ERE, IN PART, is what he wrote.

RUWEISHED, Jordan—Ruweished is a dump. It is a squalid smugglers' hamlet that sits on the rim of Jordan's eastern desert like a morsel of inedible meat that has been pushed, unwanted, toward the edge of a plate. For years, the major economic engine here was servicing the scores of dusty trucks that rumbled through each day on their way to the Iraqi border, several miles to the vacant east.

With the war, however, the border has closed, and the people of Ruweished—friendly but extremely poor—have watched in shock and awe as a fresh horde of brigands has descended on their town. These bandits do not drive 18-wheelers, but gleaming SUV's. They do not earn their living smuggling sheep, illicit drugs and guns across the border; they deal in a much more rarified commodity: the news.

Yes, that just about did justice to it. T.R. felt satisfied, even proud. He had written fairly well. For his reward—he always took rewards for writing well; it stoked some old Pavlovian instinct in the brain—he smoked one cigarette methodically and full of pleasure at the window. The window was open to the night, the night itself warm with a handsome breeze of olive groves. It seemed as if some sigh of lamentation filled the air, deep breaths of an Arabian fatigue. He could hear these breaths beneath the light wind coming through the palm trees, feel them slipping down the white stone hills that formed a bowl around Amman. The city had grown tender, it was softening, becoming beautiful: T.R. felt tender too. The sky, for instance, was an easy purple—he had never seen such color in a sky. Arriving from the border earlier that night, he had noticed that the marble of the Intercontinental's plaza seemed to ring in the white glow of the spotlights aimed at the enormous central fountain. He had no idea if such serenity was typical of Jordan, or of any Arab capital, or whether again it was the corollary of the violence raging to the east. In any case, there were hints of a heavy gust just recently expired, a sodden calm, but it was not oppressive. Down in the plaza the taxi men were out. Even now he heard them laughing. If he had never heard of desert caravans or T.E. Lawrence, T.R. could have easily imagined both from the raw materials below, which seemed to share the same cool blue of the oasis, late-night jokes and hookahs, camels fed, feet washed, the smells of cardamom, a beckoning tent with open flaps awaiting, lamb on copper trays, and a veiled young girl to serve it. He never thought his brain susceptible to such suggestions, yet there he was at the window now, walking toward the tent . . . when suddenly the phone began to clamor with a high-pitched, irritating bleat. Oasis vanished, he breathed a breath of smoke, and went to get the phone.

It was Ian Fisher. He was at the Hyatt. He was wondering if T.R. might come over for a drink. Not late—it was hardly ten o'clock—T.R. agreed, feeling saintly having filed. He was eager to meet the man who, in all likelihood, would be his partner in Iraq. T.R. had met Fisher once, very briefly, in Newark, New Jersey, when he himself was working at the bureau there and Fisher had dropped by to file a story he was sure that neither of them recalled. His recollection now was of a slim nice-looking man with short brown close-cropped hair and wire-rimmed glasses—in all, a fair description of T.R. himself. So they would make a pair of doppelgangers headed into Baghdad. It sounded right. Never distant from the pagan in his heart, T.R. smiled at this coincidental bit.

The Hyatt was a quick five-minute walk, and Fisher waited in the lobby. As he crossed the marble floor, T.R. saw at once his recollection had been right. Fisher was slight, good-looking, brown-haired, understated, and demonstrably intelligent in a cardigan and pair of khaki pants. But as they greeted one another it appeared he had the gruff, distracted manner of a young professor who was busy enough with course loads and administrative tasks to come off seeming brusque. Later, T.R. learned that Ian Fisher was not by nature brusque, just busy, although now as they shook hands, Fisher barely met his eye. Instead he checked his watch and tapped a pen against his cheek and walked across the lobby toward the bar. So abandoned, T.R. followed. Fisher after all was senior man.

They ordered drinks; an uncomfortable silence settled in. This occasionally happened when reporters met each other in the flesh. Accustomed to the anonymity of bylines, reporters oftentimes relied upon the power of their names; if their physical presence was somehow less impressive, the result was often gloom. To dissipate this gloom, T.R. brought up the story he had filed that evening. He aimed to make it funny—there were references to Donald Trump, the Arab Beach, and Swedish massage— and yet the mere mention of his labors seemed to poke and prod and slap at Fisher's nerves to the point that, when the beer arrived, Fisher gulped his with a long exhausted sigh. The drink seemed to calm him and clear the air of his anxiety. Now he started to complain about the lack of news in Jordan and the hundreds of reporters wasting time on stories no one read.

"No one reads them," Fisher said. "*We* don't even read them anymore." T.R. had indeed picked up a glumness in the press corps in Amman. It was something like a system-wide depression. Last night in the bar, the acolytes, for instance, had been planning stories, jotting in their notebooks, trying over beers to root out from the dirt of Jordan something worthwhile for the papers, something on the war. "There's a community of exiled Iraqis in Amman. If we could find them, you know, get them talking . . ." "*Newsweek* did it." "So?" "So it's been done." "So?" "So it's been *done.*" It was the sort of misery one heard in bullpens during perfect games or in the dugout, down with the reserves.

Fisher had been writing out of Jordan for a month. He had filed his share of stories, but the bosses in New York could not have cared less because the stories from Amman had not concerned Iraq. He had already racked his brain on every dispatch he could manage. He had met with government officials, talked with university professors, drank with the embassy flacks, and schmoozed the military attaché. Now he was out of tricks. Worse yet, he said, a month ago he had been in Baghdad as a backup for the great John Burns. He had been asked to stay when Burns went underground (the secret police were hunting for his hide), but with a natural human urge to save his *own* hide Fisher had requested to be sent to Jordan, where now he had spent the last four weeks in an effort to return.

"*Not* a good decision," Fisher said, shaking his head with dry remorse. Then he quoted from his own imaginary epitaph: "Ian Fisher—frequently frustrated, but mostly a real nice guy."

T.R. felt sympathetic stirrings, but he chose to listen closely and to study Fisher's face. He was learning what he could from Fisher's sigh of disappointment, from his rounded shoulders and the awful look in his eye, which was the look of a junior law partner who has gone six weeks without a restful night of sleep. T.R. was also being cautious: Politics was never far from any convocation of reporters from the *Times*. Indeed there was no way yet to know if these complaints were an invitation to complain—an invitation T.R. might accept and then regret.

The problem was that T.R. did not completely trust his peers. In some sense, he was like the Pentecostal preacher who separates the good Christ from the faulty Christians, for if he loved the *New York Times*, he had reservations toward the people it employed. Experience had taught him they were dangerous, and schizophrenic. In public they proclaimed themselves as independent spirits, pure observers, open hearts, while in private they were often skittish, insular, and as tribal as an Appalachian clan. There was, in other words, an interposing dissonance—on the one hand, they went forth with curiosity in pursuit of global truth; on the other, they were hemmed in by their own ambition and their constant maddening attempts to gauge their standing at the place. Having invested massive outlays of personal capital in working for the *Times*, they were forever pumping its stock—

as the institution rose or fell, so too did their own value. This meant any nick to the paper's reputation caused them pain. It also meant they had little patience for a life lived richly beyond the walls of Forty-third Street.

T.R., for one, believed that working at the *Times* became their cornerstone of personality—he had experienced this odd phenomenon himself. When he was introduced at parties as a *Times* reporter, instantly his interlocutor would hone in on the paper, offer an opinion of its slant, ask endless irritating questions on the placement, timing, or the bias of a story, and generally treat him like the twenty-seven years of life that went before his byline had appeared (years in which at least a few exceptional events had taken place) did not exist. It was a testament, no doubt, to the power of the *Times*. More than once, he had heard over drinks, "You don't know what the *New York Times* has meant to me. As a kid, my father read it at the breakfast table, now I read it too . . ." And while T.R. felt lucky to be part of such an institution that could so affect so many readers, he was skeptical of placing at the center of his life *a job*, to the exclusion of hobbies, passions, loves, relationships, all else—and yet there were some reporters, even many, who did exactly that.

It was just that he had never felt entirely at home at the *Times*, an entity part corporation, part empire, part religious cult, part family (the sort of family that takes summers every August at the same resort, has crests and old traditions, and makes rules about itself: "Well, that is simply not the way a *Watson* acts"). He was ready to take the blame himself and fault this on his ever-present need to stand alone, although he could not shake the feeling he was much too crass, too loud, too full of uninhibited contradictions to fit among a crowd that always seemed to be calibrating the effects of every mood. *Times* reporters, at their worst, were beehives buzzing with superiority that came from being at the *Times*, but then inferiority from knowing that the gift could be withdrawn at any moment. Thus they lived in constant fear of the next political mistake. So, yes, T.R. was being cautious, perhaps more cautious than Ian Fisher had deserved. Without quite knowing it, he had committed the crime of excess prudence, which is to miss the feint of friendship while bent in one's defensive crouch.

Their second round of beer was better. As a flush of friendliness came on in the now-dark, quiet empty bar, Fisher turned with a gambler's smile to say, "Last week, I bought the coolest fucking car."

"You *bought* a car?" T.R. was impressed. "What kind of car did you buy?"

"I bought an armor-plated Jeep."

"Where the hell did you get an armor-plate Jeep? How much did that cost?"

"Seventy-thousand," Fisher said. "I had it flown in from the Balkans. The OSCE was using it on patrol."

It seemed extravagant, to say the least, and Fisher now went on to list the other equipment he had bought, his foul mood shifting into something close to glee as he ticked off the ways he had spent the paper's money. There was, for instance, a villa in Ruweished he had rented (one could only hope from Donald Trump), a crumbling ancient pile with four rooms plus a kitchen, living room, and bath, a satellite TV, and the young Arab cousin of Ruweished's governor—named Saddam, no less—hired as a full-time guard. As well there was the gasoline, the water, food, the tents, the propane, the propane stove, the toilet paper, flashlights, tire jack, and tires—half the fun, so it would seem, was in accumulation of the gear. And in the spending of the money, too. Fisher alone had spent in such gargantuan amounts that T.R. wondered now how many millions multiplied the *New York Times* had spent in sum. For if the *Times* spent X, then CNN would surely shell out triple X, and ABC, and CBS, and NBC, and ITN—yes, the cash out-flowing from the media alone approached the astronomical. One had only to recall that This Reporter, on his first assignment overseas, with seven thousand dollars strapped in hundreds to his gut, had to wonder, what of the other thirty-score reporters covering the war? And what of the purported agents infiltrating Baghdad with their attachés of cash? Or the oilmen ready for work and waiting in Kuwait? They were doing the town in their Hawaiian shirts! T.R. still did not believe the war had been fought for profit, but he was coming to believe it had been fought *by and in defense* of profit, *by and in defense* of the long-sought amalgamated power of the U.S. dollar bill.

For truly, what lay underneath the Arab hatred of America? It was not just troops near Mecca, or support for Israel, or some old atavistic anger over the Ottoman defeat. No, it was simply they were poor and beaten, living in sandstone huts, while next door, for a month or so, the staff of CNN resided in an off-white stucco mansion with a microwave and VCR. A generation of the Arab young had come along much different from the generations come before. This new generation could be enticed by money as any other, but could also be enticed by the suicide bomb, by heavenly virgins, and by death. This generation held no faith in the modern day-to-day accumulation of wealth: Faith was reserved for the moment when the bomb went off and the angels came with treasures a thousand times more valuable than gold. Their difference lay in their elemental hatred not for America's policies or powers, but for its myths—for the country in its ideal, unreal form. After all, it was America that dressed them in the jeans and sneakers they had worn while sweltering as children, just as America produced the candy-laced rock songs that rose above the rooftops of their slums. Their appetites had been tweaked and torqued and twisted and eventually re-shaped into unnatural modes of consumption by products crowding out their markets, and impossible fantasies of *Dallas* and *Miami Vice*. They were forced beyond control to build their vision of the world (and thus their vision of themselves) on the very cash and clothes and sex of which America was made.

Yes, America had tantalized their brains with TV shows, and shaped their brains with processed food and processed movies. America had offered itself as a desirable commodity, and it *was* desirable, desirable as Coca-Cola on a summer afternoon, and slim young women on Miami Beach, and slim young girls in red Corvettes. The real young girls of course were nowhere to be found. They were as absent from the streets of Cairo as they were in Cleveland, since mainly they did not exist. Their existence was a fantasy, and the commodity a come-on, and the come-on ended at the awful moment when the sugar melted on their tongues. Still poor, still small, still living in slums, they sensed they had been conned.

In the end, this latest generation hated America for just that reason. It had been conned by advertising spots for tennis shoes and cigarettes and four-wheel drives and DVDs, and by television shows, where the most absurd retelling of the country's fantasies—and the clearest portrait of its hopes—was converted into the high-gloss products of its myths: the beautiful girl, the independent man, the life of ease and plenty.

These lies were of course well known to any American—who among them still believed a pair of tennis shoes would get you laid? But there was nonetheless proprietary interest in protecting the myth, which, if revealed as empty, could prove as damaging as any military defeat. America had not waged war to make a short-term profit; still what seemed essential was the notion of a war embarked upon to certify all future profits. Washington had gone to battle: It had gone to battle in defense of the American way.

Strange as it may sound, the point behind this thought was that the Arabs' truest enemies no longer lived within the White House or the Pentagon; they lived on Wall Street and Madison Avenue. It was the government alone that now dealt plainly with the Arabs. The Bush administration had announced that it would brook no longer any ire from the Islamic world when it could simply use its force to stem or quash or kill that ire. Unlike the American corporation, the American government set forth in no uncertain terms its willingness to break the living spine of all recalcitrant regimes.

The tactics of the media had therefore started with the premise that to get the goods they wanted most (a picture of the soldier fighting to defend this American way), it would have to look like a soldier, act like a soldier, and bedeck itself in a soldier's kit of gear. If on the way the good, clean, middle-class armadas of the press were able to test their muscles, take some fire, and feel for once intoxications of a danger that no longer touched their lives, so much the better. The ruling class in Washington was not alone in its desire for the man-making exercise of war; the chattering class was just as desirous, and just as ready to spend vast amounts to make it work.

Sitting in the bar, T.R. brought an end to all these thoughts with a long, profoundly needed sip of beer. He then turned to Ian Fisher with a question: What, he asked, should he do in preparation for Iraq?

Fisher's answer was in fact another question—five short words whose brevity belied the complications that would soon occur.

Fisher asked, "Have you met Rania yet?"

Chapter 11

A SECRET
CONVERSATION

T.R. NEVER DID CATCH Rania's last name. Like certain movie stars and figures from the Bible, she had earned that special badge of honor reserved for the famous in Amman—she was a one-name sort of girl. In fact she was no girl, but a woman in the reaches of a handsome middle age whose name T.R. had first encountered at the bar of Mama Juanita's in connection with the panoply of favors she would render for a price. Should one desire to meet the queen, Rania could arrange it. Likewise, if one desired documents to travel through a military zone, Rania could provide them in a day. Her competence in managing such critical requests, and her mystical habit of appearing to be everywhere, on everybody's lips at once, reminded T.R. of the aging Mafioso he knew in New York who had once said, when asked what he did to earn his living, "Who, me? I provide."

Rania, too, provided. The difference of course was that Rania operated not on the criminal fringe of power but in the very heart of the regime. Her father had been a well-regarded military officer and comrade to the former monarch, King Hussein, and, born to the intrigues of the palace, she had then increased her stature by marrying a wealthy businessman with ventures spread throughout the Middle East. Unlike the ordinary rut of fixers, who were often small-time grifters or local journalistic types, Rania was not only smart, but blonde, coiffed, and well-accoutered enough to be mistaken for the president of Jordan's Junior League, should such a thing exist. She was also known to possess the most spectacular set of fake breasts in the country. This was both an engineering marvel and of no small consequence to the influence she wielded in the court.

That night, settling their bar tab, Fisher had suggested T.R. contact Rania to obtain a visa for Iraq. "How much is that going to cost?" T.R. had asked.

"Well, it depends on how much work she has to do."

"What do you think? Five hundred?"

Fisher produced his finest get-real look.

So initiated to the rite of spending money, T.R. counted out an ample sum in hundred-dollar bills that night and in the morning strolled from the Intercontinental to the Hyatt—both now looking like casinos built in Vegas—on to the breakfast bar for coffee and some food. Rania was to meet him later; she would come to fetch him in the parking lot. For now T.R. was anxious to determine if Fisher was right and the Hyatt truly served a better meal.

The dining room of the Hyatt was nearly empty and the sunlight flooding in through floor-to-ceiling windows had the profound clarity that one associates with mornings by the sea. Here, the light was drier, thicker, heavier, yet the effect was much the same: The groups and singles sitting at the tables looked re-markably peaceful. It was utterly unlike the Intercontinental. In-stead of young brigades of drunken correspondents, one saw freshly shaven elders reading the *International Herald Tribune.* Perhaps they were reading their own dispatches; they certainly seemed pleased enough. Indeed, there was a pleasant feeling all around: It was not unlike the silence of the rare book room at Yale. The men at breakfast flipped their broadsheets, they sipped their coffee like English dukes. Of course! The serious reporters had been found.

T.R. resolved to change hotels at once. Even as he made this small decision, he looked up at an unfamiliar group of men enter-ing the room. The men waited for a moment in the doorway, then proceeded to the breakfast bar, where at the omelette sta-tion they commenced to load plates with bacon, sausage, hash brown, eggs—with every sort of high-caloric food. As most of the reporters had chosen meals of toast and yogurt—T.R. had himself selected Frosted Flakes—his eye was drawn to the men, who were tall, thick, imposing, and might have been union ironworkers judging by their heavy flannel shirts. They sat. Three of them tucked into their grub; the fourth meanwhile— a big broad poke of a boy with flame tattoos and a baseball cap—lit a cigarette and leaned back in his chair to breathe a cloud of smoke. The eyes of the entire room were on them now and though they surely noticed, there was no immediate re-sponse. Indeed, among themselves they hardly spoke. Their reserves of morning concentration seemed to burn for coffee, food, and cigarettes alone.

T.R. assumed they were military, or perhaps ex-military— they had that sort of looseness in their hips. They also had the

way of men inured to eating on the run—they ate one-handed
with their other hands encircling their plates. Nearly from the
day he had arrived, T.R. had heard there were tiny squads of
spooks and Special Forces in Amman; now he studied the men
to see what sort of team they made. Of the four, one was almost
certainly the leader—gray-haired, watchful, elegant, well
dressed. Of the rest, the tattooed man was both the youngest
and fittest—he had that healthy spill of muscle like an uncut
side of beef. The other two were older, in their forties, slightly
overweight. Their paunches were such that one might find
among mechanics at a stock-car race, although their faces had
that hard, rough, Confederate horseflesh that would have been
at home at any rifle shop in any southern state.

Curious as to what strange mission brought them to Amman,
T.R. put his cup down and rose to approach their table. He had
no clue what to say, but this was largely to the point. As a good
comedian will sniff the crowd and pitch his jokes according to
its mood, so too will a good reporter sniff his subject in advance
and begin the conversation with appropriate remarks. What remarks were usually dependent on the moment and the angle of
approach. While T.R. knew that he was not so good at the approach, he had done it a hundred, if not several hundred times,
and understood that conversation was akin to writing: One
began with silence and progressed against it, joking, jabbing,
teasing, earning trust in bursts. If he was none too good at this,
he still enjoyed it, for the pleasure was to joke and jab and
tease—the pleasure was to cast yourself upon the ocean of your
wit. With every word, you either gained or lost attention, either
neared or fell away from that intangible experience of truth—
you feeling me?—that hovered in successful moments overhead.

The task, of course, was infinitely harder when the subject was a stranger (which is why reporting on the clubby world of Washington was such a plum). It could be said that half the good reporter's art was making strangers talk.

Interest in this rapidly approaching talk, which obviously spooked T.R. as much as pleased him, was now shared by most of the reporters in the room. They stared at him as he rose and passed the breakfast bar. He was not surprised, nor did he mind, for there had been, he sensed, a secret conversation going on between these camps from the moment all four men had sat down with their meals. With stares alone, the reporters had been saying, "All right, soldiers, let me look at you awhile and try to divine why in God's good name you feel it necessary to participate in war—especially in *this* war. Do you really think your work is helpful, wholesome, just or have you all been brainwashed yet again by a patriotic fever that would destroy entire countries in defense of the lie that America was facing an attack?" And the soldiers saying back, "America? What the hell do you know of America? If you truly cared about America, you would have served it with your flesh. Where were you, good cowards, when America *was* attacked?" And the reporters: "We were on your television sets, and radios, and in your papers talking to your neighbors, wives, and friends. Oh, no, don't be high and mighty, sirs, for times have changed and all the battlefields you once claimed as your own have come to our cities now, and we have seen our share of blood." Then the soldiers: "So why do you hate us then, having seen the battlefield and blood? Are you so slack, so weak, so fat that you will *never* raise a fist when evil crashes at the door?" And lastly the reporters: "Hate you? We don't hate you, nor do we trust you, though, for you have lied to us so very many times." And the soldiers lastly: "But without us you would have no voice at all. How dare you speak of lies!"

Interrupting such communications, T.R. stood before their table. Now he cleared his throat.

"Good morning, gentleman," he said, and introduced himself. "I saw you sitting here and couldn't help but wonder. What exactly brought you to Amman?"

It was the leader who spoke first. "Tourism, sir. We're tourists. We're here to see the sights." Against the basso of his military monotone were snickers of evasion from his men.

But T.R. was prepared—he had expected evasion. Crowd sniffed, he understood that no straightforward method of politeness had a chance.

"Well, pardon my language at breakfast but that's a load of horseshit." Yeah! "I don't mind if you don't want to talk to me"—of course, he did—"but I'd rather not hear crap."

"That what they teach you at the *New York Times*?" It was one of the older soldiers now. "That you'd rather not hear crap?"

"Teach me nothing. I just work there. On Wednesday afternoons, I get a check."

"Whereabouts? Right there in Manhattan? And you feel safe when you bend to tie your shoes?"

"I sit before I tie them," T.R. said—and the older soldier laughed. Yes, he had them now, he had a little jazz, a little quiver in the wood, since he had shown them that a gent of the press could banter like a private on patrol. Perhaps it's what he had been after from the start: some form of evidence or necessary proof that underneath the cynical and mutually distrustful ways in which the military and the press might interact, it was conceivable to jawbone over breakfast with obscenity and jokes about New York.

Now a different conversation could begin.

"Seriously," T.R. said, "there's a lot being written on the military, but not everybody gets their fair share of ink. If you fellas are doing something interesting, you ought to let me know."

"Well, we went down to Petra last week," the other older soldier said. There was a poker player's slyness in his face. "That was inneresting, wudn't it, boys?"

The boys were occupied in contemplation of their meals.

"You been there yet?" he asked T.R.

"Can't say that I have."

"Well, everybody oughta get to Petra. All kinds of inneresting places in this country. Some outside the country, too."

"Really? And where would those be?"

"Oh, you find them if you look."

They were being coy with one another. Perhaps they were both just stubborn, or perhaps each wished to test the strength of the other's resolve. No, T.R. decided, it was dialogue—subtle dialogue. In any conversation, a reporter and his source were bound together by filaments of caution and flirtation—yes, in talks like this there was always an erotic charge. Not sexual, erotic. Every nuance was perceived, every flicker changed the course of conversation—the slightest hesitation could destroy it, a profound remark could push it into even lusher depths.

While T.R. desired to know those depths he also knew there came a time to let them go. Thus, he moved in swiftly now to shake their hands. It was nice to meet them, he explained, yes, nice indeed, but he was off, perhaps he'd catch them later for a drink.

"In the meantime," he went on, "you guys enjoy the sights."

Chapter 12

WHAT MOVIE ARE YOU STARRING IN?

THE CONVERSATION WITH the men had been most interesting, promising further interesting conversation down the road. Now, however, a dark mood threatened. As T.R. walked outside to wait for Rania, he encountered Ian Fisher.

There was nothing essentially evil meeting Fisher; rather, with all logistical brain fires burning, Fisher told T.R. he was making preparations to leave for the border that same night. For several days, Fisher had been trying to arrange a visit to an air base in the western desert of Iraq. Rumor had it that the Special Forces were engaged there in a search for chemical weapons. The arrangements had been a minor torture. A certain Major Bigelow, the U.S. military attaché in Jordan, had received a hundred calls from Fisher asking for permission to embark on the trip, but had rejected each of these requests. But Fisher had now obtained permission to approach the air base, known cryptically as R-4. There was a caveat, however: There would be no army escort, or any guarantee that the Special Forces would allow him access to the air base when, and if, he managed to arrive. It meant that Fisher ran the risk of traveling a hundred miles into occupied Iraq to find himself alone on the highway with no place safe to stay.

Nonetheless, T.R. congratulated him, since the trip would mean escape form Jordan even for as little as a day. It would also mean a byline from Iraq. And, standing in the plaza of the Hyatt, T.R. asked if he might come along.

"Actually," Fisher said, "I just spoke to the desk. They need you in Amman."

A tiny bubble of despair first slid, then detonated, deep in T.R.'s gut.

"And what exactly do they want me to do here?" T.R. asked. His stomach echoed his disappointment with a growl.

In echo of his disappointment, "Don't know," said Fisher. "I guess they want you to be on hand. I'd love for you to come along. The thought of driving through the desert by myself, not nice. I tried convincing them, but they seemed to think it better if the two of us split up."

This is about where the dark mood settled in, and T.R. began to curse the bosses in New York. He went on for a grunt or two about their micro-managerial style. When would they step aside and trust their reporters, trust the people on the ground? The people on the ground were the only ones who knew how to write about the war, though even as he grunted, T.R. recognized that he had not yet written anything about the war—of the two stories he had filed from Jordan, neither had run. The editors had killed his story on Ruweished, saying no one cared about the follies of the press. (What better follies were there than the follies of the press?) His second story had been spiked as well. (It had concerned the moneychangers of Amman who were buying up Iraqi dinars in speculation that the dinar would soar when America had won the war. Dull, until one learned the moneychangers hated the Americans, and so their hearts said, "Brave Saddam!" even as their pocketbooks were praying for a cakewalk.) Now, however, T.R. had the chance to get inside Iraq, and yet he had been ordered to remain in Jordan—the very place there wasn't any news. He therefore cursed the desk for several minutes in the hotel plaza, using a variety of gruff descriptive terms.

"Look," he said to Fisher, when his steam gave out, "if you go, I go." Even if I have to sneak across the border in the car. "

Fisher looked a tad uneasy, but gave an acquiescent nod. It was clear that despite the mandates from New York he preferred to have T.R. along.

Now Fisher went off to the Intercontinental where he planned to meet the cameraman who would accompany him to Iraq. And soon as he left, a dark gray SUV pulled up. Dim with despair, T.R. imagined that it must have been some diplomat or government official, since the SUV had tinted windows and the driver sat up front alone. With engine running, the young driver left the car and made his way around to open the door with an almost imperceptible bow. Then, a woman on a mobile phone stepped out and, studying the faces in the plaza, gave T.R. a wave. She beckoned him toward the car.

T.R. got in. "Good," the woman said, applying makeup with her free hand while the other held the phone. "So you need to see the queen?"

"The queen," he said. "No."

"Well, good. She's in a mood." She spoke into the phone—
"I'll email you back"—then turned to face him. "What was it
you needed?"

"A visa. For Iraq."

If no official introduction had been made, none was needed, for
it was obvious that Rania felt her reputation was enough to sweep
formality away. She had that sort of personality one found among
the rich: She was instantly familiar and wanted to know everything about you all at once. Driving now, she quizzed T.R. about
himself and then about the other *Times* reporters she had worked
with in the past. "Ah, Joel Brinkley, he was my first," she said with
conscious innuendo. "A wonderful reporter, a wonderful man."

Some of these men he knew in person (for it seemed that
Rania only worked with men), some by name alone. T.R. could
not help feeling underwhelming in their company—the men
she had mentioned were important men, famous men, men with
secretaries and assistants, men with reputations to uphold. In his
cargo pants and leather boots, he felt as well that he was vastly
underdressed. Rania wore a business suit that would have garnered notice in the better *boites* of Midtown; her lacquered shoes
and lacquered nails bespoke a privilege typically reserved for
chartered planes and charity events. Her frosted hair was im-
maculate, her breasts immovable, and her rings were on the
tasteful side of gaudy. If this account has wasted time on questions of her style, it is only to suggest that, like a hick arriving in
the city, or a busboy called upon to serve a dinner at Lutece, T.R.
had once more waded into waters well above his head. But the
discomfort was not entirely unpleasant—it forced him to be
keenly aware of his surroundings. In fact, discomfort in the service of awareness was one of T.R.'s more familiar mental states.

They were headed for the Iraqi embassy. When they arrived, the driver stopped the car, stepped out to open Rania's door, and T.R. followed her past two armed guards, to whom she smiled flirtatiously and bid hello, into a damp, foul-smelling room that called to mind a Greyhound station in a dirt-poor western state. A couple of shabby mustached men looked up as they came in. Hunched on broken chairs, they offered dark conspiring looks. Aside from the chairs and a coffee table with an overflowing ashtray, there was no furniture in the room, which stank of sweat, smoke, and political defeat, except a battered desk in back behind which sat a man who was something of a runtish cross between Peter Lorre and Al Franken.

Nearly at once, T.R. recognized the embassy as the sort of place he had been working in for years. It was a Bronx place, a Bath Beach, Brooklyn, place, a place for lugs and racketeers. T.R. was home, he had arrived. For this was *his* sort of place, and these his sort of people. Even now the Runt stood up behind his desk and lumbered toward them with his shirttails hanging at his gut. The way he looked exactly like a filing clerk at the Bronx Supreme Court practically brought tears to T.R.'s eyes.

"*Marhaba*," said Rania to the Runt, busying herself inside her purse to avoid the unhygienic act of shaking hands. "We're here to pick up a visa, if we could."

What she had been looking for was T.R.'s passport, which now she handed to the Runt. As no American enjoys surrendering such a thing, the echo here was *Papers, please!*—T.R. felt queasy as the Runt retreated to his desk, there to check his name against pages that had formed some sort of list. The list apparently contained the names of journalists approved for visas to Iraq, but T.R.'s name was not on the list. How could it be? He was only now applying for the visa, and not by any ordinary method. His queasiness was worsened by the fifteen hundred dollars he was carrying in cash—*that* was his method, not an application, but a bribe. Stuffed in the pockets of his pants (the more the pockets, the more the bribes?), it made him feel like a dollar sign with arms and legs.

The air inside the embassy pressed around him as he fished for the bribe, all eyes burning at his back. The mustached men on their broken chairs emitted threats and imprecations which, if silent, were nonetheless intense. Many times, in the taverns and bodegas of the Bronx, he had felt the disconcerting glow that went with being the only white for miles, but rarely had he felt the mix of threat and quizzicality that he felt now. *The enemy*—this phrase seemed plastered on his face, and yet the looks he was receiving from the men were desperate, curious, not altogether vicious in intent. If such an apprehension could be trusted, then perhaps the troops en route to Baghdad would be welcomed, since the atmosphere inside the embassy was one of fear and consternation—a general distrust, not blatant rage. If the troops were not welcomed, they were likely to encounter no grave problems, for if the embassy was any measure, the military columns moving north would find themselves in combat not with a powerful regime, but with a government unable to provide office furniture to its diplomats abroad.

Deft as it was, T.R.'s analysis was interrupted by the Runt who beckoned Rania over to address some minor trouble with the list. (Why T.R. had decided that the trouble was minor was surely due to his faith in Rania's competence, which she exhibited by smiling now and hanging up her phone.) Following behind her T.R. watched the Runt flip page by page, run his finger down the list, while Rania stood beside him saying first, "That's it," and then, "That's it." None of the names, of course, were it since T.R.'s name was not on the list—the list, he saw, was nothing but an intricate charade.

"Work with me," Rania told him, whispering in English, pointing at a squiggle on the page and then announcing with authority, "That's it. *That's* the one." The Runt, having gone through every motion, feigned the most remarkable version of relief. He smiled an Oscar-winning smile, and reached for T.R.'s hand, and shook his hand, as if to say, "How could I have been so stupid? It was right there all this time," then disappeared to his office only to return in moments with the list. Though he could not decipher what it said, T.R. clearly saw the name they had selected had been doctored: Yes, a squiggle had been added with a curlicue or two. The ink and Wite-Out had not yet dried on the page.

That night at the Intercontinental he experienced a moment's guilt thinking of the poor reporter whose name was close enough to his to have been stolen. Perhaps that man would arrive next morning at the embassy and find his visa had already been disbursed. All was fair in war, he told himself while drinking bourbon at the bar. Whiskey was a wonder at eradicating guilt.

Two nights later he and Rania once more sat outside the embassy in Rania's car. It was a dark night, and in deference to the darkness, a secret envelope had been prepared. But if the envelope contained his bribe, it also contained a *thank-you note*—a note in which T.R. had written graciously to thank the Runt for every kindness done. It broke his heart that a corrupt official wanted to be thanked in writing for illicit services performed. Once again the indication was of a crumbling regime, escape

routes planned, monies funneled into Swiss accounts—the Runt
had evidently done his sniffing and decided to get what he
could. In this respect, he had proved himself the match of
Rania, who had taken fifteen hundred dollars of her own to
make the deal. Even now, Rania stepped from the car and, high
heels clacking on the asphalt, approached the embassy to knock
on the door first once, then twice, then wait in the dark with
shifting nervous eyes, slip in through the door, and come back
minutes later with his visa. Back in the car, she told the driver to
make for the Hyatt, and just when T.R. guessed that she would
ask for money, or a cigarette, or ask to stop off for a stiff be-
calming drink, she asked instead for the brown paper bag on the
floor beside his feet. When he bent to fetch it, he discovered, it
held *Sex and the City*, all four seasons, on DVD.

Suddenly T.R. felt as if the movie he was in had changed—
the *noir* of his film noir had disappeared. The terse spook's confirmation of a finished mission never came; instead, Rania
chatted brightly now of getting home to watch her "show." It
was jarring to the senses. Still he realized that he had always
been a prisoner to just this sort of comic touch. If there were
going to be special ops and secret dealings after dark, if forgeries
were going to be swapped for bribes in Arab embassies at night,
why not a thank-you note and a DVD from HBO? Try as he
might, T.R. could not escape the comic touch. All his efforts to
be filmic, old-time, rough-and-ready, street-wise, gritty, dangerous, a connoisseur of the authentic covert arts, were inevitably
pierced, and then deflated, by shards of ordinary life.

Covering the mob, he had written much of wiretaps and
homicides; had been to prison; stood at crime scenes; attended
murder trials in which a pigeon-racing gangster had conspired

to kill informants and a petty two-bit thief. And yet he had written more about the human side of gangsters. Unsatisfied to write about their crimes alone, T.R. had felt some deep desire to write about their daily lives as well. He had visited their bars in Bensonhurst; had read and written of their court files filled with letters from adoring wives and nieces. ("I have a lot of fun with Uncle Joe. He rents fun movies for us to watch and makes popcorn when I sleep over. In the morning we have Micky Dee's for breakfast. When my dog Misty died, Uncle Joe bought me a new puppy. I will miss Uncle Joe and I love him very much. Signed, Stephanie, 8 years old.") He had even lunched in Staten Island with Anthony Spero, the acting boss of the Bonanno family, eating sausage heroes in the den of Spero's home. What this need for the human details boded for his character remained unclear, though it suggested T.R. had every instinct for the ordinary coursing through his blood. Unsure as always if he cut a finer comic or heroic figure, he cut his losses and decided he cut both.

In either case, he had lived long enough to know that whatever wisdom you accrued about yourself happened only after the fact. That is, you only noticed changes in your life once the changes had occurred. He therefore drove with Rania to the Hyatt with the solemn knowledge that perhaps it was too late to make his life a true film noir, that even if he bought a thousand visas, paid a thousand bribes, and spent a thousand nights on a thousand secret missions, he would never be hard-boiled. It was neither in his chemistry nor in his age. Spoiled son of an affluent era, he knew that he was soft, untested, yes, perhaps corrupted to the core. If he did not feel corrupted, still he was, and hated this; hated how his times had robbed him of the edge of grit, the edge of hard experience, for what of his experience was hard? It was his secret shame that he had never gone to war (Samuel Johnson: "Every man thinks meanly of himself for not having been a soldier"), had never felt that hard experience up close—that *public* hard experience—to shape him in a way that World War II and Vietnam had shaped the generations come before. The only close approximation was a terrorist attack which, horribly destructive, nonetheless had touched his generation mainly as a televised event. It brought no draft, no protests, no bloody battles in the street—its only real effect had been a distant battle fought by trained professionals which left the masses watching from the aisle. If, in London, he had hungered for the war to drive a spike of cold reality into his brain, what he truly hungered for was for the war to banish this corruption, break his bones, and grant that all-consuming sense of death-defying purpose that could make his generation into men.

Such were the maunderings that issued from T.R.'s brain—no, that issued from a DVD in Rania's car. Left to his own, he might have maundered on, connecting the disc to global economics, foreign policy, and other sins, but they arrived at the Hyatt, where, after kissing Rania's cheek—no less a force than her elegance demanded it—he exited the car.

Chapter 13

A CONVERSATION CONTINUED

So NOW HE had his visa. He was ready for the journey to Iraq. He still had no permission from the *Times*, but his determination was undimmed. He went to the bar—what else to do? Call in? He might have profited from calling in, but as a communist of sorts, T.R. often scorned the profit motive—at least where his career was concerned.

At this point several things happened at once. First, he ran into Ian Fisher in the lobby of the Hyatt. Fisher was conversing with a bearded man, Arab in appearance, or at least trying to converse—at intervals he broke away on his cell phone, speaking frantically while pacing the room. If two days earlier Fisher had appeared to burn with plans for his departure, now he looked engulfed in flame. Even as he spoke, he raised his hand to pacify the bearded man. When Fisher saw T.R. across the lobby, he approached with a final frantic phrase, hung up the phone, sighed deeply, then jammed his fingers in his hair. He was on the verge of dropping off the cliff-edge of his nerves.

"It's falling apart," he said, or some such. "The whole thing's falling apart."

What this whole thing meant was soon revealed: Fisher had arranged to travel to Ruweished with a correspondent from the *Times of London*, then to caravan together toward R–4. Now the other correspondent had backed out: His desk had ordered him to Baghdad. But Fisher couldn't go to Baghdad: Burns was there. Fisher would hardly trample on a John Burns scoop, considering that Burns was the sort to guard his stories like a junkyard dog. So Fisher was caught. And now his translator, too, was threatening to quit: The poor man's wife had assumed quite rightly that he might get shot along the way. The bearded man, meanwhile, was the cameraman whom Fisher had hired. He was willing to travel to the air base, but the *Times of London* man was not. Worst of all, the London correspondent had provided Fisher fifteen minutes' notice. He was leaving in a quarter hour for Iraq—with Fisher or alone.

Nor was that the end of it. There were reports of bandits on the road. Fisher clearly did not want to travel to the air base only to be stranded on the road as open prey to gunmen. Complicating matters was the newest rumor: Every car that crossed the border to Iraq was being sent directly on to Baghdad under escort by the secret state police. Thus, the dilemma. To cross the border now was to wind up in the capital where good sense, professional turf wars, and explicit orders from the desk had forbidden him to go. Yet not to cross was to miss the story at R–4. And worse: It was to languish one more day in Jordan where, according to ambition, instinct, and the crushing weight of boredom, one could hardly want to be.

For his own part T.R. counseled waiting. He was in no mood to linger in Amman; on the other hand, to blunder off in fifteen minutes was insane. In the morning, it would be no task, he said, to find another vehicle to form a caravan and, as for bandits and the state police, they were better dealt with by the light of day. In proof of this, T.R. brought up an old-time boxing maxim: One was typically knocked out, he said, by the punch one never saw.

This quotation seemed to work on Fisher, who agreed to change his plans. Unspoken was the implication that T.R. was now to be included in the trip. Content to let this ride, T.R. announced that he was headed for the bar. (Fisher needed to inform the cameraman of their arrangements; he also needed to inform the desk.) And as he entered the bar, the next of the several things occurred.

The bar of the Hyatt was the alcoholic opposite of Mama Juanita's. In keeping with the hotel's reputation, it was dark and elegant with jazzy music and a staff of barmen dressed in paisley vests. There, however, in their flannel shirts and baseball caps, were the men T.R. had spoken with the other day at breakfast— the older men who had impressed T.R. with their rough-hewn faces and all-American gun-shop-loving guts.

He now felt confident their previous encounter would provide a frame of reference, or at least approaching some small excuse to reawaken conversation. Still his confidence was not complete. He took a seat beside them on a bar stool. Chill winds of vast indifference blew his way.

"All right, guys," he said when the silence reached that point where he would either have to succumb to it or break away, "if you won't talk with me, will you drink with me at least?"

This produced a grudging little chuckle from the man beside him. The heavier and shorter of the two, he looked like a gambler at the Corpus Christi greyhound track.

"Well, well, well, it's the *New York Times*," the man began. "What say, Glen? Should we let him buy us beers?"

"Don't see the harm in it," Glen said.

As gin and wickedness are social greases to the upper class, so beer and insults have a similar effect among the middle. Something about the hops and malts of beer made lightning strokes of irony impossible, and as soon as he sat down, T.R. was treated to a round of ribbing about the liberal peacenik weak-kneed un-American army of mosquitoes that inhabited New York.

It was not altogether an unpleasant speech, nor was it unexpected, for it was a ritual of the oldest sort. At the moment of their meeting, city folks and country folks (or soldiers and civilians) were duty-bound to stake out separate claims, as if according to a script in turn-around since 1968. Witness the Wellfleet banker and the Chattanooga lawyer who meet in business class and then evoke the ghosts of civil war. It hardly matters if the two men are identical in terms of salary and social class; if both work for the same corporation, own the same cool cars, live in the same enormous mansions, buy the same stocks and the same slick shit from Sharper Image magazine. There was a breach, an American breach, that kept them from communicating openly without the hives of paranoia. On one side of the breach was Yankee moderation, Woody Allen, abortion clinics, arugula salad, solar panels, chardonnay, and NPR, while on the other there was southern muscle, NASCAR, hominy, shotguns, Jesus, pickup trucks, and denim shorts. By now, of course, the breach was imaginary; it was ancient, moldy, and undeserved. Still, it existed. And if there was one thing left to separate Americans, it was power: how and when and if to put the power of their country to its use. That was what these soldiers at the bar seemed to say: "All you New York liberals don't know when the time has finally come to grab a gun."*

There was some truth in what they said. T.R. knew many in New York for whom the thought of any war was fundamentally abhorrent, and yet he knew a few who stood behind the fighting in Iraq. Somehow the truth about New York had not got out, for the city—advertised as the neurotic capital of cowardly disease—was nonetheless composed two-thirds of patriotic Knights of Columbus types. (The same could be said of the pacifists in towns like Charleston and Chapel Hill—neither had *their* truth got out.) Blame the breach, or blame Manhattan's force of gravity, from which no image of the city as a part of the republic could escape. Still, the Rockaways, large swaths of Brooklyn, and all of Staten Island had more in common with Lompoc, Millersburg, and Abilene than with the island citadel they surrounded on the map.

Blood up now, shaking his head, T.R. sought to correct these men.

"Don't you think," he said, "don't you think that New York took it on the chin? We took a decent beating in September, don't you think?"

---

*Complicated, no? T.R. could easily imagine certain permutations that denied the breach—an evangelist who parked his pickup in the driveway of a solar-powered ranch house or a public television patron who, every now and then, tuned into NASCAR in his cut-off denim shorts. He could even believe that certain members of the NRA might, in the flush of a wonderful Bordeaux, eat arugula on occasion—but after that it stopped. A bright line seemed to separate those citizens who still had faith in the power of America to right the world and those who doubted that their country's power remained—or ever *was*—a force for good. Optimism versus Cynicism? Energy versus Fatigue? Faith versus Doubt? That was the axis round which spun the trouble. All else was merely costume.

"Mebbe," said the man named Glen. The other—Wade or Wayne—said, "Mebbe you deserved it on the chin."

This was hardly the admission he was looking for, and yet it was a start. He told the men that in a day or so he would be heading for Iraq. He also said that he had deep concerns about the road. He understood that they were only *tourists*—trying hard to incorporate the sound of those italics in his voice—but surely they had crossed the border in their travels, and he wondered if a man were theoretically to drive across the desert, what theoretical dangers might he theoretically expect?

A look of the smuggest pleasure passed between them—they were engaged in silent conference over how much to reveal. Of the pair, it was Glen who seemed more willing, for as Wade (or Wayne) reclined in contemplation of his beer, Glen licked his lips and crooked his shaggy head.

"You driving something armored?" he asked.

"Yes, we have an armored car."

"How 'bout a local driver?"

"No, we're driving ourselves."

However promising it was, this dialogue revealed no good advice. Before Glen could continue, Ian Fisher came to join them at the bar. Sitting down, Fisher bypassed their discussion to announce he had just spoken with the desk and it was clear for them to go. They would need a translator, though the question of the cameraman had been resolved. "Check it out," he said, with his back to the men. "The guy I was talking to before? The camerman? His name is *Jehad*, he's traveling on a *Libyan* passport. Best of all"—and here he paused in deference to his luck—"he's a trained *trauma medic*." Fisher had been counting off these wonders on his fingers; now he tapped them spryly on the bar.

"Very good," he said. "This is very, very good."

His arrival, full of excellent good news, had the effect of chilling Glen and Wade—they now retreated to their mutterings and beer. But, hoping to revive the conversation, T.R. introduced the parties—Fisher as "a trusted colleague"; the men as "tourists, quote-unquote." Again, he made a point to emphasize those delicate quotation marks since he was working on a playful sense of trust. It was a subtle trick he had used before on criminals and cops to great success, for it encouraged information by diminishing identity, thus the guilt at being fingered as a source.

But Fisher did not pick up on the trick. Perhaps he had decided that directness was the best approach; perhaps he did not care. In any case, he sat, ordered beer, and asked if Glen and Wade were former military men or still on active duty, then went on to ask if they had traveled to Iraq. Of course what he really wanted to know was if the road was safe. And those reports of bandits—were they true? In every cell, T.R. was horrified. Fisher's bluntness would destroy his careful work. He therefore blasted Fisher with an icy look, was nearly on the verge of pulling him aside—to what? explain a thing or two?—when Glen looked Fisher in the eye and said, "We're former," then with a glance at Wade went on, "and those reports you heard? Absolutely true."

T.R. felt scolded. Having gunned the engines of his outrage, now he felt the shame of cooling off. Worse yet, it soon developed that Glen and Fisher came from the same small patch of Pennsylvania—even now they were discussing Panther football and a cornfield by the state route paved to make a mall. T.R. found that he was jealous. Not of Fisher's skill. Fisher was by all accounts a skilled reporter, then again T.R. had a few tricks of his own. He was jealous because he had worked for Glen and Wade, had sweated for them, and Ian Fisher had come, without the slightest effort, and stolen them away. Do not forget. T.R. was burdened by the spirit of relentless competition; he considered these two men his turf. They were his—his turf, his men, *his guys*. Yes, that was it! He had finally found a pair of *guys*, and Ian Fisher had taken them away.

He now decided it was man-to-man. He would get more information out of Glen and Wade, and better information, and would do this in the only way that he knew how. He would outdrink Ian Fisher. If this was absurd, it was also tactical, for two days earlier, Fisher had described himself by saying, "I'm the sort of guy who can't get the bartender to look at me twice." At the time, T.R. had been impressed by Fisher's humor; now he smelled a whiff of blood. For the next two hours, he monopolized the bar; he ordered new rounds when the old were scarcely finished; he enticed his partners into ever-more athletic bouts of drinking, and, aided by the endless thirst of Glen and Wade, who drank as if to drink was no more than to breathe, and at the moment when his belly (and his bar tab) had expanded to the breaking point, Fisher finally gave in. He pushed his bar stool back, announced that they were leaving in the morning, and with that, shook hands and wandered off to bed.

Victory having come, T.R. worked to find a sober portion of his skull. If he was not polluted, he had reached that altitude of drunkenness where one has need of concentration, and stood to bring the blood cells to his brain. Glen and Wade stood up as well. T.R. was unable to detain them. They had started for the lobby when Glen turned to offer him a piece of good advice.

"The biggest problem is going to be your onesies, twosies, and threesies," Glen explained, by which he meant the tiny bands of gunmen who patrolled the road in trucks. "If you see them, well, it won't be pretty. But if you don't, you'll make it through just fine."

"Who can I thank for the information?" T.R. asked.

"Ever heard of Blackwater Security?"

"No."

"Well, me neither," came the answer, with an impish thick-faced grin.

After that, Glen said good night and went upstairs to bed. T.R went up as well. There was no great comfort in the thought that come the morning, things might not be pretty, but with the satisfaction he had finally attained, T.R. laid odds of sleeping well.

Chapter 14

A CAVALRY CHARGE

HE DID NOT sleep well. In fact, it was a lousy sleep, for he realized that having won this victory, the victory was Pyrrhic and the challenge in his head. It must be clear by now that T.R.'s head was a complicated place where the best of gusto, healthy spirit, and reactionary zeal made close-fought battle with the worst of paranoia, competition, and imaginary slights. He would have liked to blame such complications on his inexperience and claim that as a young reporter he had nothing to his name, thus everything to prove, but it was far more likely he was cranky and conflicted long before he found employment in the news.

These cranky conflicts only deepened in Ruweished, which they made for in the morning—T.R., Fisher, Nadia (whom Fisher hired as their interpreter, extending her employment to Iraq), and Jehad, the bearded cameraman—making good time over desert roads in Fisher's armored car. They arrived in Ruweished by the early afternoon and quickly settled at the house that Fisher had described. It was an elegant dump along a dumpish alley, blocks from Abu Sayef's Chicken Place. Four large bedrooms stemmed from a central hallway off of which there was, as well, a sitting room with satellite TV, a filthy muck-stained bath, and a kitchen like the kitchen in a Big Ten frat house—the dishes in the sink as if they'd laid untouched since 1963. The man who had used these dishes met them at the door as they came in. He was their guardian and watchman—a slender, dark-skinned Arab named Saddam.

Driving to the border Fisher had regaled them with a story of Saddam, how when they first had met, Saddam (the cousin of Ruweished's governor) could not decide if he desired to work for a team of American reporters or to pack his suitcase for the jihad in Iraq. Now Fisher was dressing him down for making such a mess. "You ate my *wheat bread*?" Fisher asked. "Where's the fuel we bought? Saddam, this is bad. Very, very bad."

T.R. unpacked in the spacious bedroom where, for days to come, he would sleep, read, stare at the ceiling fan, write e-mails to his wife and family, and fret at the growing understanding that the travelers would not soon be departing for Iraq. Indeed, their plan to make at once for the R–4 air base was derailed on arrival when they learned over lunch (at Abu Sayef's, of course) that the border had been closed. For many days to come, the border would close and open, close and open, like the swinging doors of a saloon, creating numerous frustrations, interventions, halts, delays, false starts, false hopes, plans made, and plans discarded. Beyond the border, these concerned their traveling partners and the general security along the western Baghdad road. After a week had passed, T.R., who was never patient to begin with, began to give up hope. He began to feel nostalgic for Amman.

The week had started well enough. Over lunch, their second day in town, they partnered with a television crew from ABC. It looked to be a promising arrangement. The crew's producer, a slim, young, dashing fellow, Daniel Harris, had put together quite a team. Armed with bottomless amounts of network money, Harris had hired a group of local roughnecks as his drivers— he referred to them quite blithely as his "goons." In fact, they were professional smugglers led by a big, dark, burly murderous man named Khalid Something, call him Khalid Khan. Khalid's thick black mustache, his enormous eyebrows, and his two-toned khaki suit brought to mind the toughest of Colombian narcotics lords. He went everywhere behind the wheel of a tank-like Chevrolet, likely with a piece strapped to his leg.

Never one to miss a trick, Harris had acquired a recently re-tired commando from the SAS as his "security consultant." He was known as Soldier Ben, a short, squat man with long blond hair and covered in tattoos. Soldier Ben was the humorless mili-tary sort, all too proud of his achievements, who looked down his nose at the reporters he was getting paid top dollar to protect. Whenever T.R. encountered him, he got the sense that Soldier Ben was saying to himself, "My God, the coin is good, but what sort of fool decides to be a member of the press." The team was rounded out by an aide-de-camp, or fixer, from Amman named Mohammad Adjlooni. Adjlooni was a master of the trade. He could extricate a journalist from any sort of bureaucratic trouble— the masculine equivalent to Rania, it was said.

Compared with such talent, T.R.'s own team had as much chance of making it to Baghdad alive as the Westfield White Sox of the Indiana Little League had in beating the 1927 Yan-kees with a no-hit shutout. Thus they had begged and browbeat

Harris to let them join his team. But there was trouble at ABC. It started with the fact that Khalid's men desired to leave at once. They were only paid while working; waiting at the border they were merely wasting time. Adjlooni and Soldier Ben desired to play it safer, since their reputation for providing good security was on the line. Harris and his cameramen were therefore caught in the middle, like a marriage counselor caught between a husband and his wife. If Khalid told them that the road was safe, one could be sure Adjlooni would proclaim it dangerous. By the same token, if Soldier Ben had spoken with a buddy and determined that the border had been closed, surely Khalid would suggest a shortcut through the desert, which the other two would then dismiss as far too risky. Beyond these arguments, there was a fundamental difference in opinion as to where to go. The *Times* crew wanted to explore the R–4 air base; ABC desired to go to Baghdad—all the way.

So as these arguments unfolded over days of waiting, T.R. read, slept, scribbled in a journal ("Oh well, this is not his war . . ."), and watched on satellite TV as the real war unfolded four hundred miles and seven hours away. The fight was on by then. The Marines were bogged in Nasariya; T.R. was bogged in a dusty border town where the evening's entertainment often meant Saddam would fetch a soup bowl from the kitchen and the lot of them got drunk placing bets on who could throw the most playing cards into the bowl. There was also pornography to keep them company. One night T.R. came home from dinner at Abu Sayef's and heard from the sitting room a round of boyish snickers. Entering the room, he found Saddam and several friends (uninvited friends) lying on the floor, eyes wide, mouths agape, staring droolingly at one wild acrobatic act of pleasure two Dutch actresses were performing on the screen. His stomach sank. Somewhere out there in the desert there were real reporters reporting on the war. Whatever problems lay ahead, he would gladly take them in an instant over this—five young Arabs in the sitting room salivating over European porn.

Of course, the problems with the border and the road were real problems: They were, in fact, nearly insurmountable. Although the infantry was moving north toward Baghdad, the western border of Iraq was still protected by Iraqi troops. These Iraqis had been left untouched by the attack, and the irony was rich, for what were they protecting, if not the flank of the American advance? It had been rumored that Iraqi border guards would let reporters pass if they could show a visa. T.R. had one, as did Fisher and the crew from ABC, although the documents would hardly be of use on empty highways, in the middle of the desert, where Iraqi soldiers and roving bands of Bedouins were likely not to give a damn about official papers stamped in Amman.

Still a few reporters, human shields, aid-worker types, and U.N. personnel had traveled out of Baghdad on the road—whenever their caravans would trundle into town, word spread like plague. Unofficial briefings would be held, often at the Arab Beach, where stories were passed around like crumbs among the starving. The reporters in Ruweished *were* starving, starved for information, starved for the facts, starved for reassurance, for the slightest good excuse to pack their bags and leave. And yet the stories they were told were typically reports of bombed-out bridges, burning tractor-trailers, roadside craters bigger than suburban homes, and armed young men in pickup trucks who shot first and never got around to asking questions.

Paralysis had therefore settled in and no one took it quite so hard as Ian Fisher. Fisher—who was thirty-six or thirty-seven, a lifer at the *Times*, employed first as a clerk, then on the metro desk, then on foreign, where he now covered the Balkans out of Prague—had reached that point in his career where sitting on the sidelines was more than an affront, it was destructive to his future. After all, his colleagues had been grabbing all the head-lines, filing from the battlefield; there they were in the shits of war and death! It was a painful thing to watch him following the coverage on the Internet each morning, for every time that Fisher read a story from Iraq, his face would sag and he would say with reluctant admiration, "Filkins sure is having a good war"—or Dwyer, or Wilson, or Myers, or any of the other dozen *Times* reporters who were over there, not here, on the border, where the best one could hope for was the promise of slipping into Baghdad unattached to any military unit, while the worst was spending one more boring deadly suicidal afternoon with lamb kebabs and french fries at Abu Sayef's. If Fisher had to pass another day there waiting for ABC to settle on a plan, he looked as if he might explode. He looked as if he might start lobbing platters of tabouleh at the wall.

To ease the tension, T.R. took to telling jokes. They were not good nor even funny jokes, but they contained the necessary patterns of diversion, and he told them to the best of his ability at breakfast, at Abu Sayef's, at the Arab Beach, and especially at night when, after tossing cards, they sat on the porch of their rented house and miserably drank warm beer to the sound of baying dogs.

"So Mrs. McGillicuddy's in a coma," he would say, his col-leagues shifting imperceptibly away from him, "and every day the nurse comes to swab her down. One day the nurse swabs Mrs. McGilicuddy's private parts and she responds . . ." By that point, the other three had thrown their towels in and left.

Still the jokes seemed to bring some focus to the disposition of their characters. If Fisher was to play the glum young warrior whose king had ordered him to man some distant outpost, T.R. played the jester—ho, is this thing on? Jehad too was something of a jester, although his humor largely ran to imitating homosexuals, which kept them entertained through the length of his performance, but never seemed to last as long as T.R.'s Borscht Belt act. Nadia, meanwhile, was solemn. Nothing seemed to help. She had given up a job with the Canadians for this, and so she read, slept, talked with her mother on the phone, and managed to embody the general state of their emotions, which ran from sad to somber to openly depressed.

All of this of course—the mad ongoing fruitless talks with Harris, the depressive atmosphere, the card games, the jokes, the drinking, the pornography, the aggravations of the border, and the tedious discussions with the army and their own desk in New York—was swept away one night when Fisher came to the sitting room and finally announced that tomorrow morning they would leave. There had been a sudden shift in plans, and there on television was the explanation—the Americans had taken Baghdad. A crowd of jubilant Iraqis even now was tearing down the statue of Saddam.

As soon as Fisher said these words, T.R. felt freshly minted. He packed, he did not sleep, or if he slept, it was only for an hour, and by six next morning they were out the door and headed for the Arab Beach. Arriving, they were met by Harris, who rushed across the gravel lot to look for Soldier Ben and then Adjlooni. In the first pale light of day, his entire attitude was saying he would suffer no more fuckups and delays.

"Did you see that footage? Jesus Christ," he said when they arrived. "Did you see them tearing down that statue? Damn!"

Coffee in hand, head wet from the shower, Harris was electrified with envy. He was missing it, the scoop, the story, Jesus Christ, the *footage!*—catching sight of Khalid, he rushed to ask the smuggler if the cars were ready to depart.

At this point there were only six or seven cars parked in the lot—Harris's fleet of bright white Chevies, with engines idling and his drivers idling too, smoking cigarettes and drinking coffee, waiting for the order to depart. Fisher parked their own car well behind this group, angled toward the road, and this was smart, for even as they waited, an enormous stream of vehicles was coming up the road.

One could see them drawing closer from a distance: SUVs, taxis, pickup trucks, Suburbans, Jeeps, sedans, vans, Cruisers, Rovers, wagons, Wagoneers, perhaps four dozen, maybe more, in all. There was a rusting Ford Granada in the pack with an Iraqi flag flapping out its door. Sweet Jesus, T.R. thought, they were coming from Amman. With the fall of Baghdad, the press corps, locked these weeks inside the capital, was streaming toward the border, streaming toward Iraq. They formed a cavalry charge of rented trucks and beaters; all their waiting and frustration had released them to the road. T.R. had the feeling he had seen all this before, this mechanized armada; yes, it was the footage from the night of the invasion, when the armored military columns rolled across the desert in a charge of their own. Now they were here, a different column to be sure, but still swept up in the same collective purpose, still accelerating in a way that made the stream seem larger than its parts, because the vehicles were moving in a stream, and one was aware that most, or many, in the stream had started leaning on their horns. There was only one main road in Ruweished and the stream had backed up for a hundred yards along the road, like traffic leaving Yankee Stadium. Even now, the first were entering the hotel lot, but not completely; the first had stopped not far beyond the entrance to the lot, which caused a bottleneck and caused the cars behind them, honking now, to move up slowly, shove, nudge, move again with no success, and finally, in the middle of Ruweished's only road, to come to a pause, and then a grinding stop.

They were stuck. It was impossible to move. It was impossible to pick out Harris in the crowd; it was also impossible to get their car onto the road, for now, from all directions, journalists were streaming toward the Arab Beach. They had parked their cars at odd angles all across the lot, jamming every possible escape. And, losing patience, Fisher nudged T.R. and muttered with a frown, "This is not—I mean it—*not* a pretty sight."

He was correct. It was bad enough to be boxed in by fifty-five or sixty new arrivals who had driven up that morning from Amman, but it was worse to imagine that their journey to Iraq would now be undertaken in a crowd. If there was something worse than storming Baghdad in a cavalry charge of newsmen, T.R. could not conceive of it. A posting in the Hartford bureau with a cut in daily pay? No. At least in Hartford one could always duck the fools.

And yet they could not quit. In the air there was the expectation of excitement. Or more than excitement: There was now momentum, it could not be denied. "We have to find Harris," T.R. said to Fisher. "We have to find a shortcut out of town."

So now they left the car and made their way toward the front of the crowd packed tightly at the hotel doors, but the reporters there were jammed too close together for a person to be found. It seemed ridiculous to search for Harris in the crowd, so they wandered off to look among the stragglers at the far end of the lot—no luck. The morning, which had started well, was promising another day of funk.

Then suddenly behind them there was movement—the crowd began to tighten at the hotel doors. For a moment T.R. thought there might have been a fight. The crowd crushed together, and the action of compression now drew others strewn throughout the lot.

From where he stood, he couldn't see a thing and yet it had to be a fight. The crowd was shouting, it was angry, there were people pressing in. Now he worked his way among the bodies. At the inner ring was a young Jordanian he recognized. This man, a waiter at the Arab Beach, was trying to address the crowd, but it was yelling at him fiercely. In a loud barrage of questions, the crowd had drowned him out.

"What's he saying?" T.R. asked the man beside him.

"It sounds like the government won't let its own citizens out of the country," he explained. "It's ridiculous! They've closed the border to their own people!" The man now cupped his hands around his mouth and shouted to no one in particular, "Watch your liberty, my friends! You're living in a fascist state!"

If this were true, it was shrewdness of the highest order. To close the border to *Jordanians* would mean that scores of local drivers, fixers, and interpreters could not leave the country for Iraq. More than shrewd, it was eminently practical. Without its local guides, the press corps would be crippled. T.R.'s instinct for conspiracy began to hum: He sensed the American military was at work.

Conspiracy or not, the news placed a devastating chill on the reporters. They began to scatter, some to their vehicles, some to the hotel restaurant, many simply wandering discussing what to do. It was only 10 A.M., and yet the day was threatening to come undone—the momentum they had built would now be lost. Then it would die. Then they would return to their villa in Ruweished for another night of cards, another night of jokes . . .

He went in search of Ian Fisher.

"Listen, do you still have the number for the information minister?" T.R.'s plan was only skeletal but starting to enact it put some muscle on the bone.

"I already called him," Fisher said. "It's no use. The border's closed. None of them are getting through."

None, indeed, if they played by Marquis of Queensbury rules, but that was an *if* available to much interpretation. T.R. considered the border closure a challenge, and of course he was susceptible to challenges. He took the minister's number, tucked it in his pocket, and walked toward the Arab Beach, where on the steps outside, he started to address the crowd.

"Hello, excuse me, folks, hello, *hey-oh!*" he said, or rather half began to shout, since in the wake of the news the crowd had dispersed. "Hello, yes, listen, I'm no government official, or anyone important. I'm a journalist like you, but I think I have a plan."

His introduction stirred a nascent curiosity among his listeners. Some small portion lent their ears.

"Look," he said, "I'm sure you know by now the government has closed the border to Jordanians," continuing to grunts of discontentment and the same man as before now shouting, "Fascists!" from the rear. "And while I agree it's not the best news we could have gotten, perhaps it's actually the worst, I think the way to handle this is basically to shove it in their face."

A sudden silence: He moved to occupy that silence, scooping up the promise of its mood.

"Right," he said, "now what I think we should do is this," surprised by his own facility and by the fact the group had grown substantially in size. "I think we should get in our cars, and drive toward the border, and present ourselves in one big mass to the soldiers at the border"—pointing down the road—"and force the soldiers there to get on the phone and call their bosses, force *those* bosses to call *their* bosses"—riffing now—"and so on, you see what I mean, until we finally reach some guy in Amman who has some power." Jesus, he could see it now, and if he had its pulse, the crowd could see it too. "I mean," he added on the surge of seeing this take place, "what good does it do for us to hang out here at *this* establishment?" to which there came an easy swell of laughter. "So let's just go. In fifteen minutes we should get in our trucks. What do you say? Fifteen minutes and we leave?"

Consensus emerged that this was a plan, and the crowd began to wander toward their trucks. But it was only half the plan. Wandering off himself, T.R. dialed the number of the Information Ministry. He asked for the minister by name and was surprised to get him on the phone.

"Good morning, Mr. Adwan, sir," he said.

The minister said good morning. He sounded worried and alert, but asked how he might help.

"I'm standing in Ruweished, sir, with perhaps a hundred journalists and need to ask a favor."

"Yes?"

"I need you to close your eyes and picture something, sir. Could you do that, sir? Close your eyes?"

"My eyes?" Adwan seemed concerned.

"Yes, sir, your eyes. I need you to close your eyes and picture, I don't know, sixty vehicles of every shape and size. Are you doing that, sir? Are you doing that for me?"

"I don't understand what this is—"

"Please, sir. Picture, if you could, those vehicles. Now picture them in one big mass driving toward the border . . ."

"Sir, the border is closed, there is nothing—"

"Mr. Adwan, please. The vehicles are headed for the border. They are backed up on the road. They are stretched out for a hundred yards, and now they start to honk their horns. All sixty. Can you hear them, sir? Can you hear them honking their horns, sir?"

"Sir, I told you—"

"In another fifteen minutes, Mr. Adwan, these vehicles will leave Ruweished. Fifteen minutes after that, they'll be waiting at the border."

"But, sir, I must insist—"

According to his plan, he then hung up the phone.

Chapter 15

THE BORDER

IT WAS SOMETHING longer than a fifteen-minute ride. No matter. The point had been made.

The border post, when it appeared, was no more than a pillbox in the road. A single sentry manned the post, and a few yards off the shoulder of the road stood a corrugated shack where two more sentries with automatic weapons squatted in the dust. As the vehicles approached, the first guard moved from the pillbox; as the others rose in bafflement, he studied the line of cars. He stood in the road, firmly, with his rifle to his chest. The cars pulled up no more than fifteen feet in front of him; they stopped. If there would be a confrontation, it would happen here between these stubborn parties; it would happen on the road between the opposition of their needs.

The cars came to a halt. They waited. The sentry stood. It almost felt like the high-school prom and summoning the courage to ask some girl to join you in a dance. The fear, T.R. knew, would vanish with the first few steps. He looked at Fisher, then at Nadia and Jehad. "Come on," he said. "Let's check it out." Then he opened the door. "Let's see what's going on."

They had stopped in the road some ten or fifteen places from the front, and, leaving the car, leaving behind the chance to change his mind, he walked along the shoulder toward the post. He was not alone—a few others too had gotten out and now formed a makeshift delegation. But T.R. felt responsible. He had brought about the action now at hand.

Walking, he could feel the eyes of all the journalists in all the parked cars watching him, could feel the weight of expectation as if an accident or a grim police procedure lay ahead. And continuing to walk, he directed his attention at the sentry who awaited his approach with the dull resolve that comes from having orders one must follow, even if the orders aren't fully understood.

The sentry took a small step forward in a way that promised no retreat. To T.R.'s great embarrassment, he realized the sentry was petrified with fear. In his own fear at confronting armed guards on the border in the middle of the desert, he had failed to recognize the powerful effect a caravan of journalists might have on the man, on any man. But the sentry, he saw now, was no man at all. He was a boy, perhaps as young as seventeen. He may have never seen a journalist before; surely, he had never seen so many. He held his ground and gripped his rifle with a look of abject desolation. Perhaps he even prayed to Allah the all-merciful to make these strangers disappear.

"Stop," he said to the delegation, and raised one slender palm to halt them in their tracks.

T.R. felt sorry for the guard. Still he said, "We have spoken with the minister of information. The minister knows we are here. He knows we are going to Iraq."

"Stop," the guard repeated. His outstretched arm was trembling. His uniform hung from his bones. "Stop," he said again. It may have been the only English word he knew.

As he spoke, the other guards came up. They exchanged some words in Arabic, then one of them, an older man, took over the post as the others stepped inside the pillbox for the phone. T.R. could not tell if they were calling to request reinforcements, or if, brazen plans now working, they were notifying their superiors they would have to let the delegation pass. A hum of revving engines, testing the waters, surely testing the depths of their own impatience, sounded from the cars along the road, and at his post the older sentry seemed to fall back slightly and the delegation moved with his retreat, not advancing so much as following his steps. First his heels, then his shoulders, breached the border line behind the pillbox; edging up, the first few cars began to breach the border too, still slow, still methodical in their advance, and then a dozen cars were over. They had crossed the line, they crept along and kept moving at a cautious speed along the road, and then on a sudden swing of inspiration, suddenly accelerated, as if a starting pistol for a road race had been fired. A road race had begun—and T.R., standing on the shoulder of the road, watched in amazement as the complement of cars began to shudder past the sentries, fifty-five, then sixty in a row. The guards were stricken, they were frozen in place. They could not make it stop, and so they did not make it stop, they acquiesced, they waved the cars along the road, and it was only after half the cars had passed that T.R. saw his own car waiting for him on the shoulder of the road, and jogged up in a semi-run to join them, opened the door, and Ian Fisher in the driver's seat called out, "Jump in!"

His chief impression now was of a motley horde of vehicles passing by in some bright blur of sunshine, and he shouted back, "I'm in! Keep going! Don't lose our place." As Fisher did keep going, a manic energy entered the car, they swerved toward the road again and into line with the wild adrenal excitation of a getaway attempt—a getaway that must succeed. A bloom of happiness began to blossom in his chest. He hollered, almost hooted, in his great excitement and surprise, "Holy shit, there it is! Iraq is down the road!"

Down the road, indeed, some hundred yards ahead, there was a huge steel dark-gray awning, or pavilion, whatever it was, it did not matter, they were speeding toward it now, they were nearly there. They had made it just this far, and without some new technology or gear, but on the spirit of their wits and guts alone, and the experience of racing through the desert seemed the culmination of that spirit. T.R. felt it burning in his hair, he felt it in his teeth. He was entering forbidden territory now and would get to know how that would feel.

BOOK THREE

IRAQ

Chapter 16

NECESSARY LIES

Because the telling of a story—any story—is supposed to be a seamless process (moving forward at its own sweet pace), the teller must at times resort to lies to sweep it toward what is often called the point. A storyteller, like a lover, never likes to lie, but, lover-like, he is occasionally tempted. He knows it sometimes serves his purpose to omit some inconvenient portions of the truth.

This temptation is all the more dangerous when the story is personal. Readers of a memoir, expecting the unvarnished truth, can pick up the turpentine odor of a lie at fifty yards. So the writer must be careful, scrupulously careful, in choosing his lies. It is best he avoid them altogether. If already told, he must confess.

So T.R. now confesses to a lie. He did not, as was suggested, arrive at his plan to cross the border on his own; rather he took the germ of the idea from Charlie LeDuff. In what had clearly been a moment of crisis, he had called LeDuff in Turkey from Ruweished and had taken his advice to storm the border, when he could, no matter the cost. He had taken such advice before (once, on Charlie's counsel, he had told an editor to go to hell) and the result had not been happy. It had required T.R. to conjure up an anger that he had not rightly felt.

Despite his strengths, T.R. did not possess LeDuff's facility for anger, or his temper, or even his faculty for wounded pride, and when all was counted, T.R. as a rebel upstart always seemed infected with a hint of the pretender. Some faint whiff of doubt in his demeanor suggested he was far less rebellious than he claimed. Speaking to the editor that day, he had not been pleased with his own performance. (In the newsroom, his voice had been too faint, too polite; he had been too much of the good boy when he said, "Oh really? Go to hell," and should have simply said, "Fuck you!") He could imagine LeDuff, a rabble-rouser, part-time prima donna, full-time imp, and owner of a temper that was easily provoked, tearing up the bosses—but when he had done it, T.R. detected in his own voice some undeniable betrayal of his roots. Before authority, as always, he became the nice bar mitzvah boy from Shaker Heights. He could not rid himself of the desire to please. So T.R. tended to be skeptical of LeDuff's advice—it rarely fit his personality to size. In Ruweished, however, threatened with the possibility of being locked out at the border and another month of living in the *Times*'s dumpy house without the solace of a story, he had taken the advice. This, however, was more exception than rule.

In the spirit of confession, nor was this the only lie he told. He had also fibbed about his getaway attempt. One might recall a "huge steel dark-gray awning or pavilion" looming on the road, implying that the structure lay across the border in Iraq. It did not. If T.R. has given that impression, he asks to be excused, none the least because the chaos on the road was intense. The line of cars had been advancing toward an unknown destination—the action was dispersed; disorder followed in its wake. A few cars had tried to cut ahead, took to the shoulder, ran through sand, their tires kicking up a spray of dust. To this confusion was the added threat of what the guards might do when they arrived at the structure—no one seemed to know and so the caravan rushed on. When, finally, at the gates of the pavilion, it was clear the soldiers there would not let them pass, the whole armada shuddered to a halt. "What the hell?" T.R. had roared from the front of the Jeep. "Aren't they letting us in?" But the soldiers were dressed in the blue and gray of Jordan's Special Forces, not Iraqi green.

"Holy shit, we haven't left the country yet!"

Indeed, they had only passed the initial checkpoint. There was another checkpoint yet to pass. Beyond the pillbox on the road there lay a hundred yards of desert, and beyond those hundred yards there was a customs post where Jordanian inspectors would now spend hours examining their cars.

And so there came a period of waiting as the sixty vehicles each in turn nudged forward into the pavilion, cut their engines, and submitted to a search. Two armed soldiers approached each car to study every nook and cranny, root through luggage, peer beneath the seats, get down on hands and knees to examine the chassis for God knew what—maybe smuggled ammunition, maybe bombs. Meanwhile, the reporters formed an angry line inside a large, low, sweltering Quonset hut where behind a set of windows travel documents were being checked. It was bureaucracy at work—Middle East bureaucracy. And, deflated by their failed escape, the journalists lined up to show their passports like a line of bettors at the OTB.

What saved this mess from chaos was that most of the reporters knew each other. After all, they had spent weeks together waiting, drinking, planning, and commiserating in Amman. Gathered in the stifling desert shack, there was the soul-numbing feeling one experienced at certain New York press events: a hunger for the action to begin and, in the meantime, idle chat.

"Did you hear that what's-her-name's in Baghdad?" "Who?" "You're gonna surf this beach!" "Rhym Brahimi." "Charlie don't surf." "She's hot." "You think?" "I love the smell of napalm in the morning." "Annanpour is hotter." "Jesus, she's a man!" "I stay here in this room . . ." "So what?" ". . . and I get weaker . . ." "Are you saying you like men?" "I'm saying you're an errand boy . . ." "I'm saying I'd fuck her." ". . . sent by grocery clerks . . ." "You would?" ". . . to collect the fucking bill . . ."

Waiting for his number to be called, T.R. stood among these men. They were mostly in their middle to late thirties and passed the time by quoting films on Vietnam. It was something of a small obsession. Whether it was due to some unquenchable nostalgia for the past, or whether they were starved for history, or simply ignorant of history, or whether to the contrary they felt some real connection to the war in Vietnam, it hardly mattered. T.R. understood—he, too, had always felt the weight of Vietnam. It was a touchstone, a challenge. It seemed to overshadow any mystery that he had ever known. And yet the irony was strong because, for all his interest and obsession, he did not know much about the war beyond what Hollywood had taught him. And that was a selective lesson—selective at best.

At the cineplex, he had learned to love the grunt in Vietnam because the moral burden of the war had been humped through the jungle by the grunt. The grunt was Laurence Fishburne, the grunt smoked pot, and if the grunt killed babies, if he burned down villages, and slaughtered gooks, the grunt had been sent to Vietnam because the draft board sent him, so the grunt was innocent—he danced to the Doors on the bows of swift boats simply to survive. T.R. had also learned to hate the government through film, or at least that part of the government that sat in air-conditioned rooms in Saigon flipping through the pages of its files. It was quite possible that his populism had begun with the cinematic notion that the government was idiotic, cruel, barbaric, clueless, and absurd while the grunt was funky, the grunt was cool. What was lacking in this lesson was the taste of history. The films he saw had taught him nothing of the threat from China (real or perceived), nothing of the sweats of LBJ, and nothing of the downfall of the French. Dien Bien Phu? Well, gezundheit!

Now he heard his name called out, and turning, spotted Ian Fisher in the crowd. Fisher was approaching with that hot parental energy he always brought to the task of keeping his team in line.

"Are you ready?" Fisher asked. "The rest of us are done."

T.R. was not ready, nor was he calm. His group had already forced its way through the bureaucracy; he alone was still behind. And so he shoved his way to the front, jostling bodies. The lazy sense of being at a press event had vanished—now it was a scrum, the rush was on.

"I need my passport stamped," he told the man behind the window.

"Sir, you must have wait in line."

"Please, my group is leaving. I need this stamped at once."

His brusqueness worked some magic on the man, who stamped him with a sullen look and sent him on his way. They stepped outside the Quonset hut. A vast array of press cars sat beneath the metal awning; the awning sat beneath a hard blue, cloudless desert sky. Up the road, running east of the awning, were miles of desert, not the black rocks that he had seen before, but honest, open desert. It felt as if the light had changed or the air around him had a newfound clarity. And instantly, he was alert, awake—perhaps the light *had* changed—but also distant from his body, as if this were a film he was watching of himself. T.R. felt gentle in his arms, legs, stomach, chest, and groin, felt as if the deep frustrations of the last few weeks had finally dissolved. Sentimental soul, he even felt an on-rush of forgiveness for the forces that had stopped him—the *Times*, Mr. Adwar, the man behind the passport desk. (Of course, he did not know that scores of reporters had already crossed without their passports stamped and that waiting to obtain one had been pointless. Then again, his visa purchased in Amman was pointless, too— it had been issued by the old regime.)

They were coming out from the Quonset hut between the vehicles parked in a jam beneath the awning, and off to his right were shallow trenches in the desert that he guessed were military bunkers. Later he was told they were missile silos the Americans had buried in the sand.

The Jeep was waiting for them on the shoulder. Nadia sat in back in her protective vest; Jehad sat up front in his. T.R. felt as if he had not seen them now for several weeks, but even as he climbed inside the Jeep he did not greet them, did not say a word. There was hardly any fellowship inside the Jeep; instead there was the feeling of distinct and silent bodies each pursuing thought-lines of their own. Moments later the team from ABC arrived, and Harris, its producer, stopped beside the Jeep. "Meet you on the other side," he called. And with a quick wave and a smile, he pulled ahead, and, Fisher following, they crossed into No Man's Land. Soon they approached the shadows of a massive metal arch. Bowed and slender, it was not unlike the Gateway Arch, except atop it sat a giant portrait of Saddam. By now T.R. was absorbing every image with the vivid physical intensity that accompanies those first few moments when a man is not sure if he is dreaming or awake—the shapes and colors of ordinary objects seem distorted by a funhouse mirror of the mind; extraordinary objects, plain and all-too-real. They were passing beneath the arch into a wide asphalt border complex, filled with ruined buildings. There was even in the air some ruined tang of smoke. The complex had been looted, and the ravaged streets and buildings had a seething devastated silence that called to mind the Bronx as he had seen it first, some years ago, coming off the Bruckner into Hunts Point. It had that same dead air of quiet blight. The complex was inordinately still. Nothing in it seemed alive; nothing seemed to move.

Chapter 17

L O O T E R S

They parked the car, stepped over piles of broken glass, and walked to the nearest building they could find. It was an office, or at least the remnants of an office—desks overturned, doors kicked down, windows shattered, and the filing cabinets stripped of their files. Everywhere, in a blizzard, official papers lay about the floor, and on the walls huge portraits of Saddam were smashed in broken frames. The thought that a wild band of looters had come out here, to the middle of the desert, was astonishing, there was nothing here, no homes, no tents, no buildings—nothing for miles. And yet with each new passing room, there was more destruction, more shattered windows, more upended furniture, more smashed portraits—in one room, a wooden coatrack had been spiked through the wall like a lance. And there was more evidence, too, of the desperate urge to steal. Upstairs on the second floor, the ceiling fixtures had been stripped of bulbs.

Hoping to get such details into Fisher's story (as senior man, Fisher would be writing), T.R. went to look for him, but he quickly found that Fisher was gone. Jehad was snapping pictures of the ransacked office, Nadia roaming the halls, but Fisher was nowhere to be found. A sudden burst of panic now (none the least because with Fisher missing, he *himself* would have to write) until he spotted Fisher fifty yards away across the street. He was standing at a service station on the far side of the road.

There, a crowd of reporters had gathered at the gas pumps. At first T.R. imagined they had found a fuel supply and were engaged in some small act of looting of their own. But as he crossed the road, he saw a man in the middle of the crowd—an Iraqi in a long, white robe. Standing at his car, the man was trying desperately to fill his tank, but the crowd was swarming him. He was besieged, surrounded by a dozen yammering reporters. There was no escape. No force, not even gravity, can match the cellular attraction of reporters to a source.

They were bombarding him in English quickly translated into Arabic by their interpreters. His head shot back and forth between these camps, like a spectator at a Ping-Pong game.

"What's your name, sir?" "How much is it for the gallon?" "Are you frightened of the looters?" "Are *you* a looter? "Where do you live?" "How old are you?" "Are you married?" "Children?" "What's your occupation?" "How do you spell that name?"

Before the man could answer, a tall, thin, reedy-looking television correspondent had ordered his cameraman to stick the camera in the poor man's face.

"Yes, yes, yes, but how do you *feel*, sir?" this correspondent asked, elbowing his way past colleagues toward the man. "Please, sir, tell us how you *feel.*"

The crowd fell silent. The man looked into the dead eye of the camera—his own eye equally as dead. He spoke in Arabic. The interpreter gave his answer.

"I am one of the people with no food, no money, nothing. I have nothing," the man at the gas tank said.

The correspondent nodded gently then, as if to say, "I understand, friend. Your pain is my pain." But having got his shot he nodded at the cameraman and left.

"We're finished here. Let's move."

It may be true that to criticize the television press for being phony, coy, and cruel is not much better than to criticize a brick for being red. T.R., however, would gladly take the chance. To his mind, one could never speak too loudly of the ignorance of the television press. It was not just their brief reports, or their urge to follow herds, or even their enormous arrogance—it was a matter of their culture, of something at the center of their culture that was dead. It was not inconceivable that the process of creating television news could render its practitioners less than human. T.R. had often thought that breaking down a correspondent's image to electrons served to leach away some substance of the soul. Interviews with pen and paper at least bore traces of a human conversation—they were more organic and a certain flexibility existed when a correspondent listened with his own ears. If he did not pick up each word, at least he got the gist, the timber of the moment, the torque of the exchange. And this was crucial because it took perception and a quality of judgment—both of which were absent when a camera rolled with blind perfection and a microphone recorded everything with deaf frigidity on tape. The difference served to make a television correspondent less awake to nuance, less aware of subtlety, and less engaged— therefore more susceptible to simple explanations and the movements of the herd. If T.R. were ever to be quoted, he would rather trust his story to a man with a pen than a television camera. After all, one could hardly negotiate the whole of one's complexities before the bald exactitude of a machine.

Before he left New York, T.R. had spent a week with the Marines at a training session for reporters, and the television people had depressed him. He had bunked with one such man from CNN, Bob Franken. His quarrel with Franken had begun the very moment Franken had expressed his horror that Fox News anchors wore American flag lapel pins on the air.

"How can you be a patriot *and* a journalist?" Franken had asked. "They're mutually exclusive occupations." T.R., who considered himself both, had asked why Franken could not love his country, to which had come the answer, "America is not my country. I'm a citizen of the world."

"Like Danny Pearl?" T.R. had asked. "You *are* American, Bob, you have always *been* American, you will always *be* American— it is a nonnegotiable fact."

"My goodness," Franken had said. "I think that your employers at the *New York Times* would be horrified, horrified! to hear you say a thing like that."*

Such lack of self-awareness never failed to set T.R.'s teeth on edge. But then again, self-awareness was the first facility to die when journalists removed their own perceptions from the news.

———————

*Franken had also laid a doozy one afternoon in the mess hall when he and T.R. were discussing combat with a group of Marines. The Marines had asked how close to the fighting reporters expected to get. T.R. said the best scenario would be to trust the military. If a sergeant, or a captain, felt a mission would be too dangerous and that the presence of reporters would imperil his troops, there was no question—reporters stay behind. Once again, Franken had been horrified. "Wherever you go, I go," he told the Marines. "It's bang-bang. That's what we do in this business."

Having finished with the man at the gas pumps, the crowd of reporters started to disperse. Slowly, the border complex had begun to fill up with a second round of looters. They had come down the main road of the complex from a wilderness of desert, some in trucks, some on donkeys, some on foot. Old men hauled radiators toward their pickup trucks; young boys rode on wooden carts stuffed with coatracks, furniture, iron safes. Down the road, some hundred paces from the service station, T.R. and Fisher came upon a short, squat, bearded man behind a wheelbarrow. The wheelbarrow held a television set and two large Persian rugs.

"This is my money," he said with a smile. "Saddam Hussein robbed us."*

Soon they reassembled at the Jeep. There was T.R., Fisher, and another journalist, a dark-haired man from the L.A. *Times*, who nervously announced that pickup trucks containing bandits had been spotted on the main road a hundred yards away. The trucks, he said, were at the eastern gate of the complex, circling like hawks. He feared that soon they might approach this way.

When Harris and his crew arrived, the group decided it was safer moving forward and they headed off in numbers for the gate. Arriving at the gate, they saw it gave out on a long straight narrow highway, which gave out to open desert all the way to Baghdad, four hundred miles away.

Stopped at the gate, their trucks spaced yards apart, the travelers stared down the distance. The highway stretched ahead of them and stopped at the entrance to the highway. No one said a

---

*Grinning, this man pointed to his loot with pride and seemed not puzzled in the least that two white men should have suddenly appeared to ask him questions. Perhaps he thought it was a war and white men asked the questions in a war.

word. T.R. imagined he was looking down the throat of some huge beast—the road its tongue, the clouds above its teeth. In fact, the road was wide and well maintained. It would have made for easy driving, save the fleet of pickup trucks with armed men standing on their flatbeds that circled just within sight.

So now there was a brief discussion on how, and whether, to continue. T.R. and Fisher stood with Harris and his own crew in the road. The dark-haired man from the L.A. *Times*—his name was Michael Slackman—joined them at the last moment in a broken-down van of the sort Cheech and Chong might have driven, but with thick protective plates. He, too, stood in the middle of the road; and as they spoke, more vehicles began to pull up, pile up, beside them, until their brief discussion turned into a general debate.

The pickup trucks were not the only issue now. It was 3 P.M. and getting late. Even if they left at once and had no trouble, they would still arrive in Baghdad after dark. With the nerve ends of a dozen correspondents smoking, it was Soldier Ben who set things right.

"We spend the night here," he said. "We camp and then head out first thing tomorrow morning." So they all retreated back to No Man's Land and set up camp in the desert on the shoulder of the road.

By the time the sun went down that night a hundred journalists were camped out like weekend hikers. Some had pup tents, some lay out in sleeping bags, the rest spread their blankets on a freezing bed of sand. It was freezing in the desert and the journalists kept warm by passing bottles. At T.R.'s camp, they opened what was left of the beer. As T.R. drank with Slackman, Fisher sat in the Jeep and wrote his story—in the dark of the desert, they could see him hunched in the front seat working in the dim glow of a flashlight he wore, miner-style, strapped to his head.

All around camp, the journalists had started to relax. Trapped on the border, they drank Scotch, cooked Ramen noodles over propane; unable to progress, they listened to the short-wave radio reports about the war. Small clumps sat gathered with their radios and campfires. There was the feeling of an army on the night before a battle, drunken, camped out, trills of laughter in the night. Posses of reporters wandered through the camp to visit other posses, and they walked through the desert with the same electric energy of soldiers ready in the morning for the war.

Beyond all else it had the feeling of a Boy Scout jamboree and T.R., having had enough of such excitement as a child, wandered off to have a smoke. He walked toward the edge of camp and sat in the sand some distance from the tents—a pair of soldiers stopped him, checked his press card, let him pass. He was surprised that, here in No Man's Land, the camp was guarded by an armed Jordanian patrol.

He was also surprised to find Nadia standing in the darkness. His eyes adjusted, he could see that she was talking on the phone.

"So how's your mother?" he asked when she hung up. It seemed a likely guess.

"She's fine, worried, I don't know, she thinks I'm crazy, but she's fine." Nadia had, after all, gone off to Iraq with three strange men she had known eleven days.

"And how's your wife?" she asked. "Have you talked since we left Ruweished?"

Now she sat beside him and they smoked.

"Last we talked was a couple days ago."

"You miss her." It was not a question.

"Yes, I miss her. Talking on the phone's not easy. It's never easy on the phone."

In Amman, T.R. had treated Nadia with sly joking energetic friendliness and treated her to drinks. In the face of ambient flirtation—her looks had won her much attention—it had somehow served to set T.R. apart.

In Ruweished, they had talked of love. He had asked her if she had ever been in love—surprisingly, she answered no. A quiet night, and they were sitting on the porch outside the villa, he was drinking beer, they both had cigarettes. It had not escaped him that the moment had been full of every last romantic promise, there was romance in the darkness, in the wind, in the miles of sand, in the nighttime desert sky. But he had had no craving for romance, he simply had a craving for the truth. And in that vein, he had confessed to her that at her age, he was constantly in love, he was crazy for the stuff, he could not help himself, he fell in love with every woman, strange or known, he met. In the years that followed, he had come to see love as a pair of solitudes that touched and guarded one another. Love, he said, was powerful to the extent it saved the best in one's beloved and oneself.

Even now there was the same ripe promise—the stars were up again, the desert lay about their necks, men with guns patrolled the night. What better chance could there have been to sanctify the moment?

"Got another cigarette?" he asked. "I'm out."

She did. They smoked. It was shortly time for bed.

Later, under a blanket on the freezing sand of No Man's Land, he rolled in his sleep and bumped a body. He did not look to check, and could not tell for certain, but the body lying next to him was hers.

Chapter 18

FOUR HUNDRED MILES

N O M O R N I N G C O U L D have been more inauspicious. Not only did he rise with an angry bladder, he pushed up from his blanket to find his lumbar column stiffer than a British upper lip. He had not slept like a rock, he had slept atop a rock, and stretched his back, stretched his legs, walked off to brush his teeth and wash his face, then lit the day's first cigarette, observing colleagues rising like a Boy Scout troop, and finally staged a morning urination behind a television truck where a well-coifed correspondent was delivering a live report on what it felt like to be standing here, *right here*, on the Iraqi border. He felt himself in healthy spirits but unprepared for the day ahead. Not that preparations could be taken for a flat dash through the desert. T.R. knew that instinct and a physical intelligence alone would see them through, which is why he wished his body did not feel as though an iron vise were turning on his spine.

When he returned to camp, Soldier Ben was laying out plans over cups of instant coffee. The convoy was to stick together at every cost and all eight vehicles, six from ABC, one from the

Times, and Slackman's Cheech and Chongmobile, were each assigned a spot. Soldier Ben would ride out a hundred yards in advance with the wiliest of Khalid's drivers, another smuggler would assume the rear, while in between all others were advised to buddy up in smaller convoys within the convoy and take as their focal point the huge white television dish atop the satellite truck. (What better beacon to carry them through danger than a television dish!) Communication would present its own problem. There was no cellular service in Iraq so now a check was made to see that each vehicle had at least one satellite phone. Of course, to use these phones would not be easy, since they needed to be pointed toward the southern sky (the satellite was orbiting up there). Soldier Ben had further ordered that their top speed hit no more than a hundred-forty. When T.R. heard that number his intestines all but leapt to his throat. He was something of a lead foot, but one hundred forty miles per hour still seemed awfully quick, even if there might be gunfire from the roadside and pickups like a Texas posse on their trail. Luckily he voiced no protest, for he quickly learned that Soldier Ben had meant *kilometers* per hour, which meant they would be moving at the easy clip of eighty. It struck him now as not quite fast enough.

It was 6 A.M., and they were finally prepared, but so was half the press corps that had spent the night in No Man's Land. In single file they drove back to the highway with a great effort to maintain integrity as one small group, although their convoy kept being infiltrated by other convoys pushing toward the road. At least fifty vehicles were trying to regain the highway at the same tight neck of sand. It was not unlike a pileup at the eastbound booths of the Lincoln Tunnel—show no aggression and you lose your spot in line. Eventually they came to the border post again—the same that yesterday had been abandoned. Now it was guarded by American troops. T.R.'s eye was drawn to the soldiers checking passports as if Iraq was an American protectorate, and they were its protectors. Yessir, yessir, you may pass. As they did pass, T.R. noticed one of the soldiers had a tin of Copenhagen and a Snickers bar peeking from his pocket. If the property master of the Military Council on Important Minor Details had been asked to outfit an American soldier, he could have done no better than to hand out candy bars and chewing tobacco. Something in those items struck T.R. as essentially American, as if the spectrum that included chaw and chocolate captured both the good-earth country flavors of American living and the wild boyish sugars of its youth.

No matter, after much congestion and delay, the pile began to loosen, the mass of vehicles to break down into smaller masses, and a flying wedge of Chevrolet Suburbans shot ahead at a breakneck pace, perhaps not wishing to be part of the charge. This left a mile-long gap between the flying wedge and what was now his own group in the second rank, inviting infiltration or attack. Still, Soldier Ben did not speed up or decrease the gap in any way, which greatly pleased T.R. He was happy to be snuggled in the middle, having gotten good advice to that effect from a retired Marine Corps colonel in New York. A friend of a friend, the colonel had informed him, "Keep to the middle. Asses in the front and back are always shot at first."

At the same time, there were dangers to consider in the middle. After twenty minutes of congestion, decongestion, breaking free along the highway, and then this quick division into staggered groups, the charge of cars had started to resemble something like a steeplechase or demolition derby. One small group of

Al-Jazeera correspondents now wove recklessly among the ranks, horn blaring, tires squealing, hands and heads out the windows, driving on some crazy jet fuel of emergency. Two more cars kept edging up like dragsters on the straightaways to cut them off from the rest of the group. The group itself was constantly expanding and contracting on the highway in an unsteady rhythm.

They were only forty minutes out of No Man's Land and already there was wreckage from the war. On the roadside were the carcasses of eighteen-wheelers bombed from above—cabs twisted, cargo haulers blackened, beached across the desert sand like whales. With Soldier Ben up front and the satellite truck still chugging in the middle, the convoy worked its best to avoid the shards of metal blown off from these semis scattered on the road.

And that was how it went: The charge, with every last tight stitch of chaos ripping at the seams, was on the road again. They slipped through the desert, a flying wedge out front, a patch of empty highway coming next, then Soldier Ben in Khalid's car with T.R.'s own car, then a dozen more, then several dozen falling in their wake. Engines gunning, craters on the shoulder, tractor-trailers twisted like the worst of broken arms, the sun just coming up. In this way, the charge of vehicles sped on for at least an hour and a half before it slowed to a crawl. An obstacle was in their way, compressing the ranks into a block. The bulk of the mass knew nothing; all they knew was that the caravan had stopped. Now they waited. Up front there was confusion, shouting—if it continued any longer, they would surely get to Baghdad after dark. But now some message worked its way from front to back. "The bridge!" people in the first few ranks were shouting. "The bridge is out!"

It was not out, not completely. There remained a narrow span undamaged by the bombing slightly wider than a truck axle. The leading vehicles approached it now, maneuvering with care. It was not a situation to admire—the concrete was broken here and there, the guardrails blown away, and iron rebar twisted like spaghetti in the road. The drop to the riverbed below was thirty-five or forty feet.

Waiting to cross, T.R.'s partners were subjected to a hyperactive round of jokes, most of which had already been told. The air in the car was anesthetized with gloom—some bright injection of amphetamines was needed. Thus T.R. began, "So what's the difference between Mick Jagger and a Scotsman? One says, 'Hey, you get off my cloud!' The other, 'Hey, Cloud, get off my ewe!' Ha, ha. How you get a nun pregnant? How? You fuck her! Ha, ha, ha!" The travelers were getting comic shock therapy. Fisher, Jehad, Nadia, even Solider Ben, whom T.R. called on the satellite phone to ask if they might stop for a Big Mac, fries, and Coke. If T.R.'s humor was manic, it was better than the deadly pall of tension in the car. Even as they inched across the bridge he was convinced that kicking life into his partners was his duty, much as Fisher was responsible for driving. That his partners seemed annoyed was obvious—and yet he did not stop. On a nerve jag, T.R. kept a steady drum-like patter and the sort of sweaty desperation that a stand-up comic will acquire after fifteen minutes have passed without a laugh. "Did you hear the one about the Arab girl getting married? How about the mobster on his honeymoon? The Jewish guy whose wife won't give him sex?" he cackled from the backseat like a death-row convict begging for life. He had told these jokes before—all of them. Not funny then, they were less so now.

"Enough already!" Jehad shouted as the Jeep now shuddered safely from the bridge. Nadia and Fisher held their tongues, but their looks of quiet gratitude suggested they agreed.

At least they were moving again. The caravan spread out, the white Suburbans burst ahead, the highway oil still hot, the sun still bearing down, and T.R.'s group of eight still riding in the center of the mass with open road ahead of them and vehicles behind. For two full hours they sped on—from T.R.'s perspective, from the windows of the Jeep, the shimmering husks of burned-out semis strewn across the sand looked as if they had been tossed haphazardly across the desert like dice.

Suddenly they stopped. It was as before, but this time there were figures in the road. A crowd of men had gathered on the highway with their arms raised, packed together, shouting. They had blocked the progress of the caravan and now had formed a checkpoint in the middle of the road. The two sides faced each other, one a line of idling trucks, the other a crowd of waving Arabs, and the point where they confronted one another was confusing, messy, urgent—neither side could understand what the other had to say.

"You must leave, you must turn back!" a man called out in English. He had shoved his way through the ranks until he stood before the trucks. "Danger is ahead!" this man was shouting. "You must leave now and turn around!"

Something bad was happening, T.R. decided. There could be no better ambush—stop the convoy with a crowd, and then attack in force. Still, the man in the road was yelling, "Turn back! Turn around! You must leave now!" and the pack of thirty men behind him was gesticulating wildly, waving them away.

A small committee of interpreters was now dispatched, and after moments it returned with news—bad news. The convoy of Suburbans that had sped ahead had pulled off the highway to refuel and had encountered some resistance in a town called Falluja. (Why they hadn't carried jerry cans of fuel was still a mystery—no matter, it was done.) One of the drivers had been shot—or shot *at*, no one knew—one was robbed, another beaten. Now the word had spread that a larger convoy was approaching. Remarkably, these men had come to warn them of attack.

"So what do we do?" asked Harris. He was asking Soldier Ben and two of Khalid's men who had gathered for a meeting near the trucks.

"We wait," the senior smuggler said. "Look at them," nodding at the gaggle of Iraqis passing now among the stalled ranks of trucks with arms flailing, telling everyone to turn around, turn back, it wasn't safe.

"What isn't safe is standing here," said Soldier Ben. "We're halfway there. If we wait any longer, we'll be getting into Baghdad after dark."

"So what? Keep moving?"

"We have no choice," said Soldier Ben. The smugglers disagreed and muttered quietly among themselves. But Soldier Ben, in perfect Arabic, cut in; soon he won them over. T.R. was impressed.

They had taken up the order to move and move they did, but it was no longer even momentarily a pleasant trip. All sense of luck and confidence had vanished with the warning, and their speed had increased greatly in proportion to the threat. There seemed no way to keep the convoy close except by speeding; and yet it was impossible to speed because the road was too strewn with debris. Beyond the fear of gunfire was the fear of puncturing a tire; beyond those fears were other fears of flipping over or running out of gas. In the middle of the desert, the convoy spread out slowly, then closed ranks, spread again, and now began to make its way, speeding, slowing, rushing, swerving, seeing figures on the road. Men with guns stood watching from atop the roadside dunes, no more than silhouettes. It seemed a certainty that any group so large, so foreign, so distinctly vulnerable and unprotected should have been attacked, but in the end their vulnerability was their shield. That after all was the crazy risk on which the journey had been founded; if they had looked like a military convoy, they would have certainly been ambushed, and yet they passed unscathed for the last hundred miles because they were exactly as they seemed—a ragtag caravan with no real notion of the dangers that surrounded them and no real understanding of the threats that marked their trail.

At any rate, moving in the center of the mass, they sped on with Fisher at the wheel, Jehad riding shotgun, T.R. tucked in back with Nadia among the fuel cans, water bottles, bags of food, helmets, armored vests, and luggage pressed against their chests, keeping ranks as best they could, while a sense of great adventure finally took hold. It felt as if they had emerged at last from underground into a great arena, wind whipped like applause—huzzahhh!—and the feeling of being alive on this bright day now broke like an ice pick to a hidden pool of happiness in T.R.'s heart in such a way that he experienced a spurt of growth, a quick release of energy so cold it burst him open even wider than the desert. If only for an instant, he could feel a bright cold love, like the brightest coldest water, for the chance to be here, be here now, and be himself. Even the air inside his lungs felt cold. He could taste it now beyond all doubt and knew with certainty that he would suffer no great harm if only he could keep it in his mouth. No, nothing bad would come to touch him. He was not religious in the least, but he was mystical about these things and here in the Jeep with Fisher, Nadia, and Jehad, he felt as if the knife blade of experience had finally cut him, and the flavor in his mouth was perhaps the tang of blood or else the tang of fear—confronted, all he had to do was drink it down.

There was one more stretch of highway, then they reached the outskirts of the city and they drove in constituted ranks down newer, better roads. Fifteen miles away, they saw quite clearly Baghdad was in flames; the long dark, skinny lines of smoke rose like a charcoal drawing in the sky—not even like a drawing, like a sketch. At last they wound through a cloverleaf, continued on the road, and pulled up to a bridge. At the entrance to the bridge, where it was widest, stood a hulking M1-A1 tank. On the barrel of the tank there was a stencil, "MOM, SADDAM & APPLE PIE," and five marines atop it dressed in beige fatigues. Two of the marines, a sergeant and his corporal, hopped down and came to stop the caravan with upraised M–16s. But as soon as they drew near, a swarm of television cameras, still photographers, pencils, notepads, shouted questions, whirring microphones, and tape recorders drowned them out.

It was exactly like those death packs of reporters that descend on sleazy junior senators, and T.R. felt pity for these young marines—trained American killers, they were utterly helpless in the onslaught of the press. By now every vehicle along the road stood empty, every camera lens stood trained, every correspondent stood around the tank. One straggling cameraman rushed by to get a shot and knocked T.R. across the back. T.R. grabbed his wrist and not so gently told him, "Bet you'll see a few more soldiers once we get to Baghdad, don't you think?" But of course they *were* in Baghdad.

They had arrived. The drive was over. They were covering the war.

Chapter 19

WELCOME TO IRAQ

IN FACT, THE caravan was already leaving. Having squeezed off some hundred dozen photos of the first marines they saw and then cajoled from them some fodder for the press mill—"Yes-sir, we were sent to liberate Iraq, yes-sir! That's Corporal William Bucklemayer, m-A-y-e-r"—they returned to their vehicles in haste and drove off toward the heart of Baghdad, a pilgrimage of Jeeps, trucks, Chevrolets, and custom-bubble pleasure vans. It was not unlike a troupe of olde Elizabethan players come to perform for the local feudal lord. (Obviously T.R. did not care for the better portion of his colleagues, but it was not unwarranted, no! Just look at them driving through the alleys of the city like a traveling goddamned minstrel show.) Returning to his car, T.R. found a tire had gone flat. The caravan had long since disappeared. This left the crew alone without protection on the streets, but with the envious, if risky, opportunity to enter Baghdad on its own.

For now they were still on the city outskirts, and the low dun-colored buildings had the tired look of tyranny. The streets were full of burning trash and the empty shops were boarded up. There was a feeling everywhere of great fatigue, lost economies, and social programs having failed—it was the same exhaustion he imagined Moscow in the seventies had had, but it was done in tones of khaki, not autumnal gray. Tire fixed, the group backed up, sped off, drove on. Soon they were passing wrecked artillery pieces lying in the fields and blackened tanks like fallen pterodactyls cluttering the road. They passed whole crowds of Iraqi men and boys standing at attention on the sidewalk, watching them pass with the wary dull appreciation of a lion in the zoo. Nearly to a man, the Iraqis on the street began to wave—short, shy, not unfriendly waves—and when the strangers in the car waved back, they began to call out slogans, some in English, some surprisingly upbeat: "America number one! George Bush number one! Welcome, USA! We love you, USA!" Wherever they had gathered, the Iraqis had an eerie mix of joy and rage—it was something like the last of the lushes stumbling home on New Year's Eve. Indeed, the Iraqis had that stunned look of midnight revelers who find that daybreak has arrived much sooner than expected. They looked up from the broken streets to watch a bright white Jeep speed by—some cheering, others waving, others merely staring as the vehicle rushed past and swiftly disappeared.

Around one corner they encountered another mass of young Iraqis on the sidewalk shouting, "USA! USA!"—some hopping up and down on one leg, then the other, fists in the air in some celebratory dance. It felt like a celebration, but for what, he thought? For the invasion? For the end of tyranny? No, it was nothing quite so rational. Perhaps it was a celebration of the promise of the moment and the understanding that the madness of the moment would consume the city now for one, or two, or seven hundred days.

Certainly there was no celebration in the Jeep. Waving at the waving crowds on the few bleak streets where the traffic slowed them on their progress to the broader avenues of town, T.R. was suddenly aware—and he was not sure how—that the Iraqis almost certainly considered this white Jeep as part of the military, part of the invasion. Even worse, perhaps the Jeep and the dozens like it that had entered Baghdad had been taken for the point of the invasion, yes, its very purpose. The tanks had come to do the dirty work and clear the way so that the media (like MacArthur in the Philippines) might now arrive. Hold on, wait a minute, whoa, but there it was, written on the faces of the mustached men and boys on every corner, waving happily and deferentially, waving with respect, as if this Jeep contained the highest rank of officer, the real top dog, no general or mere commander, but a Generalissimo, a Great Communicator. With an ancient wisdom born of the desert in their bones, these Iraqis saw it first: Who is most important? Why, he who comes to the battlefield last.

Yes, up front go the grunts, the muscle boys, too dumb, too poor, too honest to escape the dirty work, while from the rear there comes another army, better-educated, middle-class, not armed with weapons of destruction but with weapons of decision, definition, called upon to tell the world if the whole thing really worked. Remarkable! Still the question that arose was why this second army was permitted to invade. Had the military been so confident that it desired to have its cakewalk captured live and beamed across the world? Or had it rather banked on guilt—good, old-fashioned middle-class American guilt? For the Press Brigade was by and large the sons and daughters of the middle class, a class that did not sweat, and did not serve, and might be counted on to take it easy on those who did.

Of course, T.R. imagined as they passed another crowd of young Iraqis waving like a ticker-tape parade, he might again be mixing up his own fairy tale for the larger story. It was *he*, after all, who was middle class, *he* who was ashamed of never having served, so it was *he* who felt most guilty. As the business of the media became more lucrative, it also became more cautious. Joseph Mitchell was dead and gone, Breslin was gone (if not exactly dead), the trade had abandoned its working-class beginnings—it was no longer even a trade, it was truly a profession. Journalism, like the law, was studied in the finest schools, and yet the street kid did not die with his degree, he just got whacked with a wicked case of guilt. T.R. was willing to bet a ten to anybody's five that he was not alone among his peers in feeling this way interviewing some marine, same age as him. After all, one of them was headed off to war, the other into voyeuristic deeps. One could do one's duty, yes; serve the public, yes; speak the truth, of course; create that first rough draft of history. Yet this had little to do with war reporting on the level of the instincts. Down there at the bottom of it, it was all passivity—seeing, smelling, tasting, watching, standing by, none of which were active verbs.

Now they turned a corner to the heart of Baghdad. The government buildings were on fire; the streets snarled with donkey carts; there was a bite of cordite in the air, and thick black clouds of smoke, and Jeeps, and tanks, and taxicabs that lacked all doors. Over a bridge across the Tigris came a swarm of men, perhaps a hundred in all, their heads down, their backs bent, pushing carts filled with radiators, broken doors, sacks of rice, and television sets. If the feeling in this crowd was of the mask of history ripped off by desperation, torture chambers, late night confessions, early morning terrors, and a hopeless thirty years of waiting for a midnight knock at the door, the face revealed was yet another mask—frenzied, uncontrollable, and tinged with the chaotic tenderness of human liberation. Helicopters whipped above, small boys scurried after hubcaps. Car horns blared like throttled hens. T.R. stared from the Jeep at the small black eyes of an ecstatic urchin on a donkey cart. No, there was no time, not now, for anything like guilt.

"Over there!" he called. They had reached the Sheraton Hotel (familiar brand name in the middle of the vortex, strange as finding Coke cans on the empty plains of Mars). "Over there!" he called again. They were trying to enter the parking lot, and failing twice, T.R. now spotted somewhere safe to leave the car.

Backed up in a tangle, some cars leaving, others coming in, the traffic at the Sheraton was crawling. Fisher pulled from the mass to double-park some ten or fifteen paces from the curb. It was decided three of them would go inside to find a room; T.R. would stay to guard the car. When a room was found, they would come to fetch him. "Wait a minute," T.R. said with the last of his joking instincts. "If I get a ticket can I charge it to the *Times*?"

He moved up front to smoke, the traffic choked around him, but before he could relax, he was interrupted by the honking of a nearby vehicle—a white Suburban with a tall, sharp-featured Arab at the wheel. As with any case of double-parking, the Suburban had been wedged in at the curb. The driver wanted him to move, but T.R. shrugged. With traffic jamming him on every side, it was impossible to move.

Even now the traffic slowed, stalled, thickened, and congealed. The jam began a hundred yards away in Firdas Square, snaked past the Sheraton, ran along the Palestine Hotel where marines had built a razor wire perimeter protected by a battery of tanks, and then down the long broad avenue beneath a row of palm trees and the hot sun out of sight. The drivers trapped in line leaned heavily on their horns; they yelled obscenities at one another. It reminded T.R. of the Deegan on the day before Thanksgiving—all the interactive chaos of the Bronx.

Hemmed in by traffic, surrounded now on every side, all drivers losing their cool, T.R. and the man in the Chevy started shouting at each other. The man leaned out his window, and for one full minute they began to curse each other, yelling from the front seats of their cars.

"You block the road, motherfucker! Why you block the road?"

"There's nowhere to go! That's why I block the road!"

T.R. found he was cursing a face so charged with anger that it seemed to be a lightning rod collecting ions of electric hatred from the air. The driver was a good deal heavier than he was, strongly built, and with a shaved head and big tall, ropy body, looked like a rugby player save his face, which was electrified by rage. It was the face of an ogre, or an angry child.

Still T.R. could claim an edge—his guilt was coming back. His nervous system had been smoking for hours, he was utterly exhausted from the drive, and in the traces of his large intestine, his guilt had broken down to anger. It was the normal process of digestion: In the juices of the stomach, guilt turned into rage and the sense that one had much to prove. It was a cardinal rule of combat that a man engaged in a private war was an enemy to fear. And yet the Chevy driver seemed oblivious, for now he raised the stakes. First once, then twice, he nudged the bumper of his Chevy at the Jeep. When T.R. turned to blast him, he was shocked by what he saw. The Iraqis on the street had gone insane, ripping at the city as a cannibal rips at flesh, but this man's rage was burning on his face so brightly it seemed the flames were just beneath the skin. Even in the Jeep T.R. could feel the hot waves of anger blowing at his hair. If the two got any closer, one might suddenly combust. And the strangest part was that he had not done a thing to possibly deserve this. What had he done? Double-parked a car.

Nearly instantly he went into that special mode of observation that a man picks up when the challenge has been laid, a systematic high-intensity review of the opponent's strengths and weaknesses. It was an animal response that tingled like a cold front up and down the spine: One sensed immediately if the other might throw kicks or punches or, by contrast, shoot for the knees. Sitting in the Jeep, T.R. decided that the Chevy driver was a charger; he was large enough to lunge and smother his opponent in a bear hug. Quite possibly he fought best on the ground and so would do his damage on the ground in whatever way he could. T.R. stepped from the Jeep and placed the hood between himself and the other man. The Chevy driver left his own car, too, and on the streets of Baghdad, in the midst of traffic, the pair of them squared off.

"Motherfucker!" the driver shouted. "Fuck you, bad America!"

It was ridiculous. And poignant. And embarrassing. And T.R. could not help himself. He shouted back, like any connoisseur of action movies would: "Fuck me? No, my friend, fuck you!"

"You like to die, America?"

"Die? Don't you think you ought to probably fuck off?"

What a strange thing to say. Who talked like that? No one talked like that. It now occurred to him that he was criticizing his own trash talk. T.R. knew that once the talking started, there would likely be no fight. A fight was like a car crash or a post-date kiss—it happened instantly or not all.

But then the Chevy driver started to improvise. They were circling the Jeep, taunting one another, and the driver found himself beside the passenger door. On a burst of inspiration, he opened the door, reached in, and starting tossing everything he found—jackets, water bottles, notebooks, all the little knickknacks they had carried on their trip—all of it, he tossed to the street.

At first T.R. was confused. The man had reached in the Jeep with such a sense of purpose and begun to root around with such serene intent it had seemed there must be something in there he wanted to find. The very weirdness of the action froze him. There was certainly a comic aspect to it. But after the initial shock had passed he was indignant. Somehow the attack on their belongings was even more invasive, more intrusive, than a personal assault.

"Get your goddamn hands out of there!"

"You fuck off, American ass!"

A group of Iraqis who had gathered on the sidewalk now jumped in and started to restrain the man—it took a good half dozen to perform the job. Working cautiously, with two men to an arm, they finally forced the driver back inside his Chevy, then stopped traffic long enough to give T.R. the room to leave. Under their protection, T.R. pulled the Jeep ahead some hundred yards, and there sat idling along the curb again, awaiting word about the room.

It was moments later he saw the young marines across the street atop their tank, shaking heads, laughing dryly, sitting, smoking, watching in that round-the-campfire posture of the military that bespeaks fraternal ribbing and the friendliest of all sarcastic jokes. They had seen the whole thing—now they had themselves a yuck. T.R.'s face lit up like a bonfire, for he could see his silliness from their perspective—two grown men, neither armed, chasing one another like a pair of bantams through a barn. It was bad enough having given rein to his aggressive instincts. Now whatever guilt and shame lay undigested in his stomach rose again like bile beneath the smiles of these marines.

"Doin' all right there, sir?" one of them asked—that "sir" having the effect of granting him a much too early middle age. "We was gonna jump in to help, but you look like you had her under wraps."

T.R. had always enjoyed talking to soldiers. He liked the practical nature of their minds. He liked discussing cars and girls and pool. He especially liked the accents soldiers had—the Down Home drawl, the Appalachian whinny, the Tuscaloosa groove, and then the urban accents, the Bean Town burn and Brooklynese. It sometimes seemed to him that soldiers were the only class of citizen left that still spoke from a sense of place, and that they truly cared about their place. You could always peg a soldier by his accent, whether it was the hummocky lump of Frogcreek Holler, Mississippi, or the nostril whine of Mount St. Gorgeous, Maine. Whether a severely regimented military life provoked a sense of place from its recruits or whether those recruits were simply drawn from places yet to be completely flattened, bleached, anesthetized, and strip-mined by the great backhoes of the shopping mall and interstate, T.R. could hardly tell. This marine, for instance, spoke with an accent that put him in a zone between the bayou and the bourbon belt of New Orleans—and it was only possible to counter him by matching specificity with specificity, place with place.

At any rate, he looked at these marines and said, "Are any of you fellas from New York? New York? New York? New York?" He was pointing now at each of them in turn, all five answers coming back as no.

"Well, I'm from New York," he said, swelling on the instant with the city's big brass balls, "and I have never in my life seen anything like *that*. For God's sake, you double-park in New York City and you work it out. But this guy thinks that Firdas Square is the goddamn Cross-Bronx Expressway."

Through a spattering of laughter now, another marine, tall, thin, rangy, black, and chuckling like his buddies, asked T.R.: "How long you been in Baghdad, sir?"

"Fifteen freaking minutes," T.R. said.

The laughter was the good kind, not the bad, and seemed to welcome T.R. to take a seat around the campfire, join the ribbing. He would have gladly, too, except for Fisher and the rest of them approaching the Jeep. He saw at once that Fisher had that professionally worried look again, deep sweats of an internal struggle. Even Nadia and Jehad seemed a bit depressed. So reluctantly he climbed in the Jeep again and hit the engine, making ready to depart.

As he did, the first marine called out to him from the tank, "Hey, New York. Before you get going . . ."

He turned to find a bright young smiling murderous Louisiana face.

"Welcome to Iraq."

Chapter 20

R O O M S

As it happened, they were going nowhere. The Sheraton was booked, as was the Palestine. T.R. found it strange that there were no rooms only two days after Baghdad had collapsed. It was not as if the Association of Retired Catholic Seamstresses had waltzed in to rent out the El Morocco Room for its annual convention (though he later learned that an army of the press and scores of Marine Corps officers had taken rooms at both hotels, which did make for a junket atmosphere, albeit of a slightly different sort). At any rate, the Sheraton and Palestine were now surrounded by enormous bales of razor wire, and armed marines stood post at checkpoints backed by Bradleys and by M1-A1 tanks. They had cordoned off perhaps a dozen acres, all in all, creating a security zone in which the press now stood discussing operations with the officers, smoking cigarettes, taking notes, and milling about like the evening crowd at Sardi's while a great dark, heaving mass of Arabs, some in protest of the Westerners, some seeking jobs, pressed up beyond the barricades at gunpoint, shouting from without.

T.R. was passing through that mass even now on his way to the Palestine, and felt again a mix of joy and rage within the crowd, a blending he had noticed many times before in prisons, sports arenas, Harlem churches, and in certain South Bronx bars. He even felt it now within himself. After all they had come four hundred miles across the desert only to be shut out from the city's main hotels for lack of what? A reservation? Nadia was optimistic—she believed that ample money might obtain a room. Jehad had no such illusions. Fisher, meanwhile, mainly seemed concerned with tracking down their colleagues at the *Times*. Moments after passing through the checkpoint, he set about to find them in the area between the two hotels where a dozen television trucks were parked in staggered rows. Over the weeks, T.R. had come to know him well enough to recognize that Fisher's patience and his great good nature had finally reached the end of their supply. He wanted desperately to find his friends, and there was something in the way he searched the plaza now, scouring the scores of newsmen standing in the open dusty air, as if nothing could be more important than to find a fellow correspondent, which confirmed T.R.'s suspicion of himself as an amateur reporter, not a full-fledged member of the team. He was not, however, angry or insulted. Far from wanting to embark upon a story, he wanted only to soak in the juices of the last eight hours, and knew—from watching Fisher—that if he rushed to file a story, he would lose the better part of the experience and miss the chance to revel in its depths. No, he dreaded getting down to work. The joy was in the excitation of the raw experience. The rage was having to transform it into seven hundred words.

Now he remembered what he hated most about this job was breaking news. Why, then, had he assumed that war reporting would be anything *but* breaking news? Why had he fooled himself that he possessed the crispness, modesty, the sense of duty that was needed in a war? No doubt because he was an ass who craved experience. The reason he had taken this assignment to begin with was to secretly expand upon his personal reserves of knowledge and adventure—a motive hardly dutiful at all. There were no two ways about it. He had snuck his own interest into the job as slyly as a stowaway onboard a ship.

At the moment he started feeling sheepish over this, Fisher came to say he had found their colleagues, and they rushed off toward the Palestine to find a tall, distinguished-looking man in beige Bermudas, sandals, and an armor-plated vest holding court outside the lobby. Holding court was the accurate term, for the man stood in a circle of reporters, taking questions and delivering responses as though the Palestine were now his briefing room and this activity a press event.

"So you've just come out of hiding?" someone asked.

"Well, yes, one doesn't trifle with the Mukhabarat."

"And how long were you actually in hiding?"

The man to whom these questions were directed had the firm commanding look of a British sea captain who had served well in the old Napoleonic wars, but now was fighting with the admiralty to keep his ship.

"Longer than I care to think," he said.

"And now?"

"Now?" he repeated. "Now we get to work."

Through all of this, Fisher had been standing outside the circle looking in. Now he elbowed through in an effort to present himself.

"Ah, yes, Ian, splendid. When did you arrive?" Before an answer could be made, the man had moved his gaze to Nadia. "And who is this?"

Nadia introduced herself to a pair of craven eyes that seemed to assess her entire worth at once. The eyes then shifted toward T.R., and the man reached out his hand to make an introduction with a cool colonial tone of voice.

"John Burns," he said, his accent clipped as the finest hedgerow. "A pleasure to have you on the team."

The introductions went on like that for a few more minutes, then Burns turned again to Fisher. "Look," he said, "shall we meet in my room this evening? Let's say seven-thirty, eight o'clock?" It was done. Fisher was asked to spread the word among the others when he saw them. Jehad still was silent. Then they were dismissed.

They crossed the plaza to the Sheraton and went inside, Fisher to find the others, Jehad to an armchair in the lobby, Nadia toward the check-in desk to negotiate a room. T.R. had a story to file (on the drive from Jordan), which broke through any thoughts he had of simply hanging out. Time was not exactly in his favor. It was now after six. The meeting was at eight, so he would have to write within the hour, spend an hour filing—maybe more—he had never used the satellite before— then shave, shower, and change his clothes, if indeed they had a room. There had been great excitement when the desk had asked him in Ruweished to write about their travels on the road (it was the first time he had actually been *assigned* a story), but excitement withered at the thought that he might fail. One's first story from the war zone was a critical assignment, not unlike one's first appearance at the plate. Write well, and he would be considered as a man who could deliver; file a piece of junk, and he would be a rookie who had flubbed his first appearance at bat.

But as soon as he sat down to work, T.R. was interrupted. Nadia needed money. Then more money. The negotiations with the manager had reached a crucial pass. When T.R. handed her the first five hundred, he assumed it would suffice, but then she came back asking for another hundred, then a hundred more, and still she had no room.

"He's almost given in," she said. "I think."

The manager, a shady-looking fellow with a mustache, dark brown eyes, dark lips, dark fingers, nervous hands, and a great dark, falsely gracious smile, was standing at the desk now saying, "Yes, it seems there is a room, but many people have expressed great interest. Perhaps if you could offer some . . . *additional* assurance, your name could be placed at the top of the list . . ."

He had taken this one step too far. Now Nadia's eyes lit up like a laser beam and cut two holes in his face, as if to say, "Look here, rat, don't get cute with me." Within a moment, keys were in her hands. T.R. was greatly impressed.

Still he was having trouble writing. No doubt it was due to the fact he hadn't eaten anything since breakfast, tamping his hunger with a stream of cigarettes so that his throat burned and his lungs felt as if they had been roasted on a spit. He was also fighting off the loud distractions of the lobby, but no matter how he tried, this throng of officers, reporters, U.N. workers, bellhops, fixers, cameramen, and drivers tramped like a parade route through his mind. He was accustomed to writing in odd places and had written many times in cars, bars, coffee shops, commuter trains, and in the paper's newsroom with its incessant clack of keys, but never before had he experienced such dissonance.

Suddenly there was a massive thunderclap—it rocked the lobby, people froze, the street filled up with smoke. When T.R.

rushed outside to find what might have caused the blast, there was nothing but a fading cloud of dust. In Firdas Square, some twenty yards away, a car had just exploded—there it was, a smoking hulk—and yet the soldiers in the plaza hadn't moved. Coming back inside, he found the lobby had resumed its normal traffic, not an eyebrow cocked, nor a picture frame amiss. For half of one full second, T.R. wondered whether he had heard the blast at all, but then a pale young man approached him for a cig-arette—a young reporter, by his looks, exhausted, wide-eyed, obviously green as he—and said with trepidation, "Christ, that sounded close."

Upstairs in the room were further difficulties, for the room, he found, was a room in name alone. Having shelled out seven hun-dred dollars in *assurances* (which broke down to a fifty-dollar bribe, a one-hundred-fifty-dollar power fee, and then a five-hundred-dollar nonrefundable deposit for "the reservation"), T.R. had every right to expect some cozy, furnished nook in which to sleep, dress, bathe, and work. And yet among the items this room lacked were a desk, a bed, a closet, a dresser, a sink, a toilet, running water, carpet, lights, and so on, which is to say it was nothing but a cinder-block construction site with floors and four bare walls. Walking in, T.R. exploded; he slammed his rucksack at the wall. Then he sat down on the concrete floor and got to work. This was typical of him, and he could hardly say whether his behavior served or worked against his purpose. He did not know, for instance, if his anger had allowed him access to a secret store of energy that might have otherwise been hid-den, or if it jammed his concentration and drove the energy he wanted from his grasp. Or was he angry simply because he lacked control? All he knew was that the moment he exploded, he was then prepared to work, which seemed to hold the answer to the question: In his own inner makeup, anger was a spur. If put to proper uses, it could help him with a deadline. If put to ill effect, he wound up fighting Arabs on the street.

The hour of his deadline approached, the hour quickly passed. Colleagues came, colleagues went, it was clearly time to file. With masking tape, he fixed his phone to the railing of the balcony and tried to find the southern sky. There were steps to filing, none of which he'd mastered. First the phone must be securely pointed in the right direction; next the satellite connection must be made. After came a passcode bringing one in contact with the *Times* computers in New York. It was a nightmare, though not as ghoulish as the story he had written. "Car by car, truck by truck, step by step . . ."—his prose was actually that purple. Still, he lacked the luxury to care.

Already he was fifteen minutes late to meet John Burns. He had no time to shower and descended ten full flights of stairs (the elevators at the Sheraton were out), then galloped up another sixteen at the Palestine (where they were out as well) so that he knocked on Burns's door in a panting sweat like the last fat kid to finish in a gym-class relay race. Burns came to greet him, a skeptical, confused look on his face. "Ah, yes," Burns said, pausing in the doorway He had forgotten T.R.'s name.

"Sorry I'm late," T.R. apologized, "I had to file a story."

"No, no," Burns said with generosity, "think nothing of it," and turned and ushered him into the room.

Whatever shame T.R. had felt at being late was swept aside by the spectacle of Burns's room. Everywhere the room bore the traces of the deepest luxury—ripe tomatoes lay on the sink; on the coffee table were several bottles of unopened Bordeaux wine.

If there was not a Bach cantata playing, one could be forgiven having heard one. Burns's room, in its civility, seemed almost to exude the strains of Bach. T.R. had heard the stories: Burns receiving packages from Harrod's in the war zone, Burns requesting $60,000 at a drop, Burns demanding that the paper rent a house in Kabul with a swimming pool. But he was not prepared to confront such grandness in the flesh. After his own room, stepping into Burns's room was not unlike being hauled from the hole at Sing Sing to be pardoned by the warden, only to find the warden's suite had been designed by Richelieu on a budget funded by a solvent Donald Trump. Yet Burns was capable of carrying this off. On a lesser man, such luxury would have worn like false ambition; on Burns, it wore like silk.*

T.R. followed Burns from the sitting room to a smaller room in back to find the six or seven colleagues he would work with for the next few weeks. They sat on chairs and couches talking, drinking, eating, discussing the day's events, and lifted their eyes at him as he came in. A few of them he knew by sight, the rest by name—it hardly mattered. Already the process of establishing his role had begun. Before one word was spoken, it was possible to gauge a man's relation to the team, and though his days of playing baseball were behind him, T.R. had been raised in a world of Boy Scouts, Little League, and pick-up games, and the lessons he had learned came back. On a team, a man who wants

_____

*T.R.'s favorite correction to a Burns story appeared in the paper in December 2003: "An article about Christmas at Campe Ste.-Mere, a forward base of the 82nd Airborne Division in Iraq, misattributed the Ave Maria performed in a makeshift chapel. While the setting was adapted from the Prelude in C of Bach's 'Well-Tempered Clavier,' the melody is by Gounod, not Bach." Only Burns would have caught the error. Or cared.

to secure his place must act at once, show his colors instantly, and carve out space in which to operate or else risk being cast aside. Among reporters this was triply true because reporters were profound territorial beasts. (In this, they were much like waiters who depend on a busy section of the restaurant for tips.) So T.R. sat down quickly, and quickly forced his presence in the room by pulling his chair directly to the flow of conversation, then by leaning forward with his elbows on his knees. Then he lit a cigarette. No one else was smoking. His message was clear—he was here now, bold, involved. If, eventually, he blew his smoke in the direction of the sitting room, it was only to remain polite. There seemed no sense in displaying too much boldness on what would be his first full evening in Iraq.

He had walked in on a strategy session. Each reporter was giving his opinion of the stories that deserved full coverage, making cases for the particular assignments he desired. There was Burns, John Kifner, Dexter Filkins, Fisher, and himself (a sixth reporter, Craig Smith, was nowhere to be found). There were also two or three photographers about. Since Burns was elder statesman, all discussion was referred to him. Burns seemed pleased with this arrangement, not only because it was his due— he had covered every war since Vietnam and had won a pair of Pulitzers to boot—but because he also had, self-consciously or not, the irrefutable nobility of a servant to the crown. The fact that Burns could question his reporters and solicit their opinions and could order them at will—"Ian, you decamp at daybreak for Al Kindi Hospital. Should Smith show up, we'll send him off to Karbala"—was no more than an offshoot of his naturally commanding mood. At times Burns spoke to the group as though he were His Majesty's chief viceroy. "Tell me, John"—oozing

doubt—"have you kept up your contacts with the military?"
Full-faced grimace. "Yes, I see. Well, you ought to stay in touch
with them nonetheless."

Kifner took this news, as he took most news, quiet, patient,
slouching in his chair. Later he might roll his eyes at Burns, or
imitate his accent, or mock some poor decision Burns had
made—for now, his manner was polite and tempered with respect. Kifner, old dog of many battles, was equally experienced
as Burns (he had been the first reporter at the Kent State mas-
sacre) but lacked the latter's shiny British gloss. Kif was Sarge.
Burns was Sir. Therein lay the difference. "I'll hook up with
them first thing tomorrow morning," Kifner said.

"Good. Now, Dexter."

"Yes?"

"How go things in Tikrit?"

"Well, I don't know. I haven't been there in a week."

Filkins was tall, loose-limbed, somewhere in his thirties,
sandy-haired, good-looking, quietly intelligent, and wearing
khaki pants and a dirty polo shirt. T.R. knew little of him beyond the fact that Filkins was his predecessor in the Bronx. But
Filkins had not been a lifer in the borough; he had only spent a
few short months there before Afghanistan broke out. Then he
was sent to cover war. Now he was the paper's roving correspondent. Filkins was not embedded; his job was to attach himself by
hook or crook to military units and, without restriction from the
Pentagon, to get as close to the fighting as he could. This had
given him a weary edge—"What I have seen, I shall not speak
of 'til the Gates of Heaven burst . . ."—which seemed at times
like something out of Byron and at others like a put-on. Perhaps
it was a necessary cloak for someone his age.

His partner was a British cameraman named Hill, James Hill, who lived in Rome and cultivated a tempestuous, dashing, ascot-round-the-collar manner. Hill was known for taking very good, very smart, very graphic photographs of war. Together Hill and Filkins made a team, a sporting team—yes, sporting was the word—you could almost see them on a motorcycle with a sidecar cruising through the wadis. T.R. liked the two of them immensely. In fact, he liked the entire crew. He was surprised. After all it wasn't often he enjoyed the company of colleagues. He even liked the photographer who worked with Burns, a somber brooding man named Tyler Hicks. Hicks and Burns were something of a bickering old couple, steeped in mutual dysfunction, but it was magic when they worked. T.R. only hoped that given time he too might find a cameraman to partner with, and so create a team.

The team, in fact, was on his mind—these very thoughts now worked to build the pressure in his skull to make his own mark on the room. In the pit of his stomach, he could feel an almost physical desire to find his place among these men, and felt his lack of good experience with considerable discomfort—could he ever truly pull it off? He also felt the rattle of his nerves. If he did not fit in, it might go on and on. Burns must have sensed some part of this because he now directed his attention toward T.R. and offered an assignment. "Why not head to the palace in the morning?" Burns suggested. "You'll find it quite intriguing, I believe."

T.R. had no idea where the palace was, or what he would find when he arrived, but he accepted this assignment with a nod. Burns meanwhile moved on. Leaning back in his chair, he now embarked upon a speech to rouse the troops. The editors were counting on them now, he said, but that meant nothing in itself—deadlines, word counts, fancy leads, the whole insipid bag of tricks was meaningless, he said, for it would wither in comparison to one small grain of truth. As he spoke in the large dark beautifully appointed room not two days after coming out of hiding, there was a messianic gleam in Burns's eye, the glint of some old godhead. T.R. had the sudden thought that Burns, like Mr. Kurtz, had cracked and might have raised his fists to say, "War, my friends, is an undertaking fraught with peril, and yet it is the living flesh of History!"—had Ian Fisher not stood up and closed his notebook, which swiftly brought the meeting to an end. Pulling T.R. aside, Fisher frowned at his wristwatch. Then he whispered, "It's getting late. Did Nadia find a room?"

Were these the poles of the foreign correspondent? Did he go from waging battles over truth to worrying about his room? It was a harsh job, and it robbed you of your friends and family, your moorings, sensitivities, your home—did it also rob you of the better portions of your mind? For all his grandeur, Burns was missing something fundamental, something of that tender sense of ordinary life that correspondents surely gave away by moving on from one assignment to the next. They were so inured to movement that they held tightly to the habits of their movement. T.R. could practically taste the cravings Burns had had for ordinary life in the price he must have paid to have those fresh tomatoes on his sink.

At the Sheraton again, T.R. stood out on the balcony. A firefight had broken out along the river. A company of tanks and riflemen had cornered some insurgents in a large stone house on the far side of the Tigris. He could see the paparazzi flash of fire, smell the acrid bite of smoke. He had never seen such action, and might have started to romanticize it if the fighting had continued. But the tanks hit home and the upper stories of the building disappeared. And when the smoke cleared, the house was reduced to rubble. Had this really been one day? First, a steeplechase across the desert; then a fistfight in the city; now ten stories up, a fireworks display.

He soon lost interest in the skirmish. He was brooding over Burns. There was something in the man's devotion to war, his nearly papal dedication to diplomacy and politics, and then his personal attachment to the sweep of world events that struck T.R. as foreign, yet profoundly stirring. It seemed to him that Burns had some connection to the—what? the living flesh of History? Who knew, perhaps to Burns all history *was* living flesh? If Burns had shown an interest in the mating habits of the crocodile, T.R. could not have been more baffled, for his own grasp of history was infantile, it was almost nonexistent, he had not been raised that way. T.R. had been raised a middle-class midwestern Jew, and the culture that was his had taught him something, not too much, but something of situation commedies and Sunday football and a pure Ohio innocence that rarely looked beyond the borders of its yard. From his father, he had learned the old Romanian ways of hard work, trust in money, decent manners, and the immigrant's unyielding need for quiet in America. From his mother, he had picked up much about the mournfulness of Brooklyn and the ravages of alcohol. On her side was a long line of traveling salesmen, and from them he had learned about the interstate, the neighborhood, failure, and doubt. Nowhere, however, had he learned a thing of history. History had not existed in the house.

Both his parents came from troubled homes, but they survived those homes with a desire for good suburban living still intact. Like millions of Americans, they had staked their claim on a firmament of mortgage payments, tree lawns, and the promise of a decent public school. Because his father had escaped Vietnam with the telephone utility, because his mother never had to write him in Da Nang, Quan Tre, or a hundred other hellholes, and because the living flesh of history had never intervened to touch their lives, they had raised their children in the sanitary isolation that America perfects. But this had left T.R. without much feeling for the world, because the world, with all its draft cards, protests, body bags, and long nights of wondering if death would come by morning, had been banished from the home. T.R. could still remember days on end at the kitchen window when he would have bashed in his own skull just to break that horrible sweet American monotony.

Of course the irony was that a generation back his family had been soaked in the deepest history conceivable—had almost drowned, in fact. His father's family had survived the Holocaust: aunts and uncles killed at Auschwitz, seven dead, three survived. His father's father had escaped Romania in 1933 as a stowaway aboard a freighter—now that legacy seemed hardly to exist. It was the same again on his mother's side. Her father had served with the military cops in World War II, her uncle had fought at the Battle of the Bulge. But what was left? A few good stories? Some old resin of residual guilt? It was a horror that his past should disappear. Beyond his horror as a grandson, son, and eventual father, he was horrified as a reporter. How could he have reached the age of thirty-two without incorporating all this family history into his own life? It should have been the first among his subjects, his essential beat—ever more because, like many men his age, he felt a loose alliance with the past.

In the final call his hunger for the past was traceable in part to America's erasure of its own past. If his parents weren't ignorant, but merely wanted in the end to bury stubborn pain, then he would have to accept that they had sought the blandness of the suburbs, and he couldn't curse them, because they had been following the movements of the country, and how could he curse either one, parents or country, when he himself, the grandson of a stowaway, had wound up in the Boy Scouts and the Little League, with an Ivy education and a good job at the *New York Times?*

And so his estimation of a man like Burns, not to mention the marines now posted all across the city, was always set against his family history. It seemed he had always felt a bond with military men—not because of family ties but rather because he tried to hold himself to a military standard of behavior, whether it was ethics, honor, or loyalty to friends. His deepest pride was in upholding codes of patience, endurance, authenticity, and since this did not come naturally to him, and since he had no family model, he had worked very hard for very many years to surround himself with tutors.* If T.R. did not enact these values fully (or even to a third of their effect), he could not fool himself that he was not in love with them. He was in love with them. He even felt responsible to be in love.

It was now past ten o'clock. The desk had yet to call, and it depressed him—he wanted to complete his work and get to sleep. Then Hill and Filkins dropped in for a visit, and they brought along a box of MREs, Meals Ready to Eat—Beef Teriyaki, Country Captain Chicken, Cajun Rice and Beans, heavy prefab meals in heavy prefab bags. Within each bag was a smaller bag

---

*One had served with the Eighty-second Airborne. Another was the son of ironworkers. A third had been raised on a thousand-acre farm. Then there was LeDuff.

with miniature bottles of Tabasco sauce and sticks of laxative gum. America would have no constipated killers—not in this man's army. Thanks to factories in Indiana, Texas, Arizona, you could gorge, then shit, your way through a tour of world cuisine.

After dinner, it was time for bed. Of course, there was no bed. In the hallway, Nadia had found a pair of mattresses—not frames or box springs, a pair of dirty mattresses—and, in the hallway, T.R. helped her drag them toward the wall. He had scored some blankets from a colleague. They might still get some sleep. Then the gunfire started up again. He tossed and turned all night.

In the hallway, in the dark, above the city, he was sore, uncomfortable, and full of his body's own foul odors. Nor could he free his mind from thoughts of what the hell he was doing here at all. For every choice he had made along the way, he knew there were fifteen choices he had never made, never considered, never knew about, and as he fell asleep he tiptoed down the path of those decisions, which had led him here to a mattress in the hallway of the Sheraton, a $700 mattress, near the elevators, up above a thunderstorm of guns. Virgin of war, political naïf, amateur in all things historical, he nonetheless possessed some schizophrenia that gave him insight. Who else had his young man's mix of patriotic fever, immigrant distance, journalistic bitterness, and shame? If there was someone who loved the war, and hated the war, and felt the war—as he felt it—in the fibers of his brain, he wanted to meet that man, he would love to meet that man, if only to buy him a drink and, at the bar, to ask him what in God's good name he really thought.

Chapter 21

ENDLESS ASPHALT

W HAT T.R. REALLY thought was that the war was an abomination of good intention and the dangerous result of hubris in pursuit of public good. The arguments in favor of the war, and those against it, had been made a thousand times—they would yet be made a thousand times again. To T.R.'s mind, it seemed that every effort to support the war tended to ignore its consequences. Its critics, on the other hand, were largely deaf to its more reasonable rationales.

The country had invaded Iraq in thrall to a mindset that had taken root among a tiny group of men sometime around the end of the first Gulf War. This group—among them Dick Cheney, Donald Rumsfeld, Richard Perle, Paul Wolfowitz, and Douglas Feith—were from the cynical, ambitious, patriotic Hardknock School of Life, and they believed not only in the power of America, but in the power of an Evil that saw America as its foe. As a result, they formed a Fellowship: Like superheroes cloaked in the uniforms of daily life, they made their rounds as university professors, CEOs, think-tank presidents, and bureaucrats, all the while keeping one eye on the Evil that was growing in the East. Between the wars, they had no power to engage this evil and so sufficed with the occasional paper or comment in the press. Then George W. Bush was elected, and the Superheroes of the Hardknock School were brought to Washington again: The Fellowship had power. It also had the ear of an executive with a simple mind to understand the dangers of the Evil and a deep religious faith to sustain him during war.

So the Fellowship began to plan a war. The argument behind their plan relied upon the sane, if somewhat paranoid, belief that if the Evil was left to fester, it would then link up with other Evils in Afghanistan, the Philippines, in Egypt, Syria, Saudi Arabia, and Pakistan—indeed wherever Islam in its radical form had taken hold. If this collective Evil somehow got its hands on chemical, biological, or, worst of all, nuclear weapons, America might rise one morning to discover Times Square or Boston Commons or the Mall in Washington had been obliterated, an event to result not only in the deaths of thousands, if not millions—it would leave no easy enemy against which to strike back.

So the Fellowship conceived a plan to neutralize the Evil before it could attack. In the forefront of its mind, it did not have thoughts of grandeur, global domination, even greed (those came later and were more effect than cause). Instead it had a sober, complex, highly cynical concern about the safety of the country. The tragedy of 9/11 only heightened that concern—it was the final proof that waiting to respond no longer worked. It was not the catalyst for war, it was used to sell the war. Once the Fellowship surged into action and began to tell the country "We should now attack Iraq," a rationale was needed for the public,

and the Fellowship began to warn that if a war was not desirable, it was nonetheless necessary since Iraq had deadly weapons
(so they said) and the Arabs had already shown that they were
willing to attack. This warning served to stir up fear and righteous anger in the public. It also served to betray the Fellowship's enormous lack of truthfulness and trust—the stated
reasons for the war were not the honest reasons. If the honest
reasons had included that a war against Iraq would send a signal to Islamic armies that America would not take terror on the
chin, would attempt to fix a broken place in which the status
quo no longer held, and would re-situate the battle from the
homeland to the Middle East, this was never stated as a fact.
Eventually the Fellowship insisted that the war would also let
America hold up democracy as a beacon to the Arabs, but at
first, there came the lie.

Against these arguments, the best and bravest critics had con-
tended that a war against Iraq was no more necessary than desirable. Far from making the country safer, it would weaken the
American defense. War, they said, was a dangerous distraction
from Al Qaeda. The critics liked to argue over consequences.
Even if Saddam was killed or captured, they explained, his
country might be torn by civil war, for who would rule when he
was gone? The Shiite masses allied with Iran? The Kurds, who
wanted to secede? Perhaps the country might be given to the
Sunnis of the old regime? Or would America, in thrall to all
three sides, be caught in the middle like a tailback with the ball?

The critics took particular umbrage at the shifting rationales.
If the war had been designed to bring democracy, they asked,
then why not bring it to Africa or Asia? (Some might even say,
with an eye cocked to the election in 2000, why not to America

itself?) If, on the other hand, it was designed to send a signal to the Arabs, surely there were better ways to send a signal, not to mention better signals one could send. Of course the most immediate and pressing rationale had been the threat of nuclear attack, and while the wariest might still have nightmares of a suitcase bomb at JFK airport, they were justified to ask that if Iraq was going nuclear, then where, sirs, was the proof?

Beyond all else, the critics said, the war, once launched, left a poor taste in the mouth of the world. It stirred contempt at the United Nations, in Asia, South America, in the Middle East, and damaged, maybe fatally, alliances with Europe, where even now America was looked on as a demon and where untold sympathetic souls had altered their opinions of a country so in love with arrogance and blood. If the Fellowship responded that the allies were cowards and were hardly needed in a time of strength, the critics answered back that strength was fickle and depended on the backing of one's friends.

The arguments on both sides had thus devolved into cliché. The critics were shrill and said the members of the Fellowship were thugs. The Fellowship essentially dismissed the critics as a crowd of girlish men.

T.R. was an amateur. When he worked at politics at all, he worked by gut. If pressed, he would have said this gut was the sort of organ to result if one could cross the brain of Alexander Hamilton with the heart of Huey Long. He was, if anything, a Federalist with Populist tastes. The war had thus exposed his deepest schizophrenia. Like Hamilton, T.R. believed in power, in the government, in the existence of determined Evil, and in the duty of the government to use its power to eradicate that Evil—he was cynical, in other words, but only to the point where cynicism started to erode the common good. Then he became a Populist again. Cynicism, after all, was three steps from tyranny; doubt, fear, paranoia, despotism—that was the progression. Left unchecked by a mitigating force, power in the hands of cynics led to unjust wars.

If the war in Iraq was good, then it was good because it had removed a tyrant; it was good because it sought to counter Evil; it was good because the men and women fighting it believed they were fighting for a people's right to freedom (which would serve to check their nihilism and despair). The war was good because it sought to create good; the war was also good because the war stood the chance of getting better. At the same time, the war was bad because it had been based on lies; and it was bad because it might not make the country more secure—it might, at best, project an image of security. The war had not cowed Arab anger but created it. Further, on a wartime footing America now practiced the absurdities of infiltrating peace groups and seizing tweezers at its borders. Finally the war was bad because the war put to use the nation's capability for violence out of fear, not strength. It cultivated cynicism without the balm of hopefulness, leadership without humility, righteous anger without intelligence, and so had planted seeds of a profound disease. When those seeds might blossom, no one knew.

In the meantime, even as T.R. lay sleeping on his mattress in the Sheraton, the war would continue. It must continue. To end it now would be a worse disaster than its having started in the first place. How long would it continue? Again, who knew? Democracy would flourish in Iraq, or it would not. While the suspicion was the Fellowship would see to it that Iraq was governed by a friendly ruler, it was far from sure that this would put the brakes to terror. The war, at best, might delay another round of terror. Even in the first Gulf War, if the Fellowship itself had ridden into Baghdad on a team of Appaloosas, still the terror would have come, because the terrorist loved violence, violence was his lance and steed, his means of self-expression, his act of desperation; violence lit the fire in his blood. The terrorist was violent because the terrorist was evil—poor, despised, and evil—but the surest way to beat this Evil was not to war with it eternally; the surest way was to convince the Evil of a different way to live. The surest way was to make the Evil middle class. Only when the terrorist possessed a life worth living with a home worth living in, a family, and a future—only then, would he no longer strap on bombs.

There was a precedent for such a plan. What had defeated communism? Containment had defeated communism, but then again what was containment if not those factories and office parks that, in the arms race, had driven Russia broke. What was containment if not seductions of the Eastern bloc with lip-gloss visions on the far side of the Wall? Madison Avenue was containment. Wall Street was containment. What had defeated communism? Good old Corporate Strip Mall America itself.

The strip mall was T.R.'s expertise. He thought he understood it pretty well—after all, his was the first generation that could not remember life without its endless asphalt, its endless parking lots, its endless franchise stores and anesthesia. Yet if Strip Mall America had been his birthright, it had also been the graveyard of his values. Courage withered in the super-safety of the strip mall, workmanship decreased when products were designed as obsolete, honor was no longer needed when men could earn their living with a keystroke. Was it any wonder T.R. was obsessed with all things manly, challenging, and old?

He finally realized where all of this was heading, for it was heading toward the edge of dilemma larger than the fighting in Iraq. Even though he slept, he realized that there could be no happy outcome to the war. The country had embarked upon a war on terror, and it might last fifty years, it might last longer— it was now committed to a battle that could easily go on a century or more. Its endurance did not worry him. What worried him was its result. For if America chose to fight through endless war, it would lead to endless chaos, endless waste, and endless death. But if it chose to fight through middle-class seduction, it would lead to endless asphalt. And the situation was the best trade one could make. Surely no one wished to live in fear of unseen bombs, but who wished to live with the opposite of terror, with the ever-present chain store? Apparently, Americans did. The president had said as much himself—what better refutation of the terrorist than shopping? If the average American did not feel good about invading foreign countries, or sending the best young men and women off to kill, or breaking old alliances, he or she could still feel good about creating ever-larger strip malls, with ever larger food courts, with ever larger transportation hubs, so that eventually a storefront in Damascus or Riyadh would resemble an airport terminal in Tucson or Duluth. So long as the war in Iraq had been designed to make the landscape of America more common to the world, then good Americans would love it. Good Americans loved their landscape. They loved it in Detroit and Amarillo, just as they would in Cairo and Amman.

In Amman, ten days after war had broken out, T.R. had gone for drinks with Nadia and her friends, a group of wealthy young

Jordanians with fancy shoes, fancy jobs, fancy fine-tuned aristocratic manners, and fancy Western educations. Her friends had been profoundly worried over the result of this attack. They had all lived in America, they knew America, they loved America, they saw it as a second home. So almost desperately they asked T.R. about the war and why America had chosen to invade, and what it thought it stood to gain, and T.R. had done his best to answer them and felt that he had failed. All his answers had rung hollow, all but one. And that one rang absurd. In the end, he said, America had chosen to invade because the terrorist had brought his madness to the strip mall—precisely where no madness was allowed. The strip mall was the sword and shield of America, the strip mall was the waking dream that protected it from madness, even and especially from Satan's madness. And if madness paid a visit to the strip mall, rest assured the strip mall would return the favor. Yes, he had said, the strip mall would descend to the very depths of Hell itself until every inch of Hell was leveled, seized, and paved.

Chapter 22

ONE GOLD PLUNGER

THESE WERE HEAVY thoughts for sleep, and T.R. rose next morning in a worse condition than in No Man's Land. He had not changed clothes in at least three days, or brushed his teeth, or even combed his hair. His baseball cap, now calcified with sweat, was soldered to his head. In the middle of the night, he had felt a great need to use the Room, but in the hallway there had been no Room. Now he rolled from his mattress to the only comfort he possessed: another cigarette.

Burns had issued orders for a meeting at the Palestine at ten o'clock. It was now a quarter to the hour, but T.R. did not rush. Last night, leaving their initial meeting, Kifner had informed him that no matter when Burns said the morning meeting would begin, it would not begin on time. This was both a jab at Burns's managerial style (the style of a provincial governor accustomed to luxurious, late-rising mornings) and a foretaste of the necessary looseness of the foreign correspondent. There was no sense in rushing, Kifner said, especially to meetings, when a phone call from New York or an unexpected bomb might change all plans for the day. So T.R. lingered in the hallway, smoking in the first pale light of morning. The Sheraton was just now coming to life. All down the hallway there were faces in the doorways, journalistic faces—groggy, pale, dyspeptic, discontent. Apparently the press in its entirety had passed a sleepless night. Would their discomfort make for pessimistic news that day?

At ten, he walked with Nadia down ten flights of stairs, through the lobby of the Sheraton, and through the plaza in between the two hotels, the yellow dust of Baghdad thickening the air, the out-of-work Iraqis still pressed up in a mob at the wire barricades in the early heat of the early April morning two days after the fall of the regime. They flashed their press cards to the soldiers at the Palestine where, showered and well-rested, Ian Fisher greeted them with smiles—Fisher, who apparently had spent the night in comfort on a bed in Dexter Filkins's suite.

Filkins and the rest of the crew were drinking coffee at the hotel bar—a dim little alcove off the lobby even more like Casablanca than the Intercontinental. Coming in, T.R. had noticed that the final E in Palestine had been shot from the hotel's sign—it filled him with a quiver of delight. The lighting in the hotel bar was perfect: part conspiracy, part shadow, part power failure. Arab interpreters, marines with loaded rifles, Arabs in khaki robes, roughnecked drivers, fixers, exiled generals, and talking heads from CNN all sat on bar stools chatting while the burly barmen (looking as if they doubled as security) served coffee in their dirty paisley vests. T.R. drank it in with a tepid cup of coffee—there was only tea and coffee—booze, alas, had not reached Baghdad yet. Kifner in particular seemed disappointed and he muttered at his coffee cup. As he had guessed, Burns was nowhere to be found. "The Great Burns-o," he offered with the knowing sigh of every NCO. "Five more minutes and we leave."

Meanwhile, on the streets, the day was beginning. It was sunny, hot, and not yet humid in the least. The crew broke down into teams outside the lobby, T.R. partnered with a fixer and interpreter named Abu Omar, an elegant, slender, hapless, finicky old man with glasses hanging by a chain around his neck. Abu Omar had once worked as a "minder" for the Ministry of Information. He had "minded" Burns, in fact, and it was Burns who had recruited him from government snitchery to journalism work. That Abu Omar knew as little of the trade as a small-town crossing guard was only the first of his deficiencies—he was as unenthusiastic as he was ignorant of the job. T.R.'s driver, on the other hand, seemed up for anything. A big broad bruising fellow with the muscles of an NFL tight end, his name was Rafid. He was mustached and enormous. Rafid gripped T.R. by the hand outside the lobby, calling him *habibi*—baby. "*Habibi*, where we going first?" T.R. was pleased to find that Rafid was a happy thug.

So now they walked toward Rafid's car in Firdas Square and made for the palace in sunny weather that was not unlike the weather on a California morning, save the thick black smoke that burned their nostrils as soon as they crossed Jumhuriya Bridge. It was here a week ago that American tanks had made their first advance on Baghdad. Now the bridge, which spanned the Tigris at the center of the city, was congested with a lunatic parade of looters dragging sofas through the traffic and maneuvering their donkey carts between the stalled tight mass of cars stacked high with television sets. The looters were everywhere among the cars on the bridge beneath the dark black smoke. T.R. told Rafid to pull to the curb. At the railing was a vista of the city. Baghdad was burning. All down the riverbank along the waterfront the ministries were burning—huge white structures spewing charcoal clouds of smoke. The burning buildings stood along the river as they would in Rome or Paris, but were battered and demolished, some with fist holes pounded in their cinder-block facades, others struggling to rise above the river with the tired pride of old men forced to use a cane. The black smoke from every building hung above the water like a fog. From the railing of the bridge, the fog was low enough to see the vast sprawl of Baghdad laid out low beyond the buildings in a smoky reach of palm trees and patioed apartments. Thin wisps of blackened smoke rose high in the sky even that far back.

The traffic on the bridge had stalled. A hundred cars were jammed along its length. T.R. turned from the railing to the sight of two young men in sweatpants hauling an enormous pallet stacked with bags of rice between the cars; another man held a toilet bowl above his head. In the cars on the bridge, the drivers watched as dozens of looters straggled by with crates of oranges, hunks of metal, kitchen sinks, fluorescent light bulbs by the armful, broken bricks, sacks of mortar, old paving stones, and four or five gas stoves. Even now six men passed by with a refrigerator flipped on its side like a coffin.

He hopped in the car as traffic began to move. "*Habibi*, how you like Iraq?" They were headed for the palace at the far side of the bridge, but now the traffic was a swarm. Jammed for thirty minutes in a crowd of looters, the drivers on the bridge were restless—one pulled up on the sidewalk and began to drive along it, two wheels on the curb, two on the street, beside the railing. Others followed; still others wedged out of the traffic in reverse, driving backwards on the bridge. A horn honked behind them: In the road, the looters had refused to move and now a fight had broken out. The chaos was intoxicating. With the smoke in his lungs like a country compost, T.R. felt as if a jug of moonshine had been emptied in his blood.

At the far side of the bridge was an intersection with a left turn toward the palace. It was the entrance to the palace, Rafid said. They made the turn past a grove of palm trees and found that it was not the entrance to the palace—no, not yet. There was a huge brown tank in the middle of the road.

The tank swung its turret at their car.

Rafid slammed on the brakes. They were stopped in the road and no one moved. The black eye of the barrel did not move.

"American!" yelled Rafid. "Tell them you're American!"

The black eye of the barrel did not move.

T.R. slipped from the car, tags in hand, hands in the air. He approached the giant tank. There was a sergeant in the hatch and T.R. called to him that he was press.

White male, thirty-two, baseball cap, American, no threat—T.R. beamed this information at the sergeant. The sergeant waved him closer, watching skeptically as Rafid edged up in the car. Then, climbing from the tank, four soldiers in their body armor searched the car—the car was clean.

The palace was another mile behind the tank, behind a tall iron gate, and then behind a low barricade of razor wire behind which stood another squad of soldiers in their battle gear with M–16s. Passing beyond this wire with a short nod at the guards, T.R. found he was alone. Rafid had not moved, nor had Abu Omar—both were still on the far side of the wire. Now the sergeant called down from his hatch:

"Go on ahead, sir. There's no I-rakis gettin' past this line."

With that the sergeant left him with a problem. In the car, Rafid had been thrilled about the palace. He was going to see the palace. After thirty years of tyranny, the palace was a mystery, it was an emblem of the old regime—the palace *was* Saddam. Rafid had assumed that, as a Western journalist with press credentials, T.R. could get him in. T.R., in fact, had said as much—"You're with me. Of course they'll let you in." But they had not. Now T.R. would have to argue with the sergeant in the hatch.

If you have never argued with a sergeant in the U.S. Army, it is not unlike an all-day bloody workout on the heavy bag. The ruling principle is lack of give. Nonetheless, T.R. approached the tank and worked an argument along the lines of here was a man who had suffered much beneath Saddam and who deserved, far more than any member of the press, to look inside the palace— the one place he had feared and wondered at for nearly thirty years. If he was not let in, who should be? Wasn't it for men like this that we were fighting, after all?

Beneath his battle helmet, the sergeant's face was like a muskrat—wind-whipped, sunburnt, whiskery, and pinched. Clearly he did not appreciate such arguments from this reporter standing in the road beneath his tank. Orders were orders. Besides, he seemed to say, "Who the hell is *we*? *We're* not fighting anyone. *I* fight, *you* ask questions." At the same time, there seemed to be an opening. After all, it *was* for men like Rafid they had fought. Never once had T.R. heard a military man, in either Jordan or Iraq, explain his mission was to hunt down "weapons of mass destruction." It was always freedom, sir, democracy, sir, the Iraqi people, sir, deserve a better life. From his accent, T.R. guessed the sergeant came from Oklahoma or perhaps east Texas—some dry stinging place with miles of open range. What young man like that could possibly remain untantalized by a peek inside the palace? In Oklahoma terms, the palace was a mansion on the hill.

"Thirty years," T.R. began. "Guy's been waiting thirty years to see that place. Come on, Sergeant. What do you say? You'll let him in?"

"Sir, I told you once. There's no I-rakis gettin' past this line."

"I heard it's made of gold, Sergeant. Is it really made of gold?"

Now the sergeant paused. He glanced around from the hatch of his tank. Then he broke a big, bright, bashful smile.

"Yes, sir. It is made of gold. A butt-load of gold."

"Sergeant, when's the last time you saw a palace made of gold? This man"—and T.R. pointed back at Rafid at the barricade, who raised his hand and smiled—"has *never* seen a palace made of gold. And he lives here. How about it, Sergeant? Will you let him in?"

The sergeant sighed. With a last look down from the hatch of the tank, he called out to the soldiers at the barricade. Rafid passed. (Abu Omar, unenthusiastic to the end, was happy to remain behind.) As Rafid came to join T.R., T.R. reached up to shake the sergeant's hand. If the army filled its ranks with NCOs like this, he thought, it might not have a better quality of soldier, but it would surely have a better quality of man.

So now they walked along a wide, clean, open asphalt road toward the palace. The road was something like the main road at an agricultural college in Missouri. The whole compound had that pleasant landscaped college campus look. Sweeping down from either side of the road were trim green fields, like the fairways of a golf course, the smell of sod, as if they had been tended by a team of gardeners just that morning. Back in the fields were marble fountains, low white buildings made of stone, and the occasional white wooden watchtower. It was either a college campus or a lovely prison. Either way, T.R. was struck by the lack of damage. The compound had been a major military target, yet apparently the bombs had fallen with precision such that stone bunkers twenty feet off the road were blown to pieces while the date palms that surrounded them had every frond intact. The trees swayed freely over heaps of rubbled stone! One crater, twenty feet in depth, thirty wide, a nasty gash of dirt and broken stones, all tangled with twisted iron bars, sat perfectly beside an untouched marble palace. And this was not the main palace, but a sub-palace. The main palace was still another half mile down the road.

Could it be that smart bombs were smart after all? In Amman, there had been hordes of correspondents boning up on smart bombs, reading books and articles in hopes of proving smart bombs were a flawed and over-hyped technology. It was a tenet of the Western press that products of the military were an evil, or at least destructive in an indiscriminately callous way. Here, however, was a proof against such claims. If there were blasted buildings, craters in the fields, and the smell of smoke beneath the smell of cut grass, it was not as if the Huns and Vandals willy-nilly had destroyed the place. Even now T.R. and Rafid came upon a fleet of Bradleys parked outside a palace being scrubbed with a hose by a crew of soldiers in their T-shirts. The soldiers waved like college students at a car wash. Down the road were other soldiers napping in a gully with a radio—". . . lovey-dovey, lovey-dovey all the time . . ." The Steve

Miller Band! The army had preserved the palace compound, but only so the Chi Omegas might move in.

Even so, Rafid was trembling. He seemed exceedingly, excessively afraid. He looked afraid even as the Humvees passed at the rate of one per minute. With a tight frown, and a jab of his finger up the road in the direction of the palace from which the troops and trucks were coming, Rafid shook his head and said, "*Habibi*, I am frightened. This is strange."

"What are you frightened of? There's tons of Americans around."

But it was not the Americans that frightened Rafid. "No," he said with a shake of his head, "I am not supposed to be here." Then he gulped out his confession: "I am afraid we are going to see Saddam."

It seemed ridiculous until they reached the palace proper, where a wide white-pebbled plaza, like the carriage path to Fountainbleu, now opened on a pair of golden doors, and T.R. followed Rafid's gaze some forty-five feet up, where on the rooftop there were four stone busts of Saddam. Each bust, twenty, maybe twenty-five feet high, stared down at them. A stony stare, merciless. They stood in the pebbled plaza staring back.

By then, a short plump sergeant with a clipboard in his arms had scooted up beside them. As they stared in awe, the sergeant said, "Yep. G'wan take a good look, fellas. In a few more days, we're gonna bust them bastards down."

Rafid was nodding. "Bust them down," he whispered. But he did not drop his eyes.

"Shit," the sergeant said and spat. "Think that's something, come inside and get a loada the rest of this crap."

So in they went behind the sergeant with the clipboard. His tag read Wilson. Sergeant Wilson was the palace's official army guide.

Even as they stepped inside the palace with its marble floors, marble walls, marble ceilings thirty-five feet high, T.R. was thinking of Rafid. Rafid was a big strong healthy ox of a man, thick, fit, muscular—a former soldier. He had served with the Iraqi airborne in the years before the first Gulf War. Yet on his face there was a look of unsheathed terror. In the palace, guarded by a full division of American troops, Rafid could not help but tremble at encountering Saddam.

T.R. could not possibly begin to comprehend that sort of fear, a fear that brooked all rationality, a fear so buried in a man's internal organs that it could not be exhumed. When was the last time he had truly been afraid, and under what conditions? There was the typical rut of subway muggings, sidewalk crises, highway scare-ups, and hospital events, but none of these seemed even to reach the second floor of Rafid's Empire State of fear. T.R. could safely say that fear—true cold elemental fear—had been excised from his life and excised from the life of his country. Even in the worst slums of America, or in the suburbs of America, there was no fear like this.

By now the sergeant had escorted them to an inner room the size of an opera hall. Huge as it was, the room was nearly empty: There were tall, deep, gorgeously embroidered armchairs pushed against the walls and, in the center of the room, a small round wooden dais. "We call this one the Lap Dance room," the sergeant said with a wink. Crass, loud, boisterous, filled with innocent good cheer, Sgt. Wilson was a born quartermaster. T.R. had a theory that the U.S. soldier was a strange bird indeed. On the one hand, he was as admirable as any high-school quarter-back in Pennsylvania with a happy jaw and healthy skin; on the other, he possessed the worst of that secondary brand of traveling American, the U.S. Tourist, and was coarse, large, bovine, self-absorbed, and full of greed—a cruise-ship passenger with guns.

As for Sergeant Wilson, you would never wish to be alone with him after one too many beers, but as a tour guide he was fine. Leading his charges from the Lap Dance room to another bigger than La Scala, he pointed out the gold S.H. initials on the wall and then announced, in an effort to impress (as if his marked cards had indeed produced the full house he expected), "Yup, we even found a fourteen-carat gold plunger in the john." A fourteen-carat gold *plunger*? Surely, T.R. should have thought immediately of the wasteful luxuries of Saddam, of the ostenta-tions of a man who would plate his bathroom implements in gold, even as his population starved. Instead he could not beat back a vision of a bathroom in suburban Georgia with a bowl of potpourri and off-white tiles and Sergeant Wilson saying to his buddies, "Naw, don't worry if you clog the crapper. Got a gold plunger in there courtesy of Saddam." Admittedly an unkind as-sessment. Then again, like every quartermaster, Wilson had a stroke of larceny written on his face.

T.R. could see that face appearing in a story even now—a sketch of it was slowly taking shape. He could write a long de-scription of the palace through the eyes of Sergeant Wilson, Tour Guide First Class, of the Seventy-second Museum Brigade, Eighth Docent Regiment, Third Media Division. What other occupying army in the middle of a war would set aside a healthy noncommissioned officer to take reporters on a tour? T.R. could not imagine General Bonaparte, for instance, ordering his adjutants to whisk the journalists of Paris through the hallways of Versailles. That Sergeant Wilson had been dispatched like an intern at the Metropolitan Museum of Art to help reporters on their visit to Saddam's palace spoke of the impressive inroads the media had made on the military mind.

It was now inconceivable to storm the palace without a rear brigade of hacks*—it felt, in fact, as if the palace had been taken *in order* to display it to the hacks. Why? Because the media had last say in a war that might go on for a hundred years? Because the palace was a victory within that war and thus a spoil to be shown? This mingling of press and military had reached its height at the training session for reporters in Virginia, where a full colonel from the Air Force had addressed the closing forum with a speech to the effect that the armed forces had finally recognized the great power of the media. "We understand you need your information now, in real time, and we are in a prime position to deliver. We have the capability, in terms of wherewithal and technology, to get you what you want, when you want it—which is fast!" It was a snake oil pitch. Funny, too, except the media had bought it. In hock for access, the media was giving over ever more control of what it covered to the institutions that it covered. (True in Washington as well as in Iraq.) There were arguments to make in favor of allowing Sergeant Wilson to escort the press through the palace—none the least because, without him, one could never get inside—and yet one ran a risk. The military, by its nature, dominated what it touched; it was not a

---

*In the self-loathing, self-aggrandizing jargon of reporters, this was an ironic derogatory term. Reporters were "hacks" because they were not artists. But they were better than artists. Artists did not have to file on deadline from the war.

generous establishment. And so the press would have to exercise extreme restraint dealing with the military, lest the military—T.R. could imagine it—might learn a thing or two and create a news network of its own.

Yes, T.R. would deliver the ostentations of Saddam but only in the context of Sergeant Wilson and the dangers of the military's inroad on the news. Centcom might be trying to disseminate the message that its forces had defeated a regime of butchers. But here at HQ Palace, Sergeant Wilson wanted all Americans to know that Saddam unclogged the toilet with a plunger made of gold.

They now moved into the final phase of the tour and came to an office in the palace basement—mugs of undrunk coffee on the desks, abandoned coats still hanging on the rack. To Wilson, all of this was evidence of just how fast the enemy had fled, how frightened he had been. "Note the faxes in the fax machine that no one bothered pickin' up"—it had the dead ring of a practiced line. T.R. asked the sergeant how many tours of the palace he had so far given and, lighting a cigarette to signal they were done, the sergeant said, "Let's see"—in an eight-hour posting with a thirty-minute tour—"maybe sixteen, seventeen a day."

Now they all lit cigarettes, T.R. working up some joke about a gift shop. His worst sin as a journalist was glibness—he would always reach for the nearest joke. Looking for a punch line, he was slow to notice that the ash on Rafid's cigarette had grown. Unlike the sergeant or himself, Rafid wasn't ashing on the floor—it seemed to make some difference. He had looked about the office for an ashtray, but coming up without one, held his cigarette between two fingers upside-down so none of the ash would fall. When T.R. finished, he stubbed his butt on the floor;

Sergeant Wilson did the same. But Rafid with the utmost caution carried his upstairs and tossed it out the palace doors. Although he did this quietly, T.R. had noticed. He was intrigued.

Walking back to the car, T.R. asked, "So what was all that fuss about the cigarette?"

Rafid shrugged, embarrassed. "I didn't want to drop it on the floor."

Perhaps there would be many such occasions in a country built on fear, since fear—unlike the country—could not be conquered by an occupying force. Once more, T.R.'s story shuffled in his mind. He saw the plump good looks of Sergeant Wilson, and beside those looks, the fear in Rafid's face. There might just be a counterpoint in baby fat and terror. It might just speak to the future of the war.

Back at the barricade, the heat was rising. Several more reporters had arrived, mainly television correspondents with their cameras and their cables, their sound booms and attitude. The sergeant who had let them in was explaining once again that no I-rakis would be getting past this line.

T.R. and Rafid tried to pass these reporters.

"Hey, you with the press?" one of them asked, a small, slim fellow in an Oxford shirt and khaki shorts. Beside him stood a tall Iraqi lugging an enormous camera. The reporter's lips and brow were wet with sweat.

"Yeah, I'm with the *Times*."

"The *New York Times*?" Now the lips went tight and the brow began to furl. He turned to the sergeant to complain, "You let the *Times*'s local in, but you won't let ours in? Man, that isn't fair."

T.R. made for the car. Leaving the palace, Abu Omar told him that the house of Tariq Aziz, the deputy prime minister, had just been opened by the army—he had heard it from another fixer at the gate. The house was close, he said, fifteen minutes from the palace. They climbed inside the car and rushing off they went.

But even as they drove the narrow weeded path along the river to the house on Sadeh Street, they were not alone. A dozen television trucks were already lined up in the driveway with their satellite antennae. T.R. began to worry. In London, he had sworn an oath—he would avoid the pack, break left when it broke right. His instincts told him he should leave this place at once for something new. But this *was* new, it was the news, it could not be disobeyed.

What seemed worst about the news was that it forced one to abandon all things new, it forced one to avoid originality. "Feed me," said the ogre of the news. "Feed me now. By evening, no one will remember what you saw. This house will be forgotten. This golden plunger, too."

He left the car. In the driveway, the television cameras had been set up for a live shot. One reporter, tall, good-looking, almost too good-looking, in a Kevlar helmet and protective vest, introduced his story. But each time he began, his producer cut him off with a grim exhausted frown.

"Here, at the home of Tariq Aziz, prime minister of Iraq—"

"No, wait, *deputy* prime minister. Go again," the producer said.

"Here, at the house of Tariq Aziz, *deputy* prime minister of Iraq, where high-ranking officials of the Barthist, Buthist—how do you pronounce that, Nick?"

"Baathist Party. Like a bath. Go again," Nick said.

"Here, at the house of Tariq Aziz, Iraq's deputy prime minister, who is now in hiding from American officials, and where officials of the Baathist Party used to gather for expensive all-night dinners where the wine would flow all night, and the crystal goblets on the tables—"

"Wait, stop, wait," the producer said with a grim exhausted frown. "Have you ever heard of verbs? Go again."

It was not unlike an Abbott and Costello act. Yes, he thought, he could hire these two men and write a script, a "Who's on First?" for the television war. Or better, book them live at the Apollo. If every print reporter was locked in secret combat with the novel in his soul, it was possible that every television correspondent was a secret stand-up comic—even their most sober segments had the flavor of a joke.

He had his own experience with stand-up comedy not thirty minutes later. After touring the deputy prime minister's house, it was shortly time for lunch. Of course, there was no food for lunch—there was no food in Baghdad, the restaurants were closed, the markets empty, the Iraqis getting by on government supplies. But the army was awash in MREs.

There was a tank parked at the bottom of the road. He went. Five soldiers from an infantry platoon were sitting on the tank.

"Fellas, it's your lucky day," he said, feeling not unlike the bastard child of Ed McMahon. He then proposed a trade. Every member of the squad could get three minutes on the satellite phone in hock for one full box of military meals.

It worked. A skinny private, gangling, shy, with a face of painful acne, took the phone and now dialed home. He waited, but there came no answer. "Wait a minute, wait a minute, lemme call next door," he said. "They're prolly at the neighbors." Veto. He was forced to pass the phone.

T.R. had already dug into a bag of Country Captain Chicken. Rafid had a helping of the Meat Loaf. Even Abu Omar, glasses on a chain around his neck, now seemed to be enjoying one fine portion of American Mac & Cheese.

By the time T.R. had finished, the phone had worked its way to the leader of the squad, a big broad southern sergeant with a big broad southern voice. He had wandered off some paces from the tank, but not so far as to be unheard, and much to his own embarrassment, T.R. heard him saying, "Hey, baby," smiling, as his voice began to coo.

But now there seemed to be some trouble. The sergeant shook his head. He scratched his head and frowned. "What?" he frowned again. "*What?* Well, shit, baby, how was I supposed to know that? I was *in* it."

He looked back at his soldiers on the tank.

"The whole damn war's been televised," he said.

Chapter 23

M A I L

Late that night, T.R. got an e-mail from his wife.

> That is crazy . . . You shouldnt be taking the soldiers food, they
> need it. Do you still have that crazy powder stuff? Maybe theyd
> like that? Is there any way for us to send you anything? (Lani
> wants to know, and wants to know if you have an address, ahah-
> hha, seriously, she asked)

Lani was his mother-in-law. She was a sweet, blonde pious
woman who worked at a pharmacy in Cleveland—only God
knew what she thought about him working in Iraq. It was
probably of great concern to her, not so much because T.R.—
reluctant war reporter, hero to the hometown crowd, and the
fine young Jew who had swept her Catholic daughter off to
New York—was in any grave impending danger, but because
T.R. had left her daughter alone at home with worries of her
own. Nonetheless he got along with Lani, and she with him,
and it was comforting to know that she had asked for his address, even if that address was Concrete Box, Sheraton Hotel,
Baghdad, Occupied Iraq. Her concern bolstered his flagging

self-assurance—it reminded him that ordinary life existed beyond the great taxations of the war.

It was eight o'clock by now and dark outside. Dogs bayed on the Tigris. Mortar rounds exploded. Tracer fire, like burning embers, floated through the night. T.R. was in the *Times* suite of the Sheraton with Kifner, Ian Fisher, and a quantity of booze that had finally arrived in Baghdad. Working quietly by small low candles in the darkness, Kifner sat with Fisher on the balcony—Kifner with a fifth of blended Scotch, Fisher with his pipe.

T.R., drinking cans of a skunky Turkish beer that Fisher had obtained outside the Palestine that morning at a price to rival a good steak dinner in New York, continued with his letter, feeling happily more ordinary with every passing line.

I'm getting ready to go to queens with Dave, Zowie's eating a little more, I read her the riot act and I think she listened. Venus has been compulsively eating. Your mom leaves soon. Jim Walden had appendix surgery last night, very unexpected, he's ok though, but if you can, send him an email, you can do it thru me if you want. I'd understand if you didn't have the time.

He didn't have the time.* In fact, the best he could say about her news was that it struck his senses with the queerness of a

---

*This was not the lame excuse it seemed to be. Days began at seven, when he rose in the hallway on his mattress, or on the floor when he was finally allowed to crash in Dexter Filkins's suite. A morning meeting was held at nine or ten. They worked all day. Another meeting in the evening. Then they wrote, usually past midnight. Deadline was around 1 A.M. Editors could call with questions at any time.

dream. T.R. had had no dreams in Baghdad, none that he re-called, and to hear such recitation of events back home dis-tracted him—he now felt sad, nostalgic, almost interrupted. He did not *want* to feel that way, but perhaps that was the point of dreams (and therefore news from home). Both re-minded you of all the business being waged beneath the static of your nerves.

> Not much going on tonight, I'll stay in, watch a movie or just do work. Charlie told Amy he will be home in 2 weeks he thinks. I don't believe you guys. but we'll see.

Now he felt an unexpected shock of annoyance. He knew that tone. She was angry. Even more, she was trying to suppress her anger. His wife had many qualities, but she was fatally inept at expressing disappointment without a tone of accusation. And the worst of it was that she was right to accuse him. He was guilty. But guilty of what? Impatience? Annoyance? Consider-ing her letter as an interruption? She had felt him bristle six thousand miles away. No. He could not embark on the endless riddle of his marriage now. He didn't have the time.

> What else is going on? why is there no food? Are you helping/reporting on stories? that is a pretty cool thing, I like that. At least you are part of the team. I love you, please be care-ful, please. Please try to write something back to me, just so I know you are ok.
>   Bye,

And then she signed her name.

Did she have to be so lovable and pleasant? He could not return that kindness now. He opened his computer in the darkness, candles shaking on the balcony, Fisher toking on his pipe,
Kifner's tumbler clinking as he poured another drink. On the
balcony, Kifner tapped away at his computer keys—he had
drifted off and drifted back from sleep. T.R. remembered meeting Kifner. It was several years ago at Sardi's, the Broadway saloon a block behind the *Times*. The ancient barkeep had a face
like wrinkled silk; he poured Kifner's Scotch and called him
Johnny. Quite possibly, there was no one writing Kifner lovable
pleasant enervating letters. "Kif," T.R. had asked back then,
"with all you've seen, you think you'll ever write a book?" "A
book? Nah, I've got a twelve-hundred-word mind."

Now T.R.'s computer screen glowed blue like a television set
on his lap and on his beer can. He took a sip of beer and
stretched his legs. Took another sip and then he wrote.

The opulence of Sadeh Street is too much to describe.

He was already making excuses. It was a dead-end lead. Still,
it had been much—the mansions filled with chandeliers, the vil-
las with Italian marble floors, the palm tree gardens, statuaries,
porch swings, tennis courts, the Jet-Ski docks, the twenty-car
garages filled with cars.

Naturally, these homes have attracted their fair share of looters,
who have carted off the grandest antique armoires and the simplest sacks of rice, but they have also drawn a number of the
street's impoverished people, many of whom come each day not
to steal but to stare. They stare in awe at the mansions on the hill.

A little sticky, somewhat rough around the edges, but it
moved. Sadeh Street had looked like something from Bel Air—
its stucco mansions extending shadily beneath the palm trees
had the same haute California gloss. Walking past its driveways
(like the curving driveways to a Hollywood estate), T.R. had
half-expected that a limousine might pass and Douglas Fair-
banks in tuxedo might be spotted in the back with a pitcher of
martinis. Sadeh Street was luxurious and old. It was home to the
elite of Baghdad—Tariq Aziz; Saddam's two sons, Uday and
Qusay; and Sagida Hussein, Saddam's first wife. She had occupied a sprawling Mediterrean pied-á-terre with a guard shack
bigger than most of the homes of central Baghdad, but the villa
had been ransacked by a mob of looters three days after Baghdad fell. Now it was decrepit as the House of Usher—broken
bed frames, smashed chandeliers, mud-stained walls, and linens
scattered ghostlike on the floor. That morning, the gawkers had
replaced the looters. Dressed in their tennis shoes and T-shirts,
they were ordinary folk, and not unlike a crowd of tourists come
to ogle movie royalty. All they lacked, in fact, were baseball caps
and Nikons—half tourist then, half carrion bird.

T.R. went back to his notes. The notes were in the standard
thin beige notepad—it fit his pocket or his palm. He studied
them now and took a sip of beer. The writing in the pad was
practically illegible. How many times had he scribbled down a
quote to find he could not read a word? (He had said as much to
Warren Hoge.) There was a name in the pad, Haidar Something, A-R-something, Aruban or Arubay, it was impossible to
tell. He bore down on the notebook and tried to sort it out.
Aruban or Arubay—what difference did it make? All right, Mr.
Arubay, speak some words to the readers of the *Times*.

Haidar Arubay, for instance, has come to Sadeh Street at least five times in the last three days. He is a gawker, not a looter. The only thing that he has stolen is Saddam Hussein's biography—a first edition, so he claims.

"I wanted to read about his miserable life," Mr. Arubay explained.

So now he had his nut graf (it contained the story in a nut). And now he had his first good quote. What next? A change of pace. Working on the floor by candlelight, he once more flipped the pages of his notes.

M'haMMad Kamel sez: "confession" stole computer, guilty—back at mosque in bar wit champagne turns over bottle—Pol Roger > empty Kamel 23 Chateau Mouton-Rothchild same w/pol roger, turns over 1979

Looking on, Muhammad Kamel, 23, confessed that he had stolen a computer from the house just days ago, but felt so guilty he returned it to a mosque. He wandered over toward the bar. He picked up an empty bottle of Pol Roger champagne and turned the bottle over. He did the same with a depleted Chateau Mouton-Rothschild, vintage 1979.

now lunch w/ Kamel home w/Haidar w/him Sadeh S. down narrow path 10 mins to—Al-wasir st. laundry on roofs cooking smells old women doorways squatting w/younger girls—art of making lunch.

It was getting on toward lunch and Mr. Kamel told his friends that he was heading home. His house stands less than one full mile from Sadeh Street, down a narrow dirty path. This was Al-Wasir Street, where laundry hung from the low-slung roofs and women in the doorways taught their daughters the art of making lunch.

Nashet Maktouf > kam's aunt with a child naked 3 or 4—no name crying cuz he's wet w/hose & hair dripping onto concrete patch in small house Maktouf cotton dress maybe 50 55 sez: nothing we have nothing and SH has everything! scrubs kids head with palm "Evil man!"

Mr. Kamel's aunt, Nashet Maktouf, 50, was bathing a naked boy as he came in. She used a garden hose to clean him on an open patch of concrete floor.

"Nothing, we have nothing," Mrs. Maktouf cried, "and Saddam Hussein has everything!" She scrubbed her young one's head with a palm. "He is an evil man," she said.

Now T.R. was getting antsy. He had used up the better portion of his notes. Never much of a reporter, he had always preferred the craft of stringing sentences to the labor of collecting facts, and so fell back on a journalistic maxim—when the work runs out, insert oneself into the work.

He had been doing that in many ways, forms, guises, and at many levels of success for many years, first in Brooklyn, then the Bronx. Though the editors would often strike the more ridiculous of his cameos, he often managed to slip them in. It was a tawdry trick, but necessary. For whatever reason, T.R. desired to stroll like Hitchcock through the news. He had written whole stories, long stories, in which he himself had appeared as the central character—he had once produced a piece on caviar smuggling where, in essence, he had followed himself along a circuit of the city's best purveyors of the eggs: "Intrigued, a reporter wandered a few blocks east, to the Caviarteria at 59th Street and Park Avenue. There, he asked the clerk why anyone would want to smuggle such a thing."

While this might seem like self-absorption, it was not—it was a hedge against the portents and pretensions of the news. Taking cameos reached down to the depths of his impatience with a craft that often bargained personality, humor, human difference, and the funky odors of the ego in exchange for some cold standard of the authoritative voice. The voice of the *New York Times was* cold, cold enough to chill your cockles. It was a point of pride among some editors that a line on Page A1 was sonically indifferent to a line on page B8. Even on those rare occasions when the word came down to "play with it a bit," the stories often came out sounding as if Tipper Gore were reading Whitman with a cold. T.R. had always considered the reporter's job to be a proxy—proxy eyes, proxy nerves, proxy sensibility, and proxy sense of humor. Since the average citizen could no more spend a working day on Sadeh Street than at the beach, the average citizen would have to send reporters in his place. If these reporters came back in the paper sounding like a press release, what good were they? One might as well dispatch a camera in their place.*

---

*His habit of inserting his own shadow into news stories had begun on the Saturday shift. It was difficult for him to take seriously stories on the winter solstice or the West African Day Parade or men in skirts marching for their right to wear women's clothing and so, in an effort to liven things up and to interest himself and the reader, he had taken to breaking the fourth wall of the news in the same way a character in an absurdist play might step for a moment out of his role.

So now he bent above his keyboard and wrote himself into the news.

> Mrs. Maktouf was informed by a guest that Americans have a saying: a man's home is his castle. Perhaps she agreed?
>   "This is true," she said coyly. "But not all castles are the same."

Nor all news stories, he found out. When his was finished, T.R. stood, took his laptop to the balcony, found his phone, taped it to the railing of the balcony, fed the cables under Fisher's chair and typed the necessary numbers until the phone began to ring—then he was connected to New York. It took some time to get the story through, and he looked down at the soldiers on the river. Camped among the reeds in clumps of shadow, they were like a pioneer encirclement of tanks. In the darkness, all he saw were humpbacked figures. They squatted by the water in the flicker of their flames.

"Hey," said Fisher, looking up as T.R. stared at the soldiers, "tell me one good thing you saw today. You were at the palace. What was it like?"

"Room 9," T.R. responded, making reference to the crowded pressroom in the bowels of City Hall. "Too many journalists. It almost made me sick."

"But what did you *see*?" asked Fisher, his back fetched up against the railing, toking on his pipe. He was in no mood for T.R.'s asininity. Fisher had the lede-all in tomorrow's paper. He needed grist for the mill.

T.R. had very carefully avoided any chance that he would have to write the lede-all. Running down the far right column of the paper, lede-alls were the most important daily offering of news.* T.R., of course, had no idea how to write a lede-all. Lede-alls were intricate and complicated, as difficult as writing sonnets in Chinese. But as he spoke with Fisher, watched him scan the Internet for wire reports, listened as he toted up his own experiences, borrowed bits from Kifner, stole a pinch from Reuters, staged a raid on AFP, then cobbled everything together, T.R.'s eyes were opened to the methods used to make the news. He hated thinking any thought that might inspire cynicism and would hardly wish to bitch about an honest man like Fisher; still he was surprised. The premiere story in the next day's *Times* was being fashioned out of wire reports and late-night recollections from exhausted correspondents. Some were drunk, many hungry, all smelled of sweat. And yet their words would arrive next morning on the desk of Donald Rumsfeld, pristine, authoritative, crisply perfect in Times New Roman type. There would be no trace of the ugly human process that produced them. It was best they could offer. Surely, no other paper offered better. Still, the lede-all story had been heaped together in the final hours not unlike a Sunday brunch buffet.

Beyond his shock, there was naïveté. T.R. had actually believed that correspondents only wrote what they had seen. If on occasion he had printed the opinions of a bum on Gun Hill Road as if they might reflect a larger truth, he had not assumed such crassness would apply to foreign news. Fisher, of course, was not quoting bums—he had worked to amass the highlights of the day. Still, he was collecting information from whatever

---

*It was a matter of location. In an era when the city's broadsheets were placed fanned out on newsstands, the far right column, or the lede-all column, was the only column on the paper's front page that showed.

source he found. It was due no doubt to the workings of a story meant to give the global view. No journalist, not even Burns, could be everywhere at once. So perhaps the problem was not a problem of reporting, but of tone—lede-alls had the urgent tone of news. They also had the best real estate in the paper. (In that vein, they were not unlike the burger served on Fifth that runs you double of the burger served in Harlem: same meat, same bun, but a different ambience—thus a different price.) Once more, T.R. thanked his stars that he had not been called upon to write a lede-all story. He tipped his cap to Joseph Mitchell, who had said it best: "It is safe to write accurately only about the nuts and the bums."

Fisher's job was easier when Hill and Filkins returned. They had been out all day and had now come back with numerous reports. A marine from the First Expeditionary Force had been shot dead at a hospital. A cache of leather vests stuffed with ball bearings and explosives had been found in a school. It was all good news (good news being vivid news, not good) and it was now decided Filkins would assume the lede-all (Filkins having personally gathered more than Fisher's salad bar of news). Dozing, Kifner was drafted as Filkins's partner. Fisher seemed relieved. Hill, meanwhile, had the easiest work of all. Sitting down with his computer in a chair, he began to transmit pictures to New York.

T.R. rose to fetch another beer. He was content to sit in darkness with his colleagues in an atmosphere that called to mind the best of college dormitory living, with its cramped conditions, high pressure, ample booze, and intermingled smells of tobacco smoke and sweat. If he had been a fool in college, he was not so foolish now, and not—strange thought—so meaningless, for it had suddenly occurred to him that in the morning words he had written would appear on doorsteps in Milwaukee, Houston, San Diego, perhaps a chemist in Poughkeepsie would encounter them at breakfast with his toast. It was a striking thought, no less powerful for being shallow, and as always he celebrated with a smoke. His words were moving over deserts, over countries, over Jordan, Israel, above the waves and waters of a bright blue sea, past the Turks, past the pope, then over the Atlantic on a journey to New York. It *was* striking.* And yet the focus he had felt these last two days was utterly unique. Starting at the border, he had had a feeling—call it concentration, call it clarity—that could not be described. The best he could say was that a clean deep sense of purpose had invaded him, intoxicating in its cleanliness, invigorating in its calm.

For a man who often waged a battle with his nerves, this feeling of control, of self-control, possessed a rich addictive edge. Yes, he decided, there was nothing quite like filing. It was not unlike the moment after sex. Every tension, doubt, fear, movement, and anxiety was finally released. And then you smoked. There was a betting chance at even odds that he could grow accustomed to this life.

Hey,

So I've been waiting 15 minutes for this damn computer to connect—wanted to see if you had written me again—feel a little lonely tonight. No intimacy. No real talking. Plenty of people around—in fact, right now, Ian's on the balcony writing and kifner's in the room here working (I already filed, I guess I work

---

*He *was* shallow.

fast) but it's not the same as being with friends, or of course with you.

Feel depleted. It's not exactly a comfortable place to live. There's electricity only a few hours a day, the water works sometimes, there are food shortages, and you can't get beer easily. we have to walk up 10 flights of stairs because the elevators dont work.

The journalists are idiots, although the times people are okay—ian, dexter filkins (who I don't really know), john burns and kif. he's such an old warhorse. and funny as hell.

The city is strange, depressing. People here are going out of their minds. I can hear the dogs yipping down by the river now—the tigris is directly out the window. It's hot, uncomfortable, dusty . . . I feel heavy-hearted, sad . . .

At least the work is non-stop. We meet at 10 am, go out, work, write, then meet at 7 to discuss, long days that end at 1 am. It's weird working with a team—I'm not used to it, you know? Sweet contact, that's what I miss.

Anyway, want to write but very tired and this connection's acting up. Keep me in touch—with everything, babe. This place could clearly make you crazy . . .

Love,

And then he signed his name.

Chapter 24

THE CEMETERY

A FEW DAYS PASSED. They were busy and productive days. Here then is a brief report:

T.R. visited Boratha cemetery and saw so many bodies that the gravestones, crushed together in the sand, were like a mouth of broken teeth.

He visited the Shiite slum of Sadr City, where he interviewed an imam who informed him he would welcome the Americans with every comfort of his left hand even as he fought them with his right.

At the central train yard, the trains lay dormant on the tracks, and the engineers played cards; at the markets, there were more flies than food.

On the streets, meanwhile, a brisk trade in stolen telephones and television sets had now sprung up—it was somehow proof that the country would survive.

Through all of this, T.R. maintained some feeling of that high sweet sense of purpose he had felt nights before and decided that if work would save his hide, then he would work. Most of his assignments came from Burns, who liked to lean back on the couch at morning meetings (when indeed he made it to the meetings), cross his legs, sip coffee, and begin to hand out stories like a three-star general dispatching his brigades. As a rule the dangerous stories went to Filkins, the political to Kifner, Fisher got the lede-all, and T.R. got whatever was left. He did not complain about this lineup—in fact, he was grateful. T.R. was accustomed to the bottom of the order. Besides, batting last possessed an advantage. He could hit a little single and be pleased.

Best of all, of course, he was free of the assignment desk. And this was no small matter. The desk had been his whip and master in the Bronx. Arriving mornings at the office, he would sit to read the papers, drink a cup of coffee, check the mail, and then in pleasant solitude begin to plan the day, when suddenly the telephone would ring and he would answer to the single most debilitating phrase a journalist might hear—"Hold for the desk." Already the day would be in ruins, for the day would be rerouted from a lovely little feature on a Puerto Rican barber to a quick-hit daily on a driver who had killed two children in the Soundview section with his truck. Nor was it uncommon for the desk to get things wrong. There were mornings when, in fevers of disaster, the editors might call to say, "MY GOD, a Con Ed worker just fell down a SEWER HOLE in Hunts Point! They're doing a close-space RESCUE! Photo's been there for an hour! Beat it! Get there! Go, Go!! GO!!!" Flames of haste burning in his hair, T.R. would rush to Hunts Point, find the cops, find the worker, find that the worker had not fallen in the hole, but had been working in the hole, and done no more than sprain his ankle, and the close-space rescue was not a rescue at all, but a single fireman, who, having drawn the shortest straw, had shimmied down to help him out.

T.R. was not immune to the news, nor was he lazy (well, perhaps a touch); he simply knew the desk had one true goal—it had to fill the paper, stock the shelves. He could not blame the editors for avidly pursuing all disasters (underneath, there might lie headlines, after all); still, he preferred to work for Burns. Like all great generals, Burns understood the flavor of a battle. Burns knew when to stand and fight and when, in turn, to let his troops relax.

Burns had been relaxing quite a bit these days himself, spending great—perhaps inordinate—amounts of time inside his room. He had also developed an odd neurotic interest in his troops' domestic life. Shortly after their arrival, Burns had ordered Nadia to leave the *Times* suite at the Sheraton—"She may be talented and lovely, but she must pack up at once!"—Nadia was not a full-time member of the staff. Order given, it was nonetheless an order to be roundly ignored. Whenever Burns dropped by the suite (a rare occasion; still he sometimes sauntered in like a landlord come to assess the damage that his tenants might have perpetrated on the house), T.R. simply hid her bags beneath the bed. Eventually, Burns's neuroses stretched to food as well. One late April evening, Burns accused T.R. of eating his cookies. Yes, Burns had left these cookies (butter cookies flown from London in a package from his wife) on a table in the suite and thus erupted into rage when he discovered they were gone. In point of fact, Burns's own partner, Tyler Hicks, had eaten the cookies while Burns was working on a grueling story reconstructing every minor detail of the fall of Baghdad, a piece to run him several thousand words. When T.R. learned of the extent of Burns's labor, he felt sympathy for Burns, for it occurred to him that even Rommel, in his best days in the desert, had fallen prey to fraying nerves.

As for his own nerves, T.R. had begun to feel like a man who had just got over surgery. He was awake to every detail in the air, but at the back of his skull there was a dullness, huge in size, as if the mental data he collected disappeared into a large black hole. From the moment he arrived in Baghdad, every day had so electrified his senses that by now he felt as if his inner wiring was burned. Mornings, he sat with his coffee on the balcony observing smoke clouds rise above the city with the sunrise. Evenings, he stretched out on the floor and, by the candlelight, drank beer. Even at the height of day, when typically he was alert, his senses had that raw smoked quality of freshly smoldered wood.

At the cemetery, it had nearly been a problem. He had gone there looking for the dead. At the meeting at the Palestine that morning, Burns had asked T.R. to make some rough determination of Iraqi casualties, but this turned out to be a daunting, if not impossible, task. The only source for such statistics was the military, and as far as he could tell, the military (working by cliché) was inclined to let Iraqi corpses lie like sleeping dogs.*

---

*Much later, T.R. came across the following statement in an article Michael Massing wrote for *The New York Review of Books:* "I still have not heard of a single instance in which the killing of an American in Iraq has been shown on American TV." Massing then asks the necessary question as to why that is. He asserts that television news is afraid of getting "burned" by showing U.S. deaths, and therefore censors itself. T.R. offers the following support for that idea. At Mama Juanita's tavern in Amman, he watched in horror as Al-Jazeera broadcast the image of U.S. soldiers lying dead in a fly-ridden field. "Jesus," said the TV correspondent sitting next to him, swallowing his rum and Coke. "If I put that on the air, I'd be canned at the next commercial break."

So T.R.'s goal was somewhat more restrained—he would not get numbers, he would simply get a picture. This was typical of his approach. It had never been his style or method to write long stories full of figures, charts, statistics, large ideas, or recitations of the obvious or else to give some broad amalgamation of the news. More in keeping with his style, and then his talent (which was small-bore, minimal, and finely cut), was to merely take a snapshot. If anything, T.R. believed in what one had to call the Polaroid approach to news.

At first Abu Omar had attempted to dissuade him from the story. In the plaza of the Palestine, where every morning dozens of reporters, drivers, and interpreters would gather fresh from breakfast in advance of heading out, Abu Omar had stood with his glasses looped around his neck to say the story would not work. They were waiting for Rafid and their cameraman—it was almost nine o'clock. Because there were no telephones in Baghdad, the plaza between the two hotels was something of a marketplace or outdoor auction house where Western journalists could meet their hired hands and pick up local talent like construction bosses picking up day laborers in a van. The plaza served as Baghdad's central meeting place; ringed by tanks and armed marines, it was safely under guard.

"You will find no bodies in the cemetery," Abu Omar told him, shaking his elegant gray head. "There are bodies, but they have not reached the cemeteries yet. They will still be at hospitals and in the yards of people's homes."

The smile he smiled was a ministry of information smile, a smug and knowing smile, and the mode of speech he used was the stiff formal mode of the government bureaucrat. Abu Omar had survived the old regime; in Occupied Iraq he had been resurrected. An entire class of men like this existed. They were party hacks who now chased dollar bills.*

Despite the fixer's certainty, T.R. was inclined to disbelieve him. Abu Omar had been proven wrong before. Not two days earlier, he had mistakenly reported that a band of U.S. soldiers had been spotted stealing money from a bank—T.R. had passed this tidbit on. When it was found to be untrue (and nearly wrecked a lede-all in the process) Abu Omar was not apologetic. Indeed, he was offended. "Well," he had sniffed, "it is within the realm of *possibility*," as if the possible were no more than a lesser version of the facts. Moreover, Abu Omar had proved himself a miserable interpreter, for more than once he had allowed their interviews to ramble on for several minutes uninterpreted, only to say when, finally, the source had paused for breath, "This man is very sad" or else, "This gentleman is very much upset."

Now, however, as they motored through the outskirts of the city in Rafid's rusty car, T.R. began to credit Abu Omar. They had entered a quiet residential district, low suburban houses, long wide streets, rows of palm trees (almost like the Cuban quarter of Miami), went on past a factory of sorts, then took another long wide street. Though the palms were blackened from artillery, some homes smashed, some shattered, others still

---

*Both Rafid and Abu Omar were paid $150, in cash, a day. Their paymaster was Burns's right-hand man, an Iraqi known as Abu Karrar. Abu K was a shifty fellow, a big, smiling teddy bear of a man who lived in a hotel suite where he drank tea in a bathrobe. Rafid and Abu Omar despised him. They accused Abu K of skimming the payroll, which, given his smiling oily nature, T.R. did not doubt. The only time T.R. felt sympathy for Abu Omar was in his dealings with Abu K.

intact, there were no bodies to be found. It was strange, even troubling, for with the fight still on in sections of the city, where had all the bodies gone? In truth, T.R. had not seen one dead body since arriving in the city. Quite possibly, the citizens of Baghdad had claimed their dead and buried them in yards, fields, lots, and secret graves. Quite possibly, Professor Abu Omar had been right.

But then they turned a corner onto some small road with a blue mosque towering above the trees, and suddenly the smell of death was in the air. It hit his nose with a scent of rotten cherries. He recognized the smell, for if he had not seen bodies in Iraq, he had seen them many times before. One of the unspoken privileges of news reporting was a close appreciation of the corpse.

They were still some yards outside the cemetery, but the stench had crossed this distance. Thick in the air, the stench was like the portal one must pass to enter the cemetery through its high thick gothic iron gates.

Ten or fifteen cars were parked at the gates. T.R. saw it was the cars that made the stench, for on the roof of every car was a wooden coffin lashed with rope.

"Jesus," T.R. said, as they stopped at the curb. With Rafid in the lead, the four of them—reporter, driver, fixer, and photographer—climbed out.

It was a hot, bright, dusty morning. The sand beneath his feet burned in the beating of the sun, which beat down on the heads of twenty men carrying coffins into the cemetery. In teams of four, the men slid the coffins from the roofs of their cars, then carried them toward the gates. The gates were narrow and so there was a backup. Outside the gates, a line of coffins formed, carried in the arms of weeping men.

Moving toward these men, T.R. asked the first he encountered what was happening. It was an empty question, a simple question, a stupid question. Only a reporter would have asked it.

The man was short, slight, bearded, and he leaned against a younger man, his son, perhaps his nephew. Weeping uncontrollably, his chin and shoulders shook. As a coffin traveled by, shiny teardrops trembled on his cheek.

T.R. took notes as he explained, *his dead son Maath buried here last week > now dig up, Shiite custom to bury in religious ground > only temporary here "We are going with the coffin now to Abu Ghraib"*

The one thing not to do was stand in place. So T.R. looked at Abu Omar, then at Rafid. Rafid's eyes were filled with pity and disgust.

T.R. said, "Come on. Let's move." And without looking back turned his notebook to an empty page. He walked down the gates toward the next man he saw.

He was trying consciously to be a sympathetic presence, for he knew his presence here was wrong; and so he walked with a cautious step and with his head down, attempting to emit some unobtusive calm. It hardly made a difference. The men at their cars were so shellacked in grief, weeping, wailing, carrying their coffins, they hardly noticed him. And yet by turns they spoke. Slowly—or not quite slowly, since the men around him had begun to form some loose perimeter of interest—quickly now, his notes filled up with *Ali Ahmed 44 sez daughter's dead, Hassan Karrar with New Paltz Board of Education T-shirt: "All we do is bury bodies. This is war."*

Flipping back the pages of his pad, T.R. could not help thinking if he went to New Paltz (and where had *that* strange T-shirt come from?), went to ask some grieving father in the suburbs what he felt, there would be outrage, shouting matches, threats of lawyers, phone calls to the paper and the cops. But these men stood outside the cemetery gates and told him everything. They were *eating dinner>bomb hits, roof falls wife killed in the rubble* : *"even the dog was crushed"* then led him to their cars, where from the trunk, a dozen cousins were removing picks and shovels. Now they said, *"You know what these are for?"*

It was not completely unfamiliar. In the Bronx, he had gone to the projects many times reporting on murders, taking elevators five floors up to narrow hallways, knocking on doors, walking into small, dark, cramped apartments with the dishes piled in the sink, the televisions muted, shrines of Jesus candles burning on a shelf, and trembling on the sofas with their sisters were the mothers of these dead young boys, women who always seemed to wear the same dull looks and dirty shirts. "He was just about to go to college," they would say, or else, "He had a rap tape coming out." They never asked T.R. to leave. They always had another anecdote, another photograph, another aunt or uncle always had the time to find the dead boy's yearbook on a bedroom shelf and turn it to the page that showed him in his gold and crimson uniform, the one he wore when the marching band would play. Only after T.R. saw these yearbooks would he leave, and only with the same thought every time: The poor have nothing to hide because the poor have nothing but their grief.

Even now he followed a stooping man inside the gates to a beige expanse so filled with headstones there seemed no way to bury fresh remains without disturbing those already in their graves. The cemetery was a feast for the flies. Its headstones pushed to the outer walls. The man picked his way among the graves and T.R. followed until he stopped above an open hole, not three feet in the ground. He gave the bundle in his arms (for now T.R. could see it) to another man, and then began to chant for half a minute with the melancholy duty of a bugler playing *Taps*. T.R. stood some distance from the man, hands at his back, and wished he were invisible, in much the way he wished he were invisible at military funerals and firefighter funerals. And then the man retook the bundle, climbed down into the hole, and with a grimace that perhaps would never leave him, placed the body of his baby in the grave.

It was not yet ten o'clock. The sun was hot, the stench was thick, the flies were feasting, and the stooping man had started to perspire so that his sweat blended with his tears, and T.R. reached for his notebook, jotting down discreetly: *too much water on his face*. Then he put his pad away.*

A small dog trotted through the headstones. T.R. watched it watch the mourners standing at the graves. Then he left the man whose child had just been buried, walked himself among the graves, and encountered another group of men with shovels standing in another shallow grave. One old man with a turban stood in the grave waist deep. He was barefoot, digging slowly. Around him, seven other barefoot men leaned heavily on picks and shovels. They were waiting to dig the grave. A short, thick man with an embroidered cap stood above them. Dressed in robes, he held a book. Head down, eyes shut, the man rocked

---

*A part of him had wanted to believe that he would not react to grief by reaching for his notebook. But that was not the case.

back and forth and chanted from the book. As he rocked and chanted, his voice snaked up above the grave.

When the man finished chanting, T.R. asked him what it meant.

"It is the prayer of mourning," said the man, who gave his name as Khodeir Ali. Mr. Ali said he prayed for tips, at fifteen cents a prayer. He had been doing this for thirty years, more than half his life, but he had never worked so hard as in the last few days.

"Before the war, there were three, four, seven burials a day, according to the wish of God"—he bowed his head. "Now the numbers have increased to the hundreds. Already this morning we have buried fifty people."

T.R. checked his watch again. Five past ten.

Every public service in the city had collapsed. Even the gravediggers no longer came to work. The old man digging with his shovel was an engineer by trade.

"This," he said, as T.R. stood above him, "this is the first time I have ever dug a grave."

Even as he listened, T.R. knew he had to get a picture of the man. He went at once to find his cameraman, a short, young, bearded redhead with the Associated Press. The cameraman—Thorne Anderson—was taking pictures of another group of men with yet another coffin, walking backwards, snapping pictures, circling the men with that intrusive ghostly presence cameramen perfect. When T.R. went to fetch him, Anderson shook his head. "Crime," he stammered. "It's a crime." It was rare to find a journalist who wore his outrage openly, and T.R. found to his surprise that he was jealous. Anderson could use his outrage to drum up righteous anger. Without a shield of anger, T.R. was defenseless to his shame.

But he had never had the faculty for anger. He wasn't angry now and the question was, why not? If he could not be angered by an old man standing in a grave, the black flies buzzing at his ankles, body of his brother at his feet, then what would anger him? Where was his anger? Why did he feel nothing but embarrassment and shame?*

About the time these feelings started to subside, Anderson crouched low again to take another picture and the old man in the turban, setting down his shovel, picked up a small white plastic bag. The bag was remarkable for being not unlike a hundred bags that one could find in a hundred discount stores on a hundred corners of Detroit. Carefully the old man placed the bag beside his brother's body and with equal care tucked it down so that it fit in the grave.

T.R. had already turned to his interpreter to ask, "What's in the bag?"

And Abu Omar asked the question. After one long pause, he said, "His family is in that bag."

T.R. looked at the old man's face. He took a breath of air.

"Your family is in that bag?"

The old man nodded.

"How many members of your family are in that bag?"

The old man raised the fingers of his hand.

---

*Because his anger had been cut off by his comfort. The better portion of his days have been spent in a country where, if one suffered pain, it was often private pain. Public pain had been excised in America. Pain, as one might find it at Boratha, was nowhere to be found.

T.R. looked at his boots, then at the sky.

"There are five in there? Ask him who," he said to Abu Omar. "I need to know exactly who."

It was a sister-in-law, two nephews, and two nieces.

It was over. They made their way from the cemetery grounds, through the gates, and back to Rafid's car. He had filled his notebook up with miseries. But no reporting could capture one-sixteenth of the inner life of grief.

By now a second wave of press had started to arrive. Trucks were pulled up to the gates, big trucks with television dishes, satellite antennae, idling engines—mobile battle stations of the news. It was impossible to look at the trucks and not feel as if the vultures had arrived. The press was nothing now if not a vulture (the press had been mistaken as a predatory beast, but it was not—it was a carrion bird). T.R. could watch those trucks and practically determine what America would see that night—sandy headstones, old men crying, coffins lowered in the dirt, and then a cutaway of black flies buzzing in the sky.

In the car, the four of them were silent. Headed for the comforts of the Sheraton, there seemed not much to say. Abu Omar fiddled with his worry beads; Anderson clicked through his pictures on the digital display. As Rafid drove, T.R. stared out the window at the low suburban houses giving way to empty markets, empty restaurants, and the small street-corner stalls where the empty promises of stolen television sets were now on sale.

He had given way himself to the thought of going home. It was the first time he had had such thoughts—he was surprised. Not too surprised. Some end had come, some chapter had been closed. One could feel the end of things—it came on slowly, like a slowness in the blood.

He was slow enough that he failed to notice the car had stopped beside a small shop on a small avenue. Rafid had gotten out. T.R. could see him in the shop. Rafid was haggling with the owner, doing business. He had leaned over to inspect some item on the counter, now he took his wallet out, he paid, and came back to the car.

Climbing in, he turned to face T.R. across the seat and handed him a small brown paper bag.

"Please," he said. "This is yours."

Then he turned to Abu Omar for assistance: "He says it is a gift."

It was, in fact, a wristwatch—gold trim, leather band, and on its face a portrait of Saddam. T.R. tried it on. "Thanks," he said. "My wife will hate it."

It did not escape his notice that the watch read noon and already he was thinking of his wife.

Chapter 25

THEY CAN'T TAKE THAT
AWAY (FROM ME)

Back at the Sheraton T.R. took a nap. It was necessary after all that had occurred at Boratha to escape into sleep, sleep being close to death, but also to that other form of earthly inertness—laziness. There was no sense getting to work, with several hours left to file. In the last few days, T.R. had started to detect in himself the first buds of that peculiar laziness that war reporters have, a disdain for clocks and schedules that grows in a man who works on his own time, three thousand miles from the boss. He took his boots off, took his socks off, removed his shirt, and, in his cargo pants, hopped in beneath the blankets of a bed whose sheets had not been changed since the fall of the regime. He was asleep in five minutes. A nap in the afternoon was like a midday beer—it spoke of greeds and luxuries one could not resist. It was also one's last comfort in a city where the showers did not work, the power was out, and the only food one ate was chicken processed under military contract in Des Moines.

Drifting off, he thought about his wife. Whether the bed held powers of suggestion or whether he was still caught in thoughts of going home, he had started to recall the list of demands his wife had made on him before shipping out to Iraq. The first, and not the least, among them had been her request to leave behind a sample of his DNA. His wife had wanted this sample in its purest form, leaving T.R. the obligation of calling several institutions and physicians that did business in this sort of thing. A week before he left, he spent an afternoon with the Yellow Pages and found the whole thing oddly enlightening. He hadn't realized there was such an industry, so large and so widespread, and recalled wondering what reasons might exist, aside from shipping off to war, that might convince a man to place his assets in the bank. In the end it hadn't mattered, the price of the deposit had been steep, and the plan was set aside. At the time, T.R. had been relieved (for he had thought the whole thing nutty). But after a day at Boratha, he saw the wisdom in her plan.

They had been married now four years, and although they had no children, they had reached that watershed when it had started to seem as if everyone they knew was having children. That was where the DNA came in. His wife had wanted to preserve her options should anything disastrous have happened in Iraq, and though it seemed at the time that she was tempting fate and that misfortune might be brought on by the consideration of disaster, T.R. had pursued her request to the end of its line.

They rarely spent much time apart and when they did it was never for long, usually for two or three days at a time. T.R. found he missed her steady presence, for his wife was much more rooted to the ground than he; in fact, she had that good earthbound ability for female common sense. At the same time, she was a prisoner to her moods—she may have been the moodiest person he knew. There were times, when in the middle of a quarrel, he would reach out angrily to make some point, to pin her down, and find that, like a sparrow, she had flicked off to a higher branch, her mood had shifted, and his fury would be met with unexpected tenderness or his own attempts at tenderness would be answered by the blackest, most embittered rage. It was infuriating—but completely admirable. In truth he loved her moods, loved the palette of her moods, none the least because his own moods tended to evade him, much as dreams evaded him. He often thought his wife's submissiveness to mood was the symptom of a happy, healthy mind. It was not inconceivable that if his wife was pesky, bitter, raging, sweet, bored, lustful, happy, and serene within a span of thirty-seven minutes, then she was not crazy or diseased but wholly healthy. A mood was to one's internal life what a brick was to a construction project. Like a brick, a mood was the smallest unit of construction. What foreman wouldn't want to be familiar with his building at the level of its bricks?

It was natural that in the lazy climate of a nap T.R. would make the obvious connection and decide his desire to leave Iraq was actually desire to see his wife. But it was less forgivable than that. In the crassest sense, Boratha had given him a piece of what he'd come for. He had wanted to see what it had offered. Coffins, black flies, death—he had come to Iraq to find these things, and he had found them. Now he felt relaxed,* as if a gnawing hunger in his stomach had been finally put to rest. That hunger was the hunger to experience the worst of what the war could offer, and those "who had not seen it were jealous and tried to make it seem

---

*Relaxed? Strangely sated?

unimportant, or abnormal, or a disease as a subject, while, really, it was just something irreplaceable that they had missed." (Hemingway again.) Jealous? No. Diseased? Perhaps. Irreplaceable? No doubt. As T.R. rose from his nap he discovered that the shame and embarrassment of his day at the cemetery was replaced: With evening, there had come a modest sense of calm.

According to his wristwatch, it was not quite seven in the evening—Saddam's right arm was pointing at his shoes, his left arm at the sky—he was shocked he had slept so long. Even more of a shock was looking up from bed to find Alan Chin on the balcony. He hadn't seen Chin since Amman.

Rising now, still groggy, T.R. went to join Chin where Chin was sitting hunchbacked, muttering curses at a gas-driven generator at his feet. Chin was poised above the generator with a cigarette between his lips and a small steel tool in his hand. Spread out on the concrete floor, he had a look of roadside aggravation. T.R. clapped him on the shoulder with a smile.

"Know anything about generators?" Chin asked. (T.R. reached for his smokes.)

"Did you put the gas in yet?"

Chin scowled. "Of course, I put the gas in."

"What about the choke?"

"The choke?"

Choke engaged, the generator coughed, then cleared its throat.

For the next half hour, he and Chin sat happily on the balcony as Chin talked about his travels, from Jordan to Kuwait three weeks ago (where the scrum of journalists, he said, was like a spring break party in Daytona Beach), across the border up through Basra with the British, then across the midlands of the country with American divisions. The Brits, Chin said, had been terrified of the Americans; they called them Tommy, as in Tommy gun, because their first and only instinct was to shoot. For the few weeks he had been living in his car at military bivouacs: "You find the captain," Chin said, "flash your press card, and basically beg to spend the night." In all that time he had not seen a bed and had dropped some pounds from lack of food. There was a brittleness to Chin that T.R. hadn't recognized before; his body looked hollowed out like driftwood. His neck and cheeks looked thin, much as if the sun and wind had taken all the lipids from his flesh.

Even in his modest mood T.R. had expected to be jealous of Chin—jealous because his own experience had been tame in comparison. The foreign correspondent's coin was danger. Whenever two or more of them met, they bet these coins—see ya, raise ya, call!—it was exactly like a poker game. Chin had won this hand. He had just come back from living in the desert, living with the troops. If T.R. held a pair of aces—Chin held at the worst two pair, perhaps he had a flush. But T.R. felt no envy and again was surprised. Something had left him at Boratha; something had been lost, and something won.

In the happy promise that the generator might provide them power all that night, T.R. suggested a beer. He had paid a hundred dollars for a case that morning at the Sheraton. Handing Chin a can, T.R. watched Chin's entire face lit up. Chin took the beer as if it were a sacral offering and he the priest. T.R. sat on the balcony and, in the darkness with the generator humming, drank to Chin's return, and then to going home, as a feeling of camaraderie began to warm the room. For the first time since his arrival, the Sheraton began to feel like home.

Then the telephone rang. T.R. did not recognize the sound. It had never rung before.

"Is that your phone?" Chin asked. He was cracking open one more Turkish beer.

Somewhere now, it rang again.

T.R. searched until he found the phone beneath a sweatshirt on the floor beside the bed. The phone was filthy. It was coated in tobacco leaves and dust.

"Baghdad Bureau," he announced. It was the desk.

Of all the great surprises he had had that night, the most remarkable was that the desk had finally called. It was practically a minor miracle. He had spent a week in London, another three in Jordan, another two in Baghdad, but this time was the first time they had called. Such laxity was utterly unlike the editors. On metro, it would have been impossible to go one week without a hundred calls. The foreign staff, it seemed, had different rules.

"Who is it?" Chin was asking.

T.R. cupped the phone. "The desk."

"Cool," Chin said. He raised, then drank his beer.

It developed there was something of a crisis in New York. None of the reporters in Iraq had filed their stories, let alone had called. And it was after eight; deadlines were approaching. The desk had tried to find John Burns, but had no luck—he was out there somewhere in the wilderness, a combat helmet on his head, perhaps a pearl revolver on his hip. Nor could the desk find Filkins, Fisher, Kifner—and again, Craig Smith was nowhere to be found. Out of desperation the desk had called T.R. For seven seconds, T.R. felt important, felt as if the desk had recognized his talents, felt as if the editors might hand him some assignment or congratulate him on an article well done. But all they wanted was a rundown on the list of daily stories. He cracked another beer.

Still, he was too much of a good son to disappoint. T.R. knew exactly where his colleagues were and what they were doing. Kif and Fisher had the lede-all, he related, Smith was in the Shiite slums, Filkins was reporting from Tikrit. Burns meanwhile was on a goose chase following some rumor of Saddam.

"Thank you *so* much," said the editor, whom T.R. knew from Newark. "Are you having any fun?"

"Fun?" he asked. He looked at Chin, supine on the balcony, as if it were a poolside in Las Vegas. "Yes, we're having fun."

"Well, the section looks terrific," she went on. "You guys are doing an amazing job."

It was nice to hear, and yet T.R. had no clue as to the job they were doing, no clue at all about the stories appearing in print. He had not read one of them. Not from lack of interest; it was impossible to find a paper in the city, and to read the paper on the Internet was enough to drive one into epileptic fits. He had waited longer for his laptop to connect than for the worst of midnight trains; and yet it was ridiculous he had no conception of the war, no sense of its rhythms, actions, heroes, major battles, or politics, when he was in his own way interpreting those rhythms in the center of the war. (Later, this fragmentary sense of things would cause him embarrassment, for people constantly would ask him what he felt about the war, assuming that because he had reported on it, he was something of an expert. An expert on the people he had met, the places he had visited, the faces he had seen, an expert on *himself* perhaps—but not the war.) For now, however, this experience of seeing one's small corner was not entirely unpleasant. It served to reinforce a cardinal rule: The only things you owned were those you saw yourself.*

Now the door swung open and T.R. turned from the balcony as Burns entered the room in that particular way Burns had of entering a room. Think of Gielgud or Olivier appearing on the stage. There was the same grand swoon of arrival, the same unspoken message that the evening could begin. Burns had brought a bellhop from the lobby—he was short, fat, elderly, in uniform, and seemed to be attached by unseen cables to the end of Burns's arm. Burns pointed at a mound of luggage shoved against the wall, and the bellhop flung upon it instantly. It looked as though he had been fly-cast from the tip of Burns's rod.

"I'll be needing the remainder of my things taken downstairs, then up to the Palestine," Burns told the bellhop, glancing even as he issued this command at a fresh box of shortbread cookies on the sink. T.R. cringed on the balcony for half a moment, expecting new accusations he had eaten Burns's food.

But Burns had more important things in mind.

"It seems," he said, "our good friend Saddam"—it rhymed with *ham*—"was spotted two days ago at a mosque in Ad-hamiya." He stepped toward the balcony with troubled glances

---

*He never felt the wider war until he left Iraq. On his way home, in fact, he spent a day in London reading about the war. T.R. took several weeks of the paper from the bureau, hauled them up to the Crown St. James, and sat for hours in his room with stories headlined "New Stature for Rumsfeld," "Marines Killed in Najaf," and "War Coverage Creates the Fox Effect." The experience of watching the war unfold in time-lapse was not unlike comparing notes with his wife when they had talked to different people at the same party. There was a disconcerting sense of having gotten only one small fraction of a large event. What, then, of the people who had *only* read the papers, T.R. thought.

at their Turkish beer. "We ought to be prepared to follow this development at any moment. It's an absolute imperative." But underneath his speech one heard the secret line of thinking: "Thank god, these cretins haven't found the stash of wine."

Burns was removing the last of his belongings from the Sheraton to take up full-time residence in the Palestine across the street.* Eventually, he said, he would rent a house, perhaps in the Mansour district among the city's bourgeoisie. He had already found a broker and had scouted out several possible locations, but had not found the perfect place. Only Burns could find a real-estate agent in a place like Baghdad. Now he told the bellhop to remove his bags to the lobby and, there, to wait for him, no questions asked. He was not to go to the Palestine alone, he was to wait for Mr. Burns.

"Do not go without me, is that understood?" It was an absolute imperative, Burns said.

When Burns went out again, the bellhop struggled with the bags. The poor man tried to carry two in his hands and three across his back, but this turned out to be impossible—only one bag in the five possessed a strap. The bellhop attempted three or four alternatives and it was not unlike a vaudeville act, a slapstick comedy of hands and straps and bags. T.R. pitied the man and went to help him. Then his phone began to ring. "Sorry, but I have to get this." He naturally assumed it was the desk.

But a voice came booming down the line.

"ArrrrggGHGHGH! I'm going DOWN! I'm HIT!"

It was LeDuff. T.R. was delighted. "Where are you?" he cried. "Where are you calling from?"

---

*Burns, being Burns, had been living out of both rooms for a month.

LeDuff was calling from a small hotel in Nasiriya, where he had traveled with the Twenty-fourth Marines. Some weeks ago LeDuff had joined the unit in Kuwait, and now was headed north. He planned to be in Baghdad in another couple days. T.R.'s spirits soared. First Chin, then LeDuff—another pleasure of the evening. Taking the phone inside, he sat down on the balcony and asked LeDuff about his travels. LeDuff had just returned from interviewing Nasiriya's most important imam. Now he was deathly ill.

"What happened?"

"I drank a glass of grape juice. That's what happened."

T.R. knew the stuff—the stuff was utter poison. One saw it everywhere in Baghdad, in the markets and the restaurants, burbling in huge unwholesome vats on the street. Nominally juice, it had the color of a bruise, the smell of motor solvents, and the flies adored it. LeDuff had made the grave mistake of actually ingesting some.

He explained, "When the interview was over, the imam took me out on his balcony," where in the plaza at their feet there were a hundred people gathered, arms pumping, chanting wildly, and the imam raised a glass of the grape juice, shouting, "To our country! To Iraq!" LeDuff went on, "So now the whole crowd starts to yell along with him, 'Iraq! Iraq! Iraq!'" Then the imam poured another glass of juice, "and handed it to me and this time, turning to the crowd, he starts to shout, 'To Charlie!' and the whole crowd starts to follow, shouting, 'Charlie! Charlie! Charlie! Iraq! Iraq! Iraq!'"

"What could I do? A hundred people shouting. I drank the whole thing down."

T.R. hardly cared if the story was true or not. LeDuff's talent was the showman's talent, his hilarity alone could clear one's head. "But look, I've got my cousin's wedding coming up next week," and it was all the confirmation T.R. needed. Soon they were discussing his arrival and their mutual departure. They spoke about their promise made in London weeks ago. Half the case of the Turkish beer remained. So they would have that drink in Baghdad after all.

T.R. wished LeDuff good luck and soon the rest of the team arrived. First to return was Kifner, his safari vest a mottled quilt of military patches, press credentials, glory tags—one for every time he'd gone to war. T.R. had always thought that vest was reminiscent of the strange young Russian from *The Heart of Darkness:* "The glamour of youth enveloped his parti-colored rags, his destitution, his loneliness, the essential desolation of his wan-derings . . . If the spirit of adventure ever ruled a human being, it ruled this youth." Kifner was, of course, no youth, he was in his sixties, and his body had the battered look an old Jeep gets after miles of broken road. But he possessed some shadow of the flame that surely burned in him when he was young—it sometimes leapt up out of his exhaustion, leaving one to marvel at light that still remained. When he stepped toward the balcony, for instance, Kifner shouted like the first boy up on Christmas. "Great shit! A generator? Where'd you get that thing?" When Fisher arrived, he sat down and lit his pipe and gave his own perspective.

"That," he said with academic pleasure, "that is very nice."

And so they worked for two hours. On the balcony the gen-erator sputtered but their concentration drowned it out; and though the sky outside was dark, they set out candles on the floor and night stands, the whole room trembling in their glow. Above the generator the only sound was the tapping of their keyboards; even this fell silent at determined intervals as Kifner paused with a burning sigh of booze. Fisher sat on the bed and wrote his story. He puffed his pipe and tucked his chin.

At some point, Fisher got up and walked toward the dresser, pulling out an object from his bag. He plugged it into the generator. A compact disc machine.

There is a feeling that arrives when memories are made—a strain of sweetness, not unlike nostalgia, with the wakeful quality of summer mornings when the heat is low and the sunlight keen. It is not happiness, for happiness is clumsy, rude, all thumbs, compared to the tender crispness that will crackle in the body when a memory is made. One is seized by the intuition that the moment will be present in a dozen years with clarity— even in a hundred years when one is surely dead.

Some portion of that feeling came to T.R. as the compact disc began to play. It was Ella Fitzgerald paying her respects to Billie Holliday. He knew the tune—

> The way you wear your hat
> The way you sip your tea
> The memory of all that
> No, no, they can't take that away from me
> They can't take that away, from me

In the quiet room, on the quiet night, they listened. The generator put out no more than a whisper and the gunfire that had sounded off all evening had subsided with the night. It was getting on toward ten, the hour of their deadline, but they'd all stopped working. Kifner was the first to stop. He raised his head, raised his eyebrows, leaned back on the railing and smiled a devil's smile. The way he sat with his arms crossed, smiling, seemed to say that working in a quiet room at night with candles and a jazz song in the air was practically impossible—forget impossible, it was practically a crime. Already the long flat hours they had spent at work were starting to dissolve in the lovely voice that drifted through the room. T.R. glanced at Kifner and could almost read his thoughts—he was off somewhere on a reverie of other towns and other wars. Perhaps there had been other nights like this in strange exotic places when the silence overtook him and he questioned if the wild, momentous, bracingly intoxicating war reporter's life was worth the cost of feeling rootless, for it was only when a war reporter moved that he could feel his roots. Fisher, on the other hand, looked torn in two. He seemed to struggle with the music, seemed to fight it, seemed to understand that it would make him vulnerable again and pull him back to his children, wife, and home. Earlier that evening, Fisher had been sitting with his laptop and had beckoned T.R. over to admire something on the screen. It was a video clip of Fisher's family—two boys in their pajamas running through the house, "Dad, we miss you! Come home soon! We miss you! Love you, Dad!" Fisher had been pleased to show this clip, but now he listened to the music much as if the music were the sound of everything he'd lost. There was a sadness coming on in him, in all of them, a tender sadness that arrives when forgotten things come back.

T.R. sat on the floor and listened to music and thought about the music and the many times he sat at home and listened to the music—Billie Holiday, Jo Stafford, Jimmy Dorsey, Artie Shaw. Old jazz was American with swinging clarinets and boyish horns. He had always loved this music, it was *his* music, and he suddenly felt glad he had not left Iraq, for if he had left, he would have missed this night and missed the chance to recognize that old jazz reminded him of the best America, America before its shelves were stocked with plastic packages and the brain of its government with thoughts of packaged war. Old jazz was the music of a country young enough to feel its strength without the need to prove its strength, and so there was some logic that an old familiar tune in an unfamiliar country could return him to a time that he had never known, or seen, or lived in, but could hear nonetheless like a voice (a fading voice) on drifting currents of the jazz.

Chapter 26

PHONE CALLS AND PHOTOGRAPHS

IN THE MIDDLE of the night, his phone began to ring. Again. Reaching blindly from the bed, he once more found it in a pile of dirty clothes.

"Mftffft . . . whuh, yissehello?"

"Hello? Yes, hello? I'm sorry. Were you asleep? Oh gosh, you were asleep. What time is it there?"

In the darkness, T.R. strained to check his wristwatch. Saddam was performing semaphore again. With both arms pointed at the sky, his body indicated it was 2:16 A.M.

He groggily informed his caller of the hour.

"Sorry," said the caller (an editor, of course). He sounded more annoyed by the existence of different time zones in different portions of the world.

"Sorry to wake you," he said, "but it's important."

"Whuh impordin . . . ?"

"Excuse me?"

"Impordan *whuh* . . . ?"

"Well," said the editor. "You're off to Basra in the morning."

Without understanding each specific word, and with an addled brain and groggy concentration (hindered by the lateness of the hour and his previous consumption of a quantity of beer), T.R. succeeded in obtaining from the editor the following explanation for the trip. It seemed that in the complex logistics of distributing the paper's correspondents . . . *whuh?* . . . certain errors had been made, errors that resulted in a temporary lack of staff in the southern section of Iraq. There was no one in Basra, no one at all. Despite apologies, T.R. would have to go.

"I thaw whussisname . . . was in Basra."

The editor acknowledged this was true—last week. "We had to send him to the bureau in Kuwait."

"When am I supposed to be there? Issa seven-hour trip."

"Soon as you can get there." The editor explained that Wednesday morning the first meeting of the Basra City Council would be held. T.R. would need to attend this meeting. The fact that it was Monday night . . . no, *whuh* . . . already Tuesday morning, apparently was no excuse for T.R. not to attend.

He lay in bed until the sun rose, then got up to pack a bag and walked down to the Palestine to wait for Rafid and Abu Omar. He had no idea if they would care to come with him to Basra, but in the bright infringements of the morning he hardly cared. At 10 A.M., he stood outside the hotel doors. The sunlight beat down on the asphalt of the plaza, on the television trucks in the plaza, on his wet head. The plaza was already hot. At the edge of the plaza, where the bales of razor wire stacked up in a barricade gave out onto Firdas Square, a thick crowd of Iraqis marched and shouted back and forth, cursing at the soldiers on their tanks. They shook their fists at the soldiers, but the soldiers ignored them, eating breakfast. When Rafid arrived, T.R. asked him what the shouting was about.

"Money." Rafid rubbed his finger on his thumb. "Work. They want to work. But forget them, *habibi*," Rafid said. He was in a happy mood. "Where we go today?"

"We go to Basra."

Now his mood had changed. "Basra? Basra is a seven-hour trip."

When Abu Omar arrived, his mood changed as well. "Basra? Basra is a seven-hour trip."

But it was not a seven-hour trip—it was a nine-hour trip. They stopped at Abu Omar's to let him fetch a bag, stopped at Rafid's, then stopped at a small store on a quiet street to pick up water, fuel cans, and a small supply of food. Then they were off.

The landscape leaving Baghdad on the southern road was different from the landscape on the western edge of town. There, at least, a few small villages appeared to break the emptiness. On the southbound road, eleven in the morning, Rafid humming as he drove, his good mood reawakened, Abu Omar fiddling with his worry beads, T.R. in the back of the car observing how the heat of morning rippled at the asphalt with illusions of oases, there was little to command the eye except for baked-mud hovels set back in the marshlands. Parched by the sun, the marshlands were flat, and arid, and the hovels stuck out in the landscape like abandoned trailers one might see on the route from Bakersfield to Vegas. Every twenty miles or so, a ragtag group of boys appeared as if from nowhere. They stood on the highway, a small barefoot detachment. They did nothing. They did not wave, they did not smile; nor did they move. They stood and stared gazing at the traffic.

Passing one such group, T.R. turned to watch them vanish in the dust.

"Who are they? Where do they live? There's nothing out here."

"They are Shiite boys," said Rafid. He explained that with nothing more to do, these boys came out each morning to observe the traffic—traffic that had increased since the soldiers had arrived.

Even now they had begun to pass such traffic, an enormous military convoy rumbling toward Baghdad on the opposite side of the road. It was a long line of trucks that stretched for miles down the road. Out front was a wedge of armored Humvees—in these Humvees, there were soldiers standing at the triggers of their guns. When the convoy proper started—dump trucks, oil trucks, two-ton troop trucks, a small brigade of flatbed trucks weighed down with bulky canvas-covered tanks—it seemed endless too. Even as the trucks went by, T.R. thought instantly of donkeys, elephants, and armored legions leaving for the provinces from Rome. It was not every day that one stood witness to the sheer logistical dominion of the empire, but it *was* imperial—the convoy had the same unbridled sense of purpose and the awesomeness in military might. At one point T.R. checked his watch to find that seven minutes had gone by. Seven minutes and still no end in sight.

The drive went on, he dozed, he watched the convoys pass, boys appeared from nowhere on the road, there was little conversation, little to discuss. Eventually he turned back to his magazine, the *Sports Illustrated* swimsuit edition. Before he left New York, he had bought six copies of the magazine along with cigarettes, a fifth of whiskey, and a box of powdered Kool-Aid for the troops, but had consumed the latter items well before he left Amman. In the backseat of the car, he flipped the pages full of women lying half-exposed on sand. It was not distracting—in fact, it had the opposite effect. Sex had not occurred to him in weeks and yet it came back instantly: Sex was a sucker punch directly in his gut.

Soon, they were coming into Basra on a wide commercial avenue with shops and restaurants, and T.R. was surprised to find the restaurants were open, people walking on the streets, others browsing in the shops. Old men in small cafes drank tea at sidewalk tables; an early evening crowd was strolling on the Gulf. Coming into Basra was like coming into San Francisco—much less elegant, but no less calm. No tanks, no sounds of gunfire, scarcely any troops. The opposite of Baghdad, where a threat of smoky violence filled the air, the air in Basra smelled of lamb kebabs and lemons. Along its central avenue, there was a pleasant atmosphere of ordinary business. It was not unlike a small Italian village on its market day.

They parked outside a restaurant and sat down for their first paid meal in weeks, a meal of chicken skewers and pita bread, then after dinner set about to find some place to spend the night. A billboard on the highway had testified to the existence of a Sheraton. Assuming it could prove no worse than the Sheraton in Baghdad, the travelers were quickly on their way.

To assume, however, is to gamble on a wager no more certain than the favorite at the track. The favorite horse can lose; so, too, can assumptions prove unfounded. When the reporter, driver, and interpreter arrived at the Sheraton, they quickly found their wager had been lost.

The Sheraton was demolished. Where there had been a darkly elegant, brick ten-story structure with a glass lobby, residential towers, and a bow-shaped drive that swept from curb to check-in desk, there was now a smoking ruin. Half the building had collapsed to a brick pile; the other half stood teetering with bedsheets out the windows like surrender flags. In the driveway, arcing toward the lobby doors, were heaps of charred black mattresses. An iron bed frame, twisted like a skeleton, was perched atop a pile of shattered glass.

Observing this destruction. Abu Omar said, "They'll probably have a room."

Down the street was a squad of British soldiers camped at a tank. T.R. went to ask advice on where to spend the night.

"Well, yes, it's a pity," said the captain. Tall and gaunt, he was a specimen of military manners. "Frankly, your options here are fairly limited," sounding not unlike a reservation agent at the Ritz. "You are an American, I take it."

T.R. confirmed he was.

"Well," the captain added, turning cheeky. "I've a thought. Why not have a new hotel flown in?"

It was well after dusk and British jokes aside, the streets of Basra were no place to spend the night. At the car, T.R. convened a meeting to discuss their options. They could drive through Basra searching for a room; they could try another town; or, ever-present final option, they could bed down in the car.

It was at this point that Rafid shook his head.

"There is something else, but it is difficult, *habibi*."

"More difficult than this?"

"Yes." He rubbed his forehead. "I have a wife in Basra."

"Your wife lives in Basra?"

"Yes, a wife."

"*A* wife?"

Rafid nodded shyly. He apparently had two.

They soon arrived outside a small stone house at the edge of town, hauled their luggage from the car, and followed Rafid through an iron gate into a clean ground-floor apartment. It was spartanly accoutered with a kitchen, bedroom, sitting room, and bath—the bath no more than a rubber hose above a hole.

T.R. settled in the bedroom as Abu Omar, reluctant prisoner of the trip, sat down on a wicker mat before the television set that, in the lack of furniture, commanded the sitting room. Rafid, playing host, offered his guests a pair of slippers. He put a kettle up for tea.

He looked uneasy. In the car Rafid had confessed that two weeks before the war had broken out, he had left Basra, left his wife, and gone to Baghdad, where opportunities to work had been much greater—and where he had a second wife and son.

"A son?" T.R. now asked him, drinking tea in Rafid's slippers.

"Yes, *habibi*. One in Baghdad, another one back here."

Thirty minutes later there was no emotional reunion when his wife and son came home—in fact, there was no reunion, or one so muted that it qualified as none. Rafid's wife, a handsome woman in her forties, dark-haired, tired, and yet possessed of what was surely long forbearance, kissed him on the cheek, then went to the kitchen in her blouse and slacks. His son came in with the intensity of any adolescent. He went to the bedroom, and slammed the door.

Rafid rolled his eyes as if to say, "It hurts all over when the family gets involved." Over dinner of potato, salad, broiled fish, and rice, no one said a word.

T.R. excused himself to the roof. He wanted to check his mail. Yet before he hooked the laptop to the phone, the phone began to ring.

Theory: The desk had now recalled his existence.

Proof of theory: After weeks of silence, it had called three times in the last two days.

"You're not in Basra yet, are you?" asked the editor. He sound-less breathless, as if by way of sympathy he, too, had rushed off on a seven-hour trip.

"I am in Basra."

"Well," the editor went on, "there's news in Nasiriya . . ." And now an order came down that slapped at the prior orders like opposing currents in a channel. T.R. should make for Nasiriya in the morning. He should get there as quickly as he could.

New theory: Satellite phones were no less dangerous than cell phones.

Proof of new theory: Streams of obscenity from T.R.'s lips.

"Damn!" he shouted. Then, "Goddamn!" Then some rougher language he regretted instantly, for turning in the darkness, he saw that a half-dozen children, Arab children, were standing staring at him on the roof.

"Don't mind me," he muttered. "Just the office."

The children whispered quietly among themselves until a boy no more than twelve stepped forward. Small and lithe, with the bright eyes of a leader. Looking at the laptop on the roof, he pointed at the screen.

T.R. pointed back. "Yes," he said, "sit down." He gestured to the rest of them. "Come," he said. "Sit down."

So now they gathered on the roof, T.R. tapping at the keys, thinking he would find some photographs to show these boys and girls. Boys and girls liked photographs. And, eager to please, T.R. typed "BASRA" as the laptop kicked through its mechan-ics. A photograph began to form on screen.

It was six tanks in column on the streets of Basra. He shut it down.

Then he chose another, hardly better. This one showed a family by a flattened house, a dead dog lying at their feet.

The children stared at the picture. One reached out a finger and in English uttered, *dog*. They seemed to understand the facts, but not their meaning or significance. *Dog*, not *dead dog*. *House*, not *flattened house*.

T.R. felt the cruelty in his gesture and his fingers worked at the keys. He called up yet another image—an aerial view of Central Park.

"New York," he told the children in the darkness on the rooftop.

Now there was a silence, awestruck, long, impressed, and the children gathered close to study the green of Central Park, its ambience of autumn, its profound serenity and lushness, even from the air. But instead of relief, there was embarrassment and mitigated pride. He had always felt his presence as a proud American swell his body, buoy his body, he was openly emotional about America; he carried his emotions for the country like a stick, like Teddy Roosevelt's stick. But here in Basra, he could not feel happy being an American; the happiness he felt could not be shared. These Arab boys and girls would never share it and his patriotism humbled and depressed him. It had the same distasteful quality that one might feel in a limousine driving through the projects of the Bronx.

"Home?" It was the boy with bright bold eyes. "Home?" he asked again.

He was pointing at the photo, at the deepest reach of trees, and seemed so taken by the patch of green between the Ramble and the reservoir that T.R. lacked the heart to disappoint.

"Yes," he said. "Home," he said. "Yes. Home."

Chapter 27

SOME SMALL BIT
OF SAND

IT IS NOT necessary to describe the City Council meeting in the morning or the afternoon that followed in Nasiriya—the headlines that accompanied his stories will suffice. "Basra: Unruly Introduction to Democracy"—so ran the first of them. The second, which accompanied the tale of Jessica Lynch, the female private taken prisoner and then sprung free by Special Forces, read in its entirety: "Rescued Soldier's Iraqi Doctors Doubled as Her Guardians."

It was poor form when a headline, acting as the equal of a menu entry, could substitute the meal. It meant there was hack work in the journalistic kitchen. It meant, in fact, that you were serving simple fare.

Better to describe the journey back to Baghdad two days later, which became the journey home, for once T.R. returned to the Sheraton, hauling bags from Rafid's car, waiting at the checkpoint in a crowd of livid Arabs passing through the checkpoint to be frisked, then questioned by marines, he saw at once the atmosphere had changed. It was a subtle change that could be seen in the patchwork quilt of flyers taped up to the hotel doors. The flyers demanded passengers and passage from Iraq.

4th rider needed in car 2 Kuwait. Contact Sheila K. @ Palestine, room 1202.

French journalist requires space to Jordan. Immediate. M. Roucault, rm. 589.

Taking leave of his interpreter and driver, T.R. made his way to the lobby, where the atmosphere was even more profoundly changed. These last three weeks the lobby of the Sheraton had been a working hub for the journalists who gathered each morning for their daily convocations, then met come the evening over cigarettes and drinks. Now, however, great heaps of luggage to remind one of canceled flights and overnight delays were piled against the wall. T.R. was surprised to find a line of correspondents waiting anxiously at the reception desk to settle their bills. The lobby now possessed the nervous clamor of a packed hotel on Sunday morning when the dental conferences have ended. (There was, also, something of the last few days of the semester when the moving vans are parked outside the dorms.) In either case, there was an exodus of almost scriptural proportion under way. Headline at the Sheraton: Journalists in One Mad Rush to Hit the Door.

T.R. went up to the suite, shocked to find the elevators in operating order. When he stepped inside the suite, Alan Chin was sitting cross-legged on the floor.

Chin was working at his laptop, smoking. Dropping his duffel in the corner, T.R. dropped to the bed.

"The elevators are back," he said.

"And the lights are working."

"So what's the news?"

"The news?" Chin glanced from the screen. "The news? You missed LeDuff."

"Really?"

"This morning. Came in last night and left."

T.R. sat on the bed. If LeDuff had left this morning, he would arrive by six this evening in Kuwait. Check the watch: It was just past six o'clock.

"Cigarette?"

Chin tossed him one, and then a pack of matches, then they smoked.

Smoking on the bed, he asked: "How long you think you'll stick around?"

"In Baghdad? I don't know," Chin said. "At least another month."

Another month. The word sat like a tumor on his nerves. It sounded like a prison term, or cancer. It was impossible to consider, even to conceive, another month.

"Chang's coming in tonight," Chin said. "You know Chang?" Chang Lee was a *Times* photographer who had been working in the north among the Kurds.

"Coming in tonight," Chin said, "and leaving in the morning. Actually there is some news." The editors, Chin said, were shutting down the special section, Nation at War.

T.R. grew cagey. There were strategies to now consider. The cut in coverage would require a cut in staff. There was also irony. The nation would remain at war without the "Nation at War."

An hour later, he sent an e-mail to the desk:

Plan to leave Baghdad in next few days. Hope this proves amenable.

Opportunity's been great, but am needed in New York. Please advise. Hear from you soon. All best.

Then he walked to the lobby to study the flyers taped to the glass-front lobby doors. There *was* a feeling of the final days of the semester, or perhaps the week before spring break when the student center corkboard filled with notes—*1 more in car to Lauderdale* or *Daytona Beach! Seeking ride!*

At the Palestine, there was a notice from a German television crew departing in the morning for Kuwait. T.R. took the notice, stuffed it in his pocket, went upstairs, and tried the proper door, but no one answered when he knocked. He sat for a while in the lobby of the Palestine. It was dark and empty. Outside a soldier sat on a chair in the darkness, his M–16 laid thickly on his lap. He looked to be asleep. Two hotel clerks in their jackets smiled at him, shaking their heads, talking softly from behind the check-in desk. T.R. stood and went to the bar where days ago he had marveled at the cinematic lighting that resembled *Casablanca*. He ordered coffee. Two reporters, young, wearing clothes that were clean and with freshly shaven faces, stood at the bar discussing their arrival. They had arrived last night along the western road. "Got to hit the cemetery," said the first. "And the morgue." "The *morgue*." T.R. paid his bill.

At the Sheraton, Chang Lee was sitting on the bed.

"I hear you're leaving in the morning," T.R. said. "Any room in the car?"

Chang, a tall, kind, tired man, who had spent six months among the Kurds, the longest of deployments, looked at him with eyes that said, "I've done triple your assignment! You think *you've* had enough?"

And yet he said, "Of course we have a spot."

By the time he packed that night, climbed in bed beneath the sheets and found he could not sleep, and did not sleep, the door swung open, there were footsteps, then the sound of voices in the room.

"Looks like someone's leaving," Kifner said. And then: "You seen the Scotch?"

"Nice," said Ian Fisher. "Over there behind the sofa. Very nice."

He fell asleep. In the morning, on the balcony, he checked his mail but found no message from the desk and so arrived at half-past six in the lobby of the Sheraton to find Chang Lee and a second journalist, a Japanese reporter, in the asphalt crescent of the lot. They were packing their belongings in the car. T.R.'s own belongings were strapped crosswise across his back. In completion of the echo, the car that Chang had hired was a Chevrolet Suburban. Once again it was a cavalry charge, only this time in reverse.

Upstairs in the suite, T.R. left a note for Ian Fisher. In the final stages of departure, he wondered at the wisdom of this note.

"It seems formal goodbyes are not really part of the process here," the note had read.

But I couldn't leave without some version of goodbye. Thanks for all the tips and tricks and patience and the inspiration and advice. Good luck getting back to Prague. Be safe. Stay cool. Write well.

Now Chang slammed the doors, he was ready. The Japanese was ready. T.R. was ready. And the driver especially was ready, for the route from Baghdad to the border was a nine-hour drive.

Along that route in the car, the same he had traveled two days earlier, the Chevy with its big engine rushing past the mud-baked hovels off the highway, passing convoys rumbling in transit north on the highway, the empty portion of the highway where the Iraqi boys still stood staring at traffic, everything the same; T.R. in back with the weight of his duffel pressed against his legs, the laptop in his lap, a box of Burns's cookies on the seat beside him, eating Burns's cookies, which indeed he had stolen this time, offering them first to Chang, then to the Japanese and then to the driver, all of them enjoying Burns's cookies, looking at the sun get brighter in the sky and feeling the floorboards moving at their feet, he was altogether happy.

Chang had started to discuss what they would do that night. "First, a bath," he said, with a mouth full of cookies. "No, first a nap, then a bath. Then we'll go for dinner at the restaurant. Or no, we'll order dinner to the room."

And the Japanese said, "Room! Let's have dinner in the room!"

All this talk of naps and baths and rooms made T.R. think of his own room, in New York, of waking up in the room on Sunday morning well before his wife, and what it felt like to lie in bed with the windows open, limbs relaxed, staring at the curtains belled in a breeze, and how he liked to get up early for the Sunday paper from the Pakistani on the corner, and the summer evenings in that room *(on the love seat with the panderetas and the salsa music and the smell of empanadas and the old men slapping dominoes down on the street)*, and it occurred to him that it would almost be summer in New York when he returned, which meant the beach at Belmar *(skin pulled taut by the sun, floating dizziness of swimming in the waves and the long drive back on the turnpike up through the industry of Linden, which deserved a crisp cold beer that night)* or Yankee Stadium *(at Stan's or Billy's underneath the elevated train, which you could see through a notch in the right-field stands, it thrilled him every time).* As the car drove south on the same road he had traveled, everything the same, yet different for the thoughts in his head, that carried them past Basra, past Um Qassar, past the border to Kuwait where, off a highway parallel to a long pastiche of billboards, they pulled in underneath the awning of the Sheraton Kuwait. The driver helped them with their bags and each in turn shook hands.

The lobby of the Sheraton was the most luxurious lobby T.R. had ever entered. Having entered many (having now perfected the art of lobby entrance), he approached the check-in desk, withdrew his passport, displayed a credit card unused since drinking with the two old soldiers in Amman, and reserved a room. The desk clerk smiled, she was a pretty Arab woman in a two-piece suit, she handed him the key (a plastic key, a modern Sheraton Hotel key) and then informed him that the sushi bar was open late this night, a Friday night. Arranging with his partners to gather at six, he hauled his bags across the shiny marble floor. He rode the elevator fourteen stories up, got out, walked past a business center bristling with fax machines and glass, and, pausing to collect a final breath, put his key inside the lock.

To step inside a room, to enter a room, is to pass from one emotion to another, whether from the business of the study to the leisure of the bedroom or into the comfortable camaraderie of a local bar. Entering this room in the Sheraton felt like entering suspended animation. Nothing here belonged, it was empty of emotion, it was super-clean like hospitals are clean, luxurious but vacant, with a king-sized bed, expensive modern sleekly polished dark wood dressers and a sleek black wide-screen television set. The room was silent except for the humming of a thermostat, a low dull humming, more of an electric buzz. On the night stand was a complicated telephone. On the round glass table there were three remote controls.

T.R. resisted the remote controls. Instead he stood at the window. Fourteen stories down was the bright blue pan of the gulf, the water and the sunlight and the city spread on the gulf were simple. They were the simplest things in weeks.

Was it then that he began to think about the veterans flown into San Francisco only fifteen hours out of Saigon? Had they too hauled their duffel bags to rented rooms? Had they too stood at the window staring at the water? Had they too let their minds cast back like ocean-going nets and felt the company of their entire country in those rooms and then concluded that its story was their own?

T.R. stepped back from the window. He started to undress and fetched a towel from the bathroom, turned on the shower, and let the steam fill up the bath. He took his glasses off and set them on the polished surface of the dresser. They left a gritty dust of sand.

The sand had wedged its way in between the wire frame and lenses, and he worked at it in his towel with his index finger and the nail of his thumb. Then he rinsed the glasses under water at the sink and dried them with the edge of a towel. Then he got in the shower. Whatever sand was left, he would get it later. He had already worked out what he could.

ACKNOWLEDGMENTS

Thanks are due to Megan Hustad and Katharine Cluverius, without whom this book would be no more than a pile of unpublished paper. Thanks also to Raul Correa, Andy Bienen, and Charlie LeDuff for their sharp eyes and fine-tuned ears.

This book would not have existed without two people who will never get to read it. Their names are Charles Feuer and Nora Sayre.